W9-BBI-850

Angels *and* Demons

RON PHILLIPS, DMin

CHARISMA
HOUSE

Most CHARISMA HOUSE BOOK GROUP products are available at special quantity discounts for bulk purchase for sales promotions, premiums, fund-raising, and educational needs. For details, write Charisma House Book Group, 600 Rinehart Road, Lake Mary, Florida 32746, or telephone (407) 333-0600.

ANGELS AND DEMONS by Ron Phillips
Published by Charisma House
Charisma Media/Charisma House Book Group
600 Rinehart Road
Lake Mary, Florida 32746
www.charismahouse.com

This book or parts thereof may not be reproduced in any form, stored in a retrieval system, or transmitted in any form by any means—electronic, mechanical, photocopy, recording, or otherwise—without prior written permission of the publisher, except as provided by United States of America copyright law.

Unless otherwise noted, all Scripture quotations are taken from the New King James Version®. Copyright © 1982 by Thomas Nelson. Used by permission. All rights reserved.

Scripture quotations marked KJV are from the King James Version of the Bible.

Scripture quotations marked MEV are taken from the Holy Bible, Modern English Version. Copyright © 2014 by Military Bible Association. Used by permission. All rights reserved.

Scripture quotations marked NIV are taken from the Holy Bible, New International Version®, NIV®. Copyright © 1973, 1978, 1984, 2011 by Biblica, Inc.™ Used by permission of Zondervan. All rights reserved worldwide. www.zondervan.com The "NIV" and "New International Version" are trademarks registered in the United States Patent and Trademark Office by Biblica, Inc.™

Copyright © 2015 by Ron Phillips
All rights reserved

Cover design by Justin Evans

Visit the author's website at www.RonPhillips.org.

Library of Congress Cataloging-in-Publication Data:
An application to register this book for cataloging has been submitted to
the Library of Congress.
International Standard Book Number: 978-1-62998-034-8
E-book ISBN: 978-1-62998-039-3

Portions of this book were previously published by Charisma House
as *Our Invisible Allies*, copyright © 2009, ISBN 978-1-59979-523-2, and
Everyone's Guide to Demons and Spiritual Warfare, copyright © 2010,
ISBN 978-1-61638-127-1.

15 16 17 18 19 — 987654321
Printed in the United States of America

CONTENTS

Part One — Angels

Part Two — Demons

ANGELS

INTRODUCTION

O N December 20, 1857, Charles Spurgeon delivered a sermon called "The First Christmas Carol." In that sermon Spurgeon spoke of the believer and his angelic allies. He began his sermon with these words:

> Glory to God in the highest, and on earth peace, good will toward men.
>
> —Luke 2:14, kjv

It is superstitious to worship angels; it is but proper to love them. Although it would be a high sin, and an act of misdemeanor against the Sovereign Court of Heaven to pay the slightest adoration to the mightiest angel, yet it would be unkind and unseemly, if we did not give to holy angels a place in our heart's warmest love. In fact, he that contemplates the character of angels, and marks their many deeds of sympathy with men, and kindness towards them, cannot resist the impulse of his nature—the impulse of love towards them. The one incident in angelic history, to which our text refers, is enough to weld our hearts to them forever.

How free from envy the angels were! Christ did not come from heaven to save their compeers when they fell. When Satan, the mighty angel, dragged with him a third part of the stars of heaven, Christ did not stoop from his throne to die for them; but he left them to be reserved in chains and darkness until the last great day. Yet angels did not envy men. Though they remembered that he took not up angels, yet they did not murmur when he took up the seed of Abraham; and though the blessed Master had never condescended to take the angel's form, they did not

1

think it beneath them to express their joy when they found him arrayed in the body of an infant.

How free, too, they were from pride! They were not ashamed to come and tell the news to humble shepherds. Methinks they had as much joy in pouring out their songs that night before the shepherds, who were watching with their flocks, as they would have had if they had been commanded by their Master to sing their hymn in the halls of Caesar. Mere men—men possessed with pride, think it a fine thing to preach before kings and princes; and think it great condescension now and then to have to minister to the humble crowd.

Not so the angels. They stretched their willing wings, and gladly sped from their bright seats above, to tell the shepherds on the plain by night, the marvelous story of an Incarnate God. And mark how well they told the story, and surely you will love them! Not with the stammering tongue of him that tells a tale in which he hath no interest; nor even with the feigned interest of a man that would move the passions of others, when he feeleth no emotion himself; but with joy and gladness, such as angels only can know. They *sang* the story out, for they could not stay to tell it in heavy prose. They sang, "Glory to God on high, and on earth peace, good will towards men." Methinks they sang it with gladness in their eyes; with their hearts burning with love, and with breasts as full of joy as if the good news to man had been good news to themselves. And, verily, it was good news to them, for the heart of sympathy makes good news to others, good news to itself.

Do you not love the angels? Ye will not bow before them, and there ye are right; but will ye not love them? Doth it not make one part of your anticipation of heaven, that in heaven you shall dwell with the holy angels, as well as with the spirits of the just made perfect? Oh, how sweet to think that these holy and lovely beings are our guardians every hour! They keep watch and ward about us, both in the burning noontide, and in the darkness of the night. They keep us in all our ways; they bear us up in their hands, lest at any time we dash our feet against stones. They unceasingly minister unto us who are the heirs of salvation; both by day and night they are our watchers and our guardians, for know ye not, that "the angel of the Lord encampeth round about them that fear him."[1]

As we explore the mystical world of the angels, may we come to love them for their faithful service to the triune God and their tender service to us. May they be welcome in our churches, our homes, and our workplaces. May we enjoy their companionship until they carry us across the great divide to the world where there is no death.

Section One

WHERE ANGELS ORIGINATED

Chapter One

THE PRESENCE OF ANGELS

D URING OPERATION DESERT STORM IN 1991, THIRTY-FIVE
nations formed a coalition with the United States, making a
total of thirty-six nations, against Saddam Hussein to bring Kuwait
back under the leadership of the emir of Kuwait. This coalition created such a powerful force against Iraq that the air strike began and
ended within six weeks. Iraq surrendered after these bombings and a
four-day ground campaign.[1]

This operation was extremely successful because the leaders of
these countries came together, agreed on a common goal, organized
their attack, and created a fair and uniform way to direct their troops,
which promoted unity, easy communication, and a shared goal.[2]

Each of these thirty-six countries supplied troops based on their military resources. While the United States and Great Britain supplied the
most, every country supplied a particular number of troops to champion
the cause. As a result, each nation only had to supply a small amount of
resources in order to accomplish the goal of liberating Kuwait from Iraq.
The strategy was masterfully executed, and because of the formation of
this coalition, the sacrifice from each country was minimal.

Did you know that the war in Iraq was one of the longest wars in
American history? One of the many reasons for its length and com-
plexity was the absence of allies! Unlike Desert Storm, our nation had
great difficulty finding the needed support for this war, and so, alone
and exhausted, this conflict stretched years beyond what was expected.
Unfortunately, this scenario epitomizes the unhappy state of believers
living in spiritual defeat! Believers are failing to employ and deploy the
hosts of heaven surrounding them. All of the great men and women of

faith noted in the Holy Scriptures operated with the supernatural assistance of various angels.

If you haven't noticed, there is a growing fascination with angels in our society. For some reason, the possibility of supernatural encounters with angelic beings fascinates this generation. I find this astonishing because as a child of the 1960s, I was reared in an environment dominated by the denial of God and the supernatural, but today, the majority of people believe in unseen spiritual forces that can be channeled and interacted with daily.

When did this drastic shift take place, and why has it happened? As Christians, we should be keenly aware of what others are saying related to unseen forces and remember that angels assist us in ways completely unknown to us.

In their younger days, Coach Mike Dubose and his wife, Polly, had just moved from Chattanooga to Hattiesburg, Mississippi. Polly took a break from unpacking the moving boxes in their new tri-level home to put their precious two-year-old son to bed. Secure in the fact that her son was safe in bed, as he had never climbed out of the baby bed before, Polly went downstairs to continue the task at hand. Unknown to Polly, her sweet baby had climbed out of his crib, slipped outside, found his Big Wheel scooter, and disappeared. As Polly continued to get her house in order, she was totally unaware her son was in harm's way.

As she continued unpacking box after box in the lower level of her beautiful new home, Polly heard a knock at the door. When Polly opened the door, there stood a lady with her son. The woman explained she had found the boy at a busy intersection two blocks away. Now understand that Polly knew no one in Hattiesburg and had just moved to this address. Frightened and startled, Polly turned to set the boy down, then turned back to thank the lady, and there was no one at the door. The lady had just vanished.

Polly never saw or heard from that woman again. Coach and Polly Dubose believe an angel had rescued their son!

Angels are indeed our "allies." Allies are close friends who are willing to:

- Love and protect what you love
- Face a common enemy with you

- Share with you the same allegiances and loyalties
- Obey the same orders
- Make the same sacrifices
- Share similar weapons
- Operate covertly in the enemy's territory when necessary
- Keep open lines of communication
- Stay until the finish
- Operate in ranks under authority
- Move based on written agreement

Think about your own life. When living becomes difficult and you are in short supply of moral support and guidance, the instructions are simple and universal: join hands with your friends, family, spouse, and coworkers. These people are your allies. But be honest; isn't this hard to *do* sometimes? How can allies be trusted in a world full of corruption and decay? Remember the new feeling you discovered when a good friend betrayed you or when a group project fell apart because there was no cooperative effort? What about the loneliness you felt when your own family abandoned you or a loved one cheated on you with someone else? These encounters initiate all of us into the harsh realities of human nature.

Now, let's reevaluate. Isn't the idea of trusting in allies *hard* to believe? Come on, how are we supposed to trust these angelic beings in our spiritual lives? Aren't there some angels who have "fallen"? My purpose in writing this book is for us to discover that the angelic allies around us *are* trustworthy. They will not abandon us in our efforts to spread the gospel to a lost and dying world. My hope and prayer is that you realize angels are friends that help guide, protect, and minister to us so that we may endure in the cause of Christ for our lives.

The will of God consumes and possesses angels, and they passionately pursue His salvation for us. They minister to us in ways that are wholly unique from any guidance we can receive on Earth. They comfort us, speak to us, monitor the spiritual climate around us, teach us, and help us. But above all else, angels work for the Master of the universe and share in our desire to worship Him and accomplish His will. They are our allies.

Chapter Two

THE REALITY OF ANGELS

IT WAS A COLD EVENING IN GADSDEN, ALABAMA, AND DESPITE THE wintry weather forecast, I was excited to be traveling into the mountains to preach at a gathering of churches in North Alabama. The late Dr. Claude Rhea, who had sung for Billy Graham, was the featured musical guest, and I at twenty-nine years of age would follow with the message. What a fantastic opportunity for a young preacher! My wife, Paulette, wasn't quite as enthusiastic. She gave me an apprehensive look as I kissed her good-bye. "Be careful, honey. It is snowing," she warned. Not known for my driving skills, I was oblivious to her warning.

As I traveled the sixty miles north into the hills, I noticed the snow beginning to stick to the grass and fields. As I neared the church, snow had already begun to cover the road. However, to my delight, the church was full and the crowd was excited. Dr. Rhea gave a powerful testimony of his healing from cancer and delivered a stirring rendition of the popular Gaither classic "He Touched Me" as the finale to his portion of the evening. The mountain people loved it!

The atmosphere was electric when I stepped up to preach. However, the Spirit wasn't the only thing falling that night; a blanket of snow was covering the region. And because of the weather, the host pastor had asked me to be brief. As I closed the message, the congregation left quickly. I thanked Dr. Rhea for his music and bid a quick farewell to the host pastor, who was getting into his pickup truck and heading home. One man from the church asked if I needed any help getting off the mountain. With little experience driving in ice and snow, I boastfully replied, "I can handle it." As I made my way down the narrow road, my confidence soon disappeared. Snow covered everything, and visibility was difficult due to the falling snow.

The car began to skid, and I braked, sending the car into two 360s, and came to a stop perched on the edge of a steep embankment. Finally, after some time, I got the car turned in the right direction, but I realized I was in trouble. At that moment, I began to pray and ask God for help. I heard His voice speak to my spirit, "Your angel is sitting beside you." At this point in my life, I had not received the baptism of the Spirit, so the supernatural world was strange to me. I looked toward the passenger seat, and to my surprise, there was a faint glow. At first I thought it was simply a reflection from the snow, but then my spirit suddenly became alert and I realized my angel was with me.

The Lord spoke to me and said, "Command your angel to help you." I was ignorant at that juncture of scriptural instruction on the ministry of angels: "Are they not all ministering spirits sent out to minister to those who will inherit salvation?" (Heb. 1:14, MEV). I spoke to the angel and very timidly said, "Angel, would you go outside and help me not to skid and get safely home?" There was no audible response from the angel, but I knew I was safe to proceed. So I put the car in drive, and the tires gripped the road. With the faint glow now above the right fender, I came off that mountain without another slip or slide of any kind. When I came to Interstate 59, the road I was descending was closed. The state trooper who had closed that mountain road asked me how I had made it. I mumbled, "The Lord helped me…" As I began to close the window he said, "You all be careful." I looked to my right, and for an instant I saw the figure of a person sitting in the seat beside me; the trooper had seen him also. I made it safely home to my wife, who had been praying for me.

What happened on that mountain? I believe one of God's angels came out of the eternal dimension into earthly time to rescue a frightened young preacher. This was not the first time, nor would it be the last time I would experience such a presence. I recalled the two times I was protected while traveling to and from Clarke College in Newton, Mississippi. I left Montgomery, Alabama, on Sunday afternoon and headed back across Highway 80 through Selma, Alabama, and Meridian, Mississippi, to Newton, Mississippi. Between Selma and Uniontown, on that two-lane highway, I was forced off the road by an eastbound car that came over the line into my lane. I swerved onto the shoulder and went barreling toward a concrete bridge abutment at sixty-five miles an hour. With little time to react, I braced myself for the impact. A few seconds later, I found myself back on the highway, traveling west perfectly safe. I know there was no physical way I could have missed that bridge. Did an angel move the car?

Later that same year, I was traveling home with a friend in his 1965 Pontiac GTO. He was driving east between Uniontown and Selma when an eighteen-wheeler topped the hill in front of us in our lane as he passed a pickup truck. My friend turned the wheel toward the deep ditch on our right. The tire hit the soft dirt and gravel, and the car flipped over. My friend was ejected from the car and suffered a broken arm, shoulder, and collarbone. As the car rolled over three times, I felt a warm blanket cover me. Something held me safe inside that car even though I was not wearing a seat belt. If I had fallen out of the car, I would have been crushed. The car stopped upright, and gas was pouring out of the tank, but against all reason I stepped out of the car without a scratch! I looked around for the blanket that had covered me during the accident, but there was none! Who or what had covered and protected me? Was it my angel?

Dr. Craig Buettner, a family practitioner from Tuscaloosa, Alabama, and the team physician for the University of Alabama football team, was enjoying a day at the pool with his son's baseball team. Dr. Buettner and his wife, Amy, led busy lives not only with his medical practice but also as parents of five children ranging in age from five weeks to nine years old. As everyone settled down to eat with their family and friends, Amy noticed that their four-year-old son, Kennedy, was missing. They began to search the house, the pool, and the neighborhood, but there was no sign of him. Then their nine-year-old son screamed from the pool, dove in, and pulled Kennedy from the pool. Kennedy was bloated, blue, not breathing, and his heart had stopped. Dr. Buettner immediately began CPR on his little boy while Amy began to pray through her sobs. Soon the emergency crew came as Dr. Buettner cleared Kennedy's lungs and triggered a faint heartbeat.

Kennedy was soon transferred from the hospital in Tuscaloosa to the children's hospital in Birmingham, Alabama. The neurologist at the children's hospital only gave a 15 percent chance of survival for little Kennedy with no hope for a "normal" life if he did live. The doctors and nurses worked through the night with Kennedy, and by morning he was much improved. Within eight days, the boy was completely healed and went home with no brain damage at all. When Amy asked Kennedy what happened, the boy said, "An angel drew me out of the deep waters and took me to heaven, and I saw Uncle Mark and Jesus. Later the angel brought me back." Kennedy admitted that he was not afraid.

Interestingly enough, Uncle Mark had died from cancer just six months before Kennedy's accident. Uncle Mark was a deer hunter and was nicknamed "Buckmaster." Of course the angelic intervention aspect of this story is astounding; however, there are two other interesting things you should know. First, the phrase used by Kennedy "drew me out of the deep waters" was part of a scripture given to the Buettners by a close friend.

> He reached down from on high and took hold of me; *he drew me out of deep waters.* He rescued me from my powerful enemy, from my foes, who were too strong for me. They confronted me in the day of my disaster, but the LORD was my support.
> —PSALM 18:16–18, NIV, EMPHASIS ADDED

Secondly, the neurologist who helped save the boy's life was working his last day at the children's hospital; his last name was the same as Uncle Mark's nickname. Coincidence? Anomaly? No! Angels visited and saved Kennedy's life.

As the years have passed I have had countless reports and experiences with our Lord and His holy angels. Angel sightings have occurred in our services at Abba's House. Angelic interventions have been manifested on many occasions. Who are these beings? Where do they live? How do they look? How do they work? What have they done in the past? What are they doing now? What part will they play at the end of the age? How can you activate angelic assistance in your life?

The remaining chapters in this book will open your eyes to another world, the eternal dimension. You will learn that angels are a key connection to that realm for us. It is important for you to know that angelic assistance is not automatic! Angelic operation is consistent with Scripture and the heavenly chain of command. This book will fascinate you, but I hope you will move from fascination to faith, and from faith to facilitation of your heavenly resources.

Chapter Three

THE MYSTERY OF ANGELS

IMAGINE DAVID SITTING UNDER THE STARS IN THE JUDEAN wilderness after an exhausting day of herding his sheep; the splendor of the sky overwhelms him. In that moment he sees the utter insignificance of man contrasted with the mystery of God. His heart explodes in wonder and praise that God would take time to give thought to man! Beyond that David sees a God who is coming for man.

Here humanity rises to heights of glory! Our God takes notice of us, cares for us, and crowns us as royalty on Earth. However, in this psalm, David reveals to us that our universe, as vast as it is, is not the only realm where life abounds.

> O LORD, our Lord, how excellent is Your name in all the earth,
> who set Your glory above the heavens!
> —PSALM 8:1

Life exists in other dimensions beyond the earth! In fact, supernatural beings exist beyond our earthly realm. Speaking of humanity, the Bible says, "For You have made him a little lower than the angels" (Ps. 8:5, MEV). David looked heavenward and saw the majesty of God in the vastness of the created order! He looked to the earth and saw tiny man as the centerpiece and crowning glory of that order! You can hear the music of the supernatural and its rhythm soaring from his ravished soul!

There are other beings from another dimension that are moving by the multitudes across the vast expanse of our known world. These beings are not subject to the limitations of our world. Beyond our normal range of understanding is another dimension more real and lasting than anything we can imagine. The existence of another realm called "the heavenlies" where marvelous creatures both magnificent and malevolent operate is not science fiction. In this realm exist these living beings called angels, along with their dark cousins, demons. Created by God, these timeless beings have a history of their own. Remarkably, they have the ability to come and go between the eternal dimension and our world.

There are realms of reality and life beyond human reach and reason without supernatural assistance. The angels, God's hosts, are among such mysteries. Yes, these supernatural beings are found throughout the Scriptures, from the first page to the last page of the Bible.

Throughout my life, I have been the recipient of angelic assistance. Only recently has science caught up with the Bible in the area of other realms and dimensions beyond normal human perception. Living with us and beyond us at the same time are the angels of God.

THE MYSTERIOUS REALMS OF ANGELS

How old are angels? How old is creation? There is much debate among Christians about the age of the earth. To me it is irrelevant because God lives beyond the limits of the four dimensions of our existence. Time is a product of our universe and its movements, and God lives beyond these limits of human history and its time-driven record.

ANGELS ARE CREATED BEINGS

The hosts of heaven were brought to life by the Creator God. They were given a deathless, timeless existence very different from the history of humans.

> You alone are the LORD. You have made heaven, the heaven of heavens, with all their host, the earth and all that is on it, the seas and all that is in them; and You preserve them all. And the host of heaven worships You.
> —NEHEMIAH 9:6, MEV

Yahweh, the Lord, created all the "hosts" of heaven, and these "hosts" worship Him. Angels came to life at the command of God. They were commanded and they were created. (See Psalm 148:5.) These wonderful creatures are numberless. Their presence proves to us that the heavenly realm teems with energy and life.

This scripture indicates that the angels are created beings and that one of their functions is to praise and worship the Lord. Paul again affirms the fact that angels are created beings. These living beings precede Earth and humanity in the creation.

> For by Him all things were created that are in heaven and that are in earth, visible and invisible, whether they are thrones, or dominions, or principalities, or powers. All things were created by Him and for Him.
>   —COLOSSIANS 1:16, MEV

Angels were created by the Lord Jesus and for the Lord Jesus. Angels were agents of the creation of our universe.

> Where were you when I laid the foundations of the earth? Tell Me, if you have understanding. Who determined its measurements? Surely you know! Or who stretched the line upon it? To what were its foundations fastened? Or who laid its cornerstone, when the morning stars sang together, and all the sons of God shouted for joy?
>   —JOB 38:4–7

Job may very well be the oldest book in the Bible. It is full of mystery and wonder. According to the above scripture, at the dawn of creation angels were active. When I read these words, my soul trembles within me; we read and are carried back to the earliest moments of history.

Creation was initiated by a sound… "God said!" His mighty word sounded forth in what science calls a "big bang." God spoke, and the great starry host exploded in a fireworks display, the remnant of which still lights up the sky over our heads. Our sun still warms us all these ages later from that beginning blast. Watching this entire demonstration, like a family at a fireworks display, were the "sons of God," the holy angels. All of these beings shouted while Creation was being strung into place by God's hand. The stars were their orchestra as they shouted with joy!

Earth is a small planet in an average-sized solar system on the edge of a galaxy called the Milky Way. The vast expanse of the universe dwarfs our planet. In comparison, the earth would be less than a grain of sand in a large building! That perspective diminishes the significance of those of us who live on this planet.

If the visible world is all there is and life an accident, then human intelligence, achievements, and aspirations mean nothing. Solomon felt this way after exploring human existence in the present dimension and declared it to be grasping for the wind. Take a look at his words: "And I set my heart to know wisdom and to know madness and folly. I perceived that this also is grasping for the wind" (Eccles. 1:17).

Solomon understood that God has set a desire in humanity for more than what we can see in this life. His quest led him to discover the eternal dimension, a reality beyond the four dimensions of our existence. From Ecclesiastes 3:11 we see this perspective on the eternal world: "He has made everything beautiful in its time. Also He has put eternity in their hearts, except that no one can find out the work that God does from beginning to end."

He understood that God has made everything beautiful in its time. It is God who put eternity in our hearts, and the work that God does from beginning to end is on His time schedule. We should rejoice and do well in our lives, and eat and drink and enjoy the good of our labor here on Earth because it is the gift of God. Whatever God does is forever; nothing can be added to it and nothing taken from it. God does it; we should reverence and honor Him. God sees it all—past, present, and future—and we are responsible for what God has entrusted to us. Our lives are connected to an eternal world more real and lasting than the present world.

The most intriguing science fiction films of the past decade were The Matrix trilogy. These movies were fascinating as the characters were living in an artificial world they thought was real. These three movies chronicle the characters' discovery that they are really asleep to the real world, are being manipulated by evil forces, and are prisoners of this dark world. These characters who discover the unseen real world are ridiculed and mocked. Finally, in a powerful scene, the main character dies to reveal the open door to the real world.

This scenario is true of our world. It is temporary! We live in another dimension; however, we can escape the evil matrix and live in the heavenly dimension where angels operate and miracles happen. Paul made the same discovery regarding the heavenly realm and declared this fascinating truth:

> Therefore we do not lose heart. Even though our outward man is perishing, yet the inward man is being renewed day by day. For our light affliction, which is but for a moment, is working for us a far more exceeding and eternal weight of glory, while we do not look at the things which are seen, but at the things which are not seen. For the things which are seen are temporary, but the things which are not seen are eternal.
> —2 CORINTHIANS 4:16–18

There is an unseen world that is greater, more real, and more lasting than our limited existence.

UNSEEN WORLD

Quantum physics studies the origin of matter. This realm of science believes the world had a beginning; therefore, a greater world existed and still thrives beyond our cosmos. On the earth, we live in four dimensions; we live in a world with length, width, height, and time. In the natural, these dimensions limit us. Quantum physicists like Brian Greene, who wrote *The Elegant Universe*, have discovered the existence of at least eleven dimensions. All of these dimensions are moving in straight lines. This perspective of history is called "linear." God created our universe and set this line of history in motion. He created it, but He is not captive to it. God lives above and beyond our history. Knowing that there are at least seven other dimensions beyond our limited view, our perspective is broadened and our imagination captivated by dimensions we have not seen.

This is the realm where God abides! Paul called these dimensions "the third heaven." Solomon, at the dedication of the great temple, spoke of our God not limited to the heavens we observe. "But will God indeed dwell on the earth? Behold, heaven and the heaven of heavens cannot contain You. How much less this temple which I have built!" (1 Kings 8:27).

How do we reach the dimension where God dwells? Our linear history cannot reach the third heaven; these dimensions do not move in the same direction. However, His dimensions may intersect with ours. When that happens, all that is in the new (or God) dimension, according to quantum physics, becomes available in our present dimension. When these dimensions intersect, the limitations and laws of our present dimension can be altered, broken, or transformed. The limits and laws of our four-dimensional world can be suspended. Our natural order can be changed by a supernatural dimensional interruption!

A miracle is a dimensional interruption when the spiritual world breaks into our mundane existence,[1] changing our limited existence from ordinary to extraordinary. We can live in wonder again! The impossible becomes possible, and hope flourishes.

Though planet Earth is but a speck of dust in the vast ocean of the universe, the Hubble telescope proves that the four-dimensional arena in which humanity lives strains human reason in terms of size. The mega-size of creation is outdone by its awesome beauty.

When we put down the telescope and look into a microscope, we discover that one cell of the human body contains vast amounts of information. One set of twenty-four human chromosomes contains 3.1 billion patterns of DNA code.[2] It is absolutely incredible!

> I will praise You, for I am fearfully and wonderfully made; marvelous are Your works, and that my soul knows very well. My frame was not hidden from You, when I was made in secret, and skillfully wrought in the lowest parts of the earth. Your eyes saw my substance, being yet unformed. And in Your book they all were written, the days fashioned for me, when as yet there were none of them.
> —PSALM 139:14–16

Dr. Francis Collins, who sequenced the human genome and unraveled our DNA, is a Christian. He said, "The solution is actually readily at hand, once one ceases to apply human limitations to God. If God is outside of nature, then He is outside of space and time. In that context, God could in the moment of creation of the universe also know every detail of the future. That could include the formation of the stars, planets, and galaxies, all of the chemistry, physics, geology, and biology that led to the formation of life on earth, and the evolution of humans, right to the moment of your reading this book—and beyond."[3]

Long before *Star Wars*, the ancient prophets saw an end-time life-and-death struggle between the forces of darkness and the forces of light in the eternal realm. Though the war has been won by Christ at the cross, a battle rages for the soul of mankind; we are not alone in that battle. We have invisible allies available to assist us in the end time as we enforce Christ's victory.

UNSEEN BEINGS

Other beings live in the eternal dimension. These are the real ETs (extraterrestrials). Paul called this realm "the heavenlies." This realm is not geographical! This eternal dimension can be as close as one's breath! Angels live in this realm but are allowed to cross over into our four-dimensional world! Our Lord Jesus came out of that realm into this realm to reveal to us the way home! Angels move interdimensionally in order to operate on our behalf. Angels, without number, accompany us now.

In this exciting time in history, angelic activity and involvement are on the increase as we move toward the climax of history. Two worlds, the spirit realm and the physical realm, are on a collision course that will culminate in Christ's return.

Chapter Four

THE VARIETY OF ANGELS

How does God operate in our world? He moves through people and angels! In this chapter we will consider some of the different varieties of angels we find in the Bible.

THE HOSTS

Earlier I shared that angels are called "hosts." This name has to do with the vast numbers of these spiritual beings available to serve! How many angels are there? No one except God can count them: "The chariots of God are twice ten thousand, even thousands of thousands" (Ps. 68:17, MEV); "...an innumerable company of angels..." (Heb. 12:22, MEV); "...numbering ten thousand times ten thousand, and thousands of thousands..." (Rev. 5:11, MEV).

The point is that there are plenty of those wonderful friends available at just the right moment to help us. This was certainly true on the evening of March 6, 1996, as a fierce storm blew into East Tennessee. Dana and Julie Harding had almost completed building their 3,700-square-foot two-story home. The lower level housed Dana's recording studio and business, while their family lived on the second level.

Dana and Julie had done much of the work during the construction of their dream home, along with the help of friends and family. The house was 98 percent complete; all that was needed were gutters, drainage, and some backfill work.

When they went to bed that spring evening, a storm was starting to brew. By 3:45 a.m., it had reached full force. "There was a huge clap of thunder that shook the house and woke me up," recalled Dana, a very sound sleeper who had actually slept through an earthquake once. "Something inside of me told me to go to the basement. I looked out the window, and it looked like a waterfall coming off of the roof—a solid sheet of water."

Dana went down to the then-unfinished recording studio. "We had just moved in four days before, and the studio space was just a big, open room." Except for a couple of support walls and some boxes stacked against the east wall, there was nothing there. Dana walked across to the opposing wall and looked at it. First, shock gripped him, then horror set in as he saw the first signs of impending disaster.

"When I looked at the wall," Dana said, "I saw a crack beginning to form." The crack was about five feet up the ten-foot block wall and was running horizontal the entire length of the fifty-two-foot foundation wall. When the rain came off of the roof, it poured down along the foundation of the new house. Several tons of loose fill dirt unexpectedly settled instantly and created a trap for the water where it could not escape from around the foundation. More water poured off of the roof with no place to go other than to put extreme amounts of pressure on the foundation walls—walls that were never meant to withstand the untold tons of water pressure being exerted on them.

Dana ran up the stairs and woke Julie with the news that the walls were cracking. Julie got out of the bed, put on a robe, sat down on the couch, and began praying. Dana was immediately on the phone with Mike, his good friend and builder, who assured him that he was on the way. Within ten minutes, Mike was there, assessing the situation.

"This is really bad. I'm going to get my work van [with all of the tools], and I will be right back," Mike declared.

The crack in the wall had opened up to about a half-inch and showed no signs of stopping. To make matters infinitely worse, the thirty-two-foot end wall was beginning to show signs of stress and was beginning to crack as well. As Mike flew down the dark, wet streets, formulating a plan of action in a mind that had gone from peaceful sleep to waking nightmare, Dana went out into the maelstrom to attempt to divert the potential disaster that was coming, fighting the rain, mud, wind, cold, and the desire to fall facedown in the mud and scream.

But all the while, Julie prayed.

And God showed up.

Actually, to be more precise, He sent His angelic messengers. As Julie sat inside praying, wide-awake at this point, she suddenly had a vision. "I saw the downstairs, and there were angels standing around the perimeter, lining the walls of the basement." She initially thought that they were there to support the walls so they would not cave in. As their true purpose was revealed, the reality of the situation became even more miraculous.

At about 4:30 a.m., forty-five minutes after the whole series of disastrous events began, Mike pulled back into the driveway with his work van. A cold, wet, and muddy Dana met him as they walked into the basement (the house was built into a hill, so one end of the house actually had an outside door, with three sides being predominantly underground). When Mike saw the wall and the crack that had tripled in size since the time he left, he exclaimed, "Get Julie out of the house NOW!"

Dana sprinted up the stairs, picked Julie up, and got her out into Mike's still-running van. Mike escaped right behind them. Then it happened...

Within sixty seconds of their getting out of the house, the entire fifty-two-foot span of foundation wall collapsed. A tidal wave of mud, rock, water, and various other objects came flooding into the basement. As Dana stood in the rain and watched his dreams cave in with the wall, he recalls thinking, "God, if the whole thing is coming down, just let me be in there when it does."

Now, normally in such a situation, once one wall caves in, the house above it would, at the very least, sag several inches. This would create a chain reaction of cracked drywall, broken tile, misaligned doorways, broken glass, and a host of other problems.

However, since the far end wall had extreme amounts of pressure against it, was cracking, and had already lost one side support wall, once the end wall collapsed, the house would basically shift, and the whole thing would cave into the hole that had been the basement. "I was at my wit's end. I was just waiting for the other shoe to drop," Dana recalls.

It never did.

Julie later realized that although she thought the angels in her vision were there to keep the walls from collapsing, they were, in fact, holding the house up. God supernaturally showed her the angelic hosts who were there protecting them from what could have been a catastrophic loss. The end wall, as damaged as it was and with as much pressure as it was bearing, never let go. The side of the house that was suddenly left with no support under it sagged less than three-eighths of an inch. There was virtually no damage to the inside of the house. "Unless you knew exactly where to look," Dana stated, "there was no damage. In fact, all of the damage that was done was hairline fractures in drywall joints and a couple of bathroom tiles that have almost unnoticeable fractures in them. Basically, the kind of stuff that would have happened over time as the house settled anyway."

Over the next several hours, as the cavalry of friends and workers arrived to help, the house was shored up, and the situation was downgraded from "life-threateningly dangerous" to "how many wheelbarrows full of mud can you remove from a basement?" Through the whole experience, and to this day, Dana is still amazed: "Through the whole day and through all of the chaos, Julie was the rock. I was exhausted and ready to throw in the towel, but God had given Julie the vision and had allowed her to see that the angels were there protecting us and supporting us. There was peace in her that, at the time, I didn't understand. I could only see in the natural the chain of events that happened and what the logical conclusion *should* have been. God showed Julie what the true reality of the situation was."

Just as Jacob had a dream of angels, so did Julie at Sea Level Studios, and their home still stands. By the way, my daily radio program is recorded in that miracle place! The hosts are available to us all.

ANGELS

The "hosts" are also called "angels." The English word *angel* comes from the Greek word *aggelos*, found in the original New Testament. This word means "a herald or a messenger."

In the Old Testament the word translated "angel" is *malak*, which means "a message sent." This, of course, indicates that God uses angels to communicate. In a later chapter, we will see how we can receive faith and direction from these amazing allies.

Allies are supernatural creatures of high intelligence. They are a part of our kingdom family. In Hebrews 12:22 we read of an "innumerable company of angels" gathered with the church at worship. Obviously the angels are God's "communication specialists" to Earth.

All of us are aware of the financial meltdown in late 2008. Two weeks before the crisis broke, I was praying in my basement study when I felt a breeze and a presence in the room. As I prayed, I heard in my spirit a voice saying, "Make your retirement safe!" Instead of obeying the angelic visitor, I called my representative at our Christian retirement agency, and he advised against moving the money. Consequently I experienced loss, as did most of the country. I am firmly convinced that God sent an angel to advise me, and I did not listen.

SONS OF GOD

Angels are also called "sons of God." This title is primarily used in the Old Testament, and it speaks of their relationship with God the Father. "Again there was a day when the sons of God came to present themselves before the LORD" (Job 2:1, MEV).

Angels are the "unbegotten" sons of God, while Jesus is the "only" begotten Son of God (John 3:16). Those of us who are Christians are now also "sons of God." "Beloved, now we are the sons of God" (1 John 3:1). God is Father to us all, and we are part of an eternal cosmic family.

CHERUBIM

Some angels are called cherubim; they guard the throne of God upon the earth. It appears, from what we read in Scripture, they accompany God when He manifests Himself on Earth. "He rode on a cherub, and flew; He flew swiftly on the wings of the wind" (Ps. 18:10, MEV).

Cherubim are first mentioned in Genesis 3:24 when they are placed east of Eden to guard the way to the tree of life. This is very interesting because the word *cherubim* comes from an ancient word that means "great, mighty, and gracious to bless!"[1] These are clearly the attributes of God! There at Eden it would seem that these cherubim are hostile to humans in that they guard the way to the tree of life.

On the contrary, they are exhibiting grace, for if Adam ate of that tree, he would be cursed to live in an aging body forever! It was grace that set the cherubim there for us.

I believe Adam and his family brought their offering to the gates of Eden where these cherubim were stationed. Here, a blood sacrifice was offered by our ancient family. It is interesting to see later in Scripture that cherubim of beautiful gold adorned the holy of holies around the bloody mercy seat in the tabernacle and temple. They also adorned the ark of the covenant. These beautiful creatures were a reminder of all that was lost beyond the garden gate and man's need for a Savior.

The real cherubim abode in the tabernacle when the cloud of glory, called the Shechinah, appeared above the mercy seat. Angels guarded the presence of God. When God was not honored, angels were activated to defend God's throne.

> I will meet with you there, and I will meet with you from above the mercy seat, from between the two cherubim which are upon the ark of the testimony. I will speak with you all that I will command you for the children of Israel.

—EXODUS 25:22, MEV These cherubim later appear in the Book of Ezekiel, chapter 10, where they are described as having four faces, wings, and wheels as a means of conveyance. This would seem to go along with the idea of God's chariot drivers transporting God's throne on the earth!

Later these same beings are observed in Revelation 4 and are called "living ones," in English, and in Greek, *zoon*, from which we get our English word *zoo*. Cherubim are angelic forces related to the planet Earth and its creative order. The four faces exhibit this truth as the number four traditionally represents the earth in early times.

In the next chapter, I will discuss Lucifer, who was the chief cherub, how he became Satan, and how that affects Earth.

SERAPHIM

Some of the heavenly beings are called seraphim. This is only found in Isaiah 6 when the great prophet had his transforming vision. Isaiah's king and cousin, Uzziah, had died, and the prophet went into the forbidden holy of holies! In his grief, he needed a word from God even if he died in His presence. Upon entering the holy of holies, Isaiah saw the Lord high and lifted up in majesty and glory! In this place, seraphim worshipped God crying, "Holy, holy, holy." As Isaiah looked upon this scene, he was provoked to confess his own unworthiness. A seraph brought a coal of fire from the altar where the blood sacrifice burned and placed it upon the prophet's lips, cleansing him and redirecting his life.

Seraphim means "burning ones"; it would appear there is a direct link between these angels and the manifest presence of God. These are the beings that set our hearts on fire for God's holiness, His presence, and His power! (See Isaiah 6:1–7.)

MICHAEL

Michael, whose name means "who is like God," is mentioned in both the Old and New Testaments, where we discover he is the commander and chief of the angelic armies related to Earth. In the Book of Daniel, it is Michael who came to the aid of the angel who was warring against the demonic prince of Persia for two weeks in order to answer Daniel's prayers. (See Daniel 10:13.) Michael is also found in Revelation 12:7 at the end of the age as the one who casts Satan and the fallen angels out of the heavenlies. In today's vernacular, Michael would be known as the secretary of war!

GABRIEL

This mighty angel shows up to answer prayer, interpret dreams, and release the word of God. If Michael is secretary of war, then Gabriel is vice president of communications. He interpreted dreams for Daniel on two separate occasions. Gabriel also brought the word to Mary that even though she was a virgin, she would bear a child, Jesus, the Son of God. Gabriel said of himself that he "stands in the presence of God" (Luke 1:19, MEV). This indicates that, along with Michael, Gabriel is the highest rank of angelic authority.

Could this angel have a special assignment to watch over salvation? In Isaiah 63:9 we read, "In all their affliction He was afflicted, and the angel of His presence saved them" (MEV). Some believe the angel of His presence is the preincarnate Christ; clearly this angel is not but is Gabriel.

ANGEL OF THE LORD

The term "angel of the Lord" is mentioned sixty-three times in Scripture. Like the angel of His presence, many believe this angel is the preincarnate Christ. This is impossible as this angel also appears twelve times in the New Testament. This angel and the angel of His presence could possibly be the same being. This angel carries an awesome anointing, so much so that God's presence is recognized then worshipped whenever this angel appears. This leads me to believe this angel is God's accompanying angel.

The angel of the Lord has mighty power. He knows and operates for the people who dwell in the presence of God. It was this angel that stayed the hand of Abraham from killing Isaac...that stretched his sword over Jerusalem, causing its destruction in David's day...that killed 185,000 of the Assyrian army in one night...that ordered the watching angels to do surveillance of the whole earth in Zechariah. Also we see the angel of the Lord directed the heavenly choir over the shepherds' field in Bethlehem, appeared to Joseph and Mary to guide them to safety in Egypt, and struck Peter to awaken him and lead him out of prison.

PRINCIPALITIES, POWERS, THRONES, AND DOMINIONS

These are titles of angels who rank over regions, nations, cities, and communities. These can be either good or evil beings. There is a struggle in the invisible realm, known as the heavenlies, between angels of light and those of darkness. This struggle is affected by our prayers. In a later chapter we will say more about the fallen angels. Angels are organized into ranks and operate in a military fashion. Also, all angels have names, distinct personalities, and specific assignments.

As the church comes to the end of herself and realizes the impossibility of her task, the threat of demonic terror, and the rising opposition of a secular society, she will engage the supernatural resources available from God. The church will discover an open heaven, and the hosts, the angelic armies, will come to our aid!

Billy Graham has said, "Angels belong to a uniquely different dimension of creation that we, limited to the natural order, can scarcely comprehend. In this angelic domain the limitations are different from those God has imposed on our natural order. He has given angels higher knowledge, power, and mobility than we; they are God's messengers whose chief business is to carry out His orders in the world. He has given them an ambassadorial charge. He has designated and empowered them as holy deputies to perform works of righteousness. In this way they assist Him as their creator while His sovereignty controls the universe. So He has given them the capacity to bring His holy enterprises to a successful conclusion."[2]

Let us get to know these friends and allies so we may enlist their aid in the great mission to which we are called. Angels are waiting for our call.

Chapter Five

THE APPEARANCE OF ANGELS

I N 1994 OUR CHURCH BEGAN EXPERIENCING AN OUTBREAK OF angelic sightings. This continues today. Angels walked into a youth gathering one Wednesday night. They were described as ten- to twelve-foot-tall beings glowing in amber and white.

In our previous sanctuary, on two occasions angels exploded balls of fire in the sanctuary that were both visible and loud. On one of these occasions, it was directly over my head, occurring as I rebuked demonic forces. On the other occasion, a layman, whose teenagers were on drugs, took authority over the enemy in our pulpit, and again angelic fire was manifested. This happened in Scripture to Manoah in the Book of Judges, chapter 13, as the angel of the Lord ascended in the fire!

Later, there appeared two angels on the platform who have now moved into our new sanctuary with us. Both stand slightly behind me and to my right hand. One is a towering figure who stands almost the height of the building; the other is smaller and stands nearer and is known as our "joy angel." On many occasions, those who also stand to my right may find themselves tickled or laughing for no apparent reason; this has happened to me dozens of times. Although these angels are not visible to everyone, those who see in the spiritual realm have observed them. Even those who cannot see them have experienced their ministry. Jennie Griesemer had such an experience; I will let her tell you in her own words.

Although more than fifteen years have passed, the memory is still strong and clear in my mind of the day I "saw" an angel.

Morgan and Kayla were both just toddlers, buckled securely in their car seats behind me. It was our errand day, and I was diligently completing my tasks. Our next stop was to deliver some products from my small direct sales business to a new customer who lived in Grant Estates off Dietz Road in Ringgold, Georgia, where we lived at the time. She had instructed me to leave the products on her front porch and for no reason was I to go into the fenced backyard. "We have a Chow dog back there who is very vicious. He has even bitten family members," she warned, "so just leave the order by the front door. It will be fine."

I drove into the subdivision and up a steep ridge to a secluded cul-de-sac where my customer's home stood alone surrounded by woods. After parking in the driveway, I grabbed the box of products, headed up the sidewalk, up the front stairs, and onto the front porch where I deposited my load by the front door. Turning to leave, I froze in panic at the top of the stairs, for at the bottom of the steps stood that Chow dog, teeth bared, growling viciously, and poised to attack. Fear swept over me, but I was not unprepared for this moment. God had me on a journey, and it was time for an object lesson.

"No temptation has overtaken you except such as is common to man; but God is faithful, who will not allow you to be tempted beyond what you are able, but with the temptation will also make the way of escape, that you may be able to bear it" (1 Cor. 10:13).

Through the Bible teaching of a man named Kenneth Copeland, God had been instructing me in the nature of fear and faith. I had come to understand that fear is the same spiritual force as faith, but moving in reverse gear. Whereas faith is produced by hearing the Word of God, fear comes by hearing and believing wrong things. Fear is a twisted form of faith; it is faith in the enemy's ability to harm. No wonder Jesus instructed repeatedly, "Fear not." Fear and faith are mutually exclusive and, like forward and reverse gear, cannot operate in the same heart at the same time.

Like a big red flag, the awareness of fear reminded me that I must not yield to it. By the grace of God, I declared aloud, "I WILL NOT FEAR!" As quickly as the force had swept over me, it retreated. With a clear mind now, I responded with faith in the Word of God in my heart (Ps. 91:9–11; 103:20; Heb. 1:14). I spoke aloud what God in His mercy had abundantly stored up in my heart over the preceding weeks and months of training: "Angels, I charge you in the name of Jesus to move this dog down the sidewalk, put him back in his fence, and let me pass safely back to my car."

Suddenly, the fierce eyes of that animal, which until that moment had been intensely fixed on me, popped open. I saw a stunned look in his eyes. Then his head was pressed down to the sidewalk as if an invisible hand had taken hold of his neck. He responded with a growl of futile resistance as the invisible hand turned him 90 degrees to face down the sidewalk. As the invisible hand dragged him, the dog growled and pulled against the force that moved him away from me. I followed behind the animal, pointing the way, thanking God for His angel of protection. "Thank You, God, for Your angels. Thank You for hearkening to my voice. Keep going, now. Put him in that back fence..."

At the end of the sidewalk, the captive dog turned left toward the back gate, and I turned right to get into my car. Safely inside the car, the adrenaline that had pumped through me left me a bit weak, and I began to tremble. I had seen an angel. I couldn't tell you what he looked like, but I saw him. Like the wind when it unfurls a flag, I saw the angel by the force of his action on that dog. Indeed, angels are "ministering spirits sent forth to minister for those who will inherit salvation" (Heb. 1:14).

As we look through Scripture and history, angels appeared in many different ways. Angels are not all alike in their appearance and function. In Scripture, angels often took on the appearance of men. Some angels have wings; others do not. Angels seem to be able to assume whatever shape is necessary to perform their function. Angels often act as we do—eating and drinking, talking and singing. Yet they appear as wind or fire; they also appear as spirits.

Angels are spirit beings.

Angels seem to have a spiritual body suited for the heavenly dimension. A spiritual body is not subject to the limitations of our earth suits or bodies. First Corinthians 15:44 says, "It is sown a natural body, it is raised a spiritual body. There is a natural body, and there is a spiritual body" (MEV).

Our bodies as they are cannot access the spiritual dimensions.

Angels and demons can pass through what we call solid objects and are not limited to our space and time.

It would appear the angels operate in a spiritual body not subject to the laws of nature in our four-dimensional realm. Our bodies in the afterlife will be like the angels: "For in the resurrection they neither marry nor are given in marriage, but are like angels of God in heaven" (Matt. 22:30, MEV).

Angels are soldiers.

As we have observed, angels are called "hosts" more than any other title given to them. The word for "hosts" is translated by some as "angel armies." Angels have access to weapons in the spiritual realm. As we have already observed, angels are mighty soldiers in the heavenly realm. Recall in Daniel chapter 10 that Daniel saw and heard the words of the angel after three weeks of fasting and prayer. The appearance of the angel was "clothed in linen, whose loins were girded with the fine gold.... His body also was like beryl, and his face had the appearance of lightning, and his eyes were like lamps of fire, and his arms and his feet were like the gleam of polished bronze, and the sound of his words like the sound of a tumult" (Dan. 10:5–6, MEV). Daniel alone saw, described, and heard the declaration of the angel. The angel had been hindered by the prince of Persia. The battle between the two had waxed strong and delayed the angel from coming to Daniel. It was only when Michael the archangel came to assist and fight with the enemy that Daniel could hear the heavenly message.

In this passage the curtain is lifted momentarily to reveal the heavenly battles that angels, demons, and believers are engaged in. Not only did the angel fight in the heavens for Daniel, but he also then comforted, reassured, strengthened, and instructed Daniel on the end times.

Angels are mighty in battle and take up the cause of believers and of Israel. The battle is the Lord's, and it rages in the invisible realms.

Angels operate in the supernatural realm.

Paul describes angels as "mighty" in 2 Thessalonians.

> ...and to give you who are troubled rest with us when the Lord Jesus is revealed from heaven with His mighty angels.
>
> —2 THESSALONIANS 1:7, MEV

When translated from the Greek, this word *mighty* is *dunamis*, which means "innate supernatural power." These mighty angels, by their very nature, are miracle-working beings full of God-given power and might. Angels are agents of miracles and the supernatural power of God even in our day!

Angels are swift in their movements.

On closer observation angels seem to move at the speed of thought; sometimes they move so quickly they simply "appear" on the scene. They are not limited by our time or history as they soar through our atmosphere and the solar system; they are truly the ultimate UFOs.

> Then I saw another angel flying in the midst of heaven, having the eternal gospel to preach to those who dwell on the earth, to every nation and tribe and tongue and people.
> —REVELATION 14:6, MEV

Man envies the angels, for we long to fly! From the Wright brothers' first attempts to the emerging technology that enables us to live in space, man has a compulsion to explore beyond the confines of our four dimensions as the angels do. Neil Armstrong, commander of the Apollo flight that put the first man on the moon, said, "Pilots take no special joy in walking. Pilots like flying."[1] We all, whether given opportunity or limited by life's circumstances, long to soar in that heavenly dimension. One day we will fly with the heavenly hosts.

Angels are strong.

Angels appear as strong, tireless creatures who, as we read in Revelation 4:8, do not rest day or night from their worship. Angels have an anointing of strength that flows in the atmosphere of worship; unlike us, they do not tire in war, worship, or ministry.

Angels are systematic.

Angels do not deviate from order or rank. They operate according to the commands of God, knowing their purpose and ministry as they remain faithful in the execution of these duties. There is no doubt that you may have trafficked with angels. You may not have recognized them, as many times they take on human form and cannot be distinguished from humans, but they were in your company.

Chapter Six

THE CONFLICT OF ANGELS

I N THE MONUMENTAL WORK *EARTH'S EARLIEST AGES*, G. H. Pember declared that there was a primeval earth that experienced colossal catastrophe.[1] Pember convincingly proves that something happened between Genesis 1:1 and Genesis 1:2 that made the earth "without form, and void." In Isaiah 45:12, Isaiah declares that God did not make the earth "without form, and void." What occurred on Earth before the planting of the Garden of Eden? Could there have been a world in which a cherub named Lucifer ruled and covered the earth from a land called Eden? In the prophetic lamentation to the king of Tyre, God speaks through Ezekiel to describe this ancient world and its anointed leader, the angel Lucifer.

Ezekiel 28 takes us back, beyond our history, to a land of Eden prior to the garden. Lucifer is described as "the seal of perfection, full of wisdom and perfect in beauty" (v. 12). Furthermore, we are told, while still perfect, he ruled over a land called Eden. "You were in Eden, the garden of God" (v. 13). In that garden, this angel king was covered in great wealth and also surrounded by a vast amount of musical instruments. In fact, Lucifer was created to be the covering of God's new planet, Earth. "You were the anointed cherub who covers; I established you; you were on the holy mountain of God; you walked back and forth in the midst of fiery stones" (v. 14). Here was a creature created perfect by God to rule over the primeval earth, to lead its creatures in worship, and to release the creative resources of God from the fiery stones to all on Earth. Lucifer was anointed for that high purpose, yet Lucifer committed iniquity even though he was created perfect. "You were perfect in your ways from the day you were created, till iniquity was found in you" (v. 15). This word *iniquity* means "to twist or pervert." Lucifer began to crave the worship for himself! God cast Lucifer out of his leadership role: "Therefore I cast you…out of the mountain of God; and I destroyed you, O covering cherub, from the midst of the fiery stones" (v. 16). God cast Lucifer out because of pride: "Your heart was lifted up" (v. 17).

Isaiah confirmed this prophetic word, giving us another account of this momentous event. "How you are fallen from heaven, O Lucifer, son of the morning!" (Isa. 14:12, MEV).

Lucifer's fall took place in the ancient Eden. When he fell, the old earth was destroyed as if an asteroid had hit! All life was abolished, and the earth became without form and void. In that rebellion one-third of the angelic hosts fell with him.

> Then another sign appeared in heaven: There was a great red dragon with seven heads and ten horns, and seven diadems on his heads. His tail drew a third of the stars of heaven, and threw them to the earth. The dragon stood before the woman who was ready to give birth, to devour her Child as soon as He was born.
> —REVELATION 12:3–4, MEV

Notice that these angels fell to the earth; this was a part of that ancient catastrophe. Lucifer became Satan, the archenemy of God and His purpose for man! Satan desires the Creator's position, pre-eminence, people, and power. He wants to sit on "the mount of the congregation" (Isa. 14:13, MEV). Satan and the fallen angels desire to dominate the worship of the people of God!

GOD'S PLAN IS MAN

God came again to the ruined planet, made it habitable, and planted a garden in the same place—Eden. He then created man, but lurking in that garden was a serpent possessed by Satan. A new king of the earth had come, and Satan came to usurp man's position. Adam and Eve fell, and consequently, all humanity fell, leaving fallen humanity and hosts of demons to inhabit this earthly dimension.

As the second Adam, Jesus Christ would die and be raised from the dead in order to defeat Satan and the fallen angels and also to redeem fallen humanity. God would create a new humanity in Christ.

THE CHARACTERISTICS OF THE ENEMY OF GOD'S PLAN

Though the battle has been won, we still face the dark forces of Satan until the end of the age. Notice the characteristics of these dark forces:

Demonic features

The Bible speaks of these fallen angels as sinners. These created beings were involved in wars and conspiracies against the Most High: "For if God did not spare the angels that sinned, but cast them down to hell and delivered them into chains of darkness to be kept for judgment..." (2 Pet. 2:4, MEV).

They are all rebels by nature. They are evil and fierce. These unholy angels exhibit wickedness, iniquities, and unlawful deeds under the angel of darkness. Psalm 78:49 says, "He cast on them the fierceness of His anger, wrath, indignation, and trouble, by sending angels of destruction among them."

Demonic function

Demons are organized into ranks called principalities, powers, rulers of darkness, and spiritual forces of wickedness. These powers are associated with demonic possession and witchcraft as they influence human beings. Even in Shakespeare's *Macbeth*, Lady Macbeth invoked the powers of evil, the "murdering ministers" and "sightless substances" that "wait on nature's mischief."[2] Scripture reveals their nature this way.

> For our fight is not against flesh and blood, but against principalities, against powers, against the rulers of the darkness of this world, and against spiritual forces of evil in the heavenly places.
> —EPHESIANS 6:12, MEV

Demons live to thwart Christians from fulfilling their purpose. Operating in stealth, they secretly seek to subvert the will of God. In 1 Timothy 4:1, these evil ones are called deceitful and seducing spirits as well as the spirits of error: "Now the Spirit expressly says that in latter times some will depart from the faith, giving heed to deceiving spirits and doctrines of demons."

"And no wonder! For even Satan disguises himself as an angel of light" (2 Cor. 11:14, MEV).

They operate in deception particularly where truth is rejected. By doing this, demons work destruction on the earth and cause grave trouble by manipulation.

Demonic forces already bound

Some ranks of fallen angels were so vile God has bound them in chains of darkness.

> Now it came to pass, when men began to multiply on the face of the earth, and daughters were born to them, that the sons of God saw the daughters of men, that they were beautiful; and they took wives for themselves of all whom they chose. And the LORD said, "My Spirit shall not strive with man forever, for he is indeed flesh; yet his days shall be one hundred and twenty years." There were giants on the earth in those days, and also afterward, when the sons of God came in to the daughters of men and they bore children to them. Those were the mighty men who were of old, men of renown.
>
> —GENESIS 6:1–4

Some demons cohabitated with women, and the offspring of the union created giants on the earth. These giants could be the source of the so-called gods of mythology of the ancient world. In the New Testament they are called "the angels that sinned" (2 Pet. 2:4, MEV).

These angels left their own house, took up residence in human hosts, and bred a hybrid race of wicked, vile humans.

Christ's preaching to them

Peter speaks of Christ preaching to "the spirits in prison." Here Jesus Christ came during the three days He was absent from Earth after His crucifixion and prior to His resurrection.

> By whom He also went and preached to the spirits in prison, who in times past were disobedient, when God waited patiently in the

days of Noah while the ark was being prepared, in which a few, that is, eight souls, were saved through water.

—1 PETER 3:19–20, MEV

We know that these certain demons were confined by God. Though the word *preach* is used in the passage, it is not *evangelion*, which means "to preach the gospel," but *kerusso* in Greek, which means "to proclaim or announce." This passage is directed to demons. There is no gospel preached to men after death. "As it is appointed for men to die once, but after this comes the judgment" (Heb. 9:27, MEV).

Furthermore, there is no special prison for humans who sinned in Noah's day. Jesus Christ died and descended into Hades. He dropped off the dying thief in paradise and went to the place of torments. He announced His victory to these confined demons: "…who has gone into heaven and is at the right hand of God, with angels and authorities and powers being made subject to Him" (1 Pet. 3:22, MEV).

In the realm of eternity the enemy's most powerful demons were totally humiliated: "Having disarmed authorities and powers, He made a show of them openly, triumphing over them by the cross" (Col. 2:15, MEV).

Jesus, at His ascension, emptied paradise of the Old Testament saints and sealed up hell with its wicked forces.

Angels and demons

The good news for all of us is that there are two angels for every demon. They are often referred to as the angel armies. These faithful allies have been battle-tested and proven in the timeless ages of the past. Today angels stand with us to enforce the victory of the Son of God, while our defeated enemy is subject to all who believe in Christ. God will one day restore our planet, and a new Eden will be ours where together with the angels of glory we will glorify our Father and His Son, Jesus Christ!

HOW ANGELS
OPERATE

Chapter Seven

WORSHIP—ANGELS AROUND THE THRONE

O N MY FIRST MISSION TRIP TO HUEHUETENANGO, GUATEMALA, I experienced angelic accompaniment in worship. Hundreds of us were gathered in the convention center and had been worshipping through music and singing for forty-five minutes when I noticed round orbs of light moving overhead. I also heard sounds in addition to our voices and instruments that were angelic in nature. In those moments I was lifted into a deep intimacy with God; I began to cry, "Holy," and weep.

Angels are first and foremost worshippers of the living God! They were created to worship, as were we! Perhaps the oldest narrative in all of Scripture is the Book of Job. In God's rebuke of Job, we catch a glimpse of the ancient past.

> Where were you when I laid the foundations of the earth? Tell Me, if you have understanding. Who determined its measurements? Surely you know! Or who stretched the line upon it? To what were its foundations fastened? Or who laid its cornerstone, when the morning stars sang together, and all the sons of God shouted for joy?
>
> —JOB 38:4–7

Angels shouted as God the Father brought His creation into being. They were not silent observers of the great works of the Father; they responded with singing and shouting as His mighty power stretched into the vast universe.

Scripture enthusiastically accounts angels blessing and worshipping

God our Father: "Bless the LORD, you His angels, who are mighty, and do His commands, and obey the voice of His word" (Ps. 103:20, MEV).

Angels are watching activities in the life of the church. First Timothy 5:21 lets us know that they will not operate when we violate what the Holy Spirit has charged us to do: "I charge you before God and the Lord Jesus Christ and the elect angels that you observe these things without prejudice, doing nothing with partiality."

CHURCH GATHERING AT THE END OF THE AGE

As we move toward the end of the age, angelic appearances will become more frequent. In Hebrews, there is a biblical picture of church gatherings that most of us have missed. I am convinced this describes worship shortly before Jesus comes to claim the church at the end. In our worship, the dimension of glory—the heavenlies—breaks through and commingles with us. Could it be that the scene described in Hebrews 12 is a picture of the church gathered on Earth rather than heaven?

> But you have come to Mount Zion and to the city of the living God, the heavenly Jerusalem, and to an innumerable company of angels; to the general assembly and church of the firstborn, who are enrolled in heaven; to God, the Judge of all; and to the spirits of the righteous ones made perfect; and to Jesus, the Mediator of a new covenant; and to the sprinkled blood that speaks better than that of Abel.
>
> —HEBREWS 12:22–24, MEV

True worship brings "the heavenly Jerusalem" to our gatherings. We are gathering with an "innumerable company of angels."

Note the following truths. First, the church will not be afraid of the manifest presence of God. When you read the record of Moses in Exodus 19, essentially the Israelites were afraid of God's presence. They had seen His mighty judgment on Egypt, and fear took hold of them. Many people today are afraid of God's powerful, glorious presence.

> So on the third day, in the morning, there was thunder and lightning, and a thick cloud on the mountain, and the sound of an exceedingly loud trumpet. All the people who were in the camp trembled. Then Moses brought the people out of the camp to meet

with God, and they stood at the foot of the mountain. Now Mount
Sinai was completely covered in smoke because the Lord had
descended upon it in fire, and the smoke ascended like the smoke
of a furnace, and the whole mountain shook violently. When the
sound of the trumpet grew louder and louder, Moses spoke, and
God answered him with a voice.

—Exodus 19:16–19, MEV

God came down, but the people would not draw near. Notice it was
the third day! This event was celebrated at the Feast of Pentecost. At
this encounter they received the law but missed God's presence. They
told Moses in essence, "Don't ever do this again!"

Another "third day" came fourteen hundred years later. As prophesied, on this third day Jesus rose from the dead. At the Feast of
Pentecost, forty days later, God's power shook the earth again. This
time the Spirit's manifestations were welcomed by the early church.
Unfortunately many in the church today are afraid of God's presence.

Look at this passage from Hebrews again and see what the end-
time church gathering should look like: "But you have come to Mount
Zion and to the city of the living God, the heavenly Jerusalem, to an
innumerable company of angels" (Heb. 12:22, MEV). Seven points are
identified in Hebrews 12:22–27 that show us what the end-time church
gatherings will look like. They are:

1. Angels gather with the kingdom church to give glory
   to God.

2. Intensified worship: Mount Zion was where David
   placed a choir and orchestra for thirty-three years, the
   length of Jesus's life on Earth. Their praise was offered
   continually. When the end-time church gathers, praise
   and worship go to the next level.

3. Innumerable angels join in the worship; in fact, there
   will be too many angels to count!

4. Worship breaking through to the other dimension and
   heaven kissing the church: The separation between the
   spiritual realm and this world are blurred and breached

in the kingdom church: "To the general assembly and church of the firstborn, who are enrolled in heaven; to God, the Judge of all; and to the spirits of the righteous ones made perfect" (Heb. 12:23, MEV).

5. God speaking a fresh word about the last days through the prophetic ministry: Angelic assistance will release the prophetic word to the end-time church. The kingdom church will experience direct revelation from heaven's mercy seat. Angels will watch over that word and release it through the church: "See that you do not refuse Him who is speaking. For if they did not escape when they refused Him who spoke on earth, much less shall we escape if we turn away from Him who speaks from heaven" (Heb. 12:25, MEV).

6. The church shaken to its foundations so that everything unnecessary is taken away: "Whose voice then shook the earth; but now He has promised, saying, 'Yet once more I shake not only the earth, but also heaven.' Now this, 'Yet once more,' indicates the removal of those things that are being shaken, as of things that are made, that the things which cannot be shaken may remain" (Heb. 12:26–27).

7. The church receives kingdom truth and releases kingdom power to evangelize the end-time world.

Notice that all of this happens with the presence and assistance of an "innumerable company of angels." Understand this: we should expect and embrace more angelic contact in the last days. A shaking has already begun, and angel sightings are taking place where the kingdom is breaking through.

This should not surprise us since angels are always observed near the Old Testament temple worshipping continually. Since our bodies are the temples of the Holy Spirit, our hearts become the holy of holies when we enter into intimate worship. Angels are drawn to passionate worship. When we come together in the church assembly, we should be cognizant that these glorious beings who are older than time are gathering with us. They are still giving God all their worship! What angels did at the beginning they are still practicing eons later at the end of the age. They are praising God the Father and His Son, the Lord Jesus Christ. John describes a heavenly scene in Revelation 5 where he saw and heard the voice of many angels, living creatures, and the elders worshipping around the throne. In verse 11 he indicates this massive assembly was "ten thousand times ten thousand, and thousands of thousands" (MEV). They worshipped with a loud voice.

As John Paul Jackson describes the scene in his book *7 Days Behind the Veil*, "The reason all Heaven keeps repeating, 'Holy, holy, holy,' is not because that's just what they do up there, strumming along with their little golden harps. 'Holy!' is a witness to what God has just done. Every time God acts, the act is holy, and so the angels and every other heavenly creature bear witness to that holy act and cry out 'Holy!'"[1]

As allies with the angels, we cannot remain silent as we experience the mighty works of God. We too must shout His praises, for He is worthy. If the angels, who are not recipients of the saving grace of Jesus Christ, never stop worshipping, how much more should we hasten to give Him all our praise!

Chapter Eight

DESTINY—ANGELS AMONG THE NATIONS

OUR LORD JESUS CHRIST WARNED THAT IN THE LAST DAYS there would be "wars and rumors of wars." He also encouraged believers not to be afraid. He then said, "Nation will rise against nation, and kingdom against kingdom" (Matt. 24:6–7, MEV). Among the nations and kingdoms of the earth there will always be conflict. Hidden in these words of Jesus is the war between the dark forces of Satan and the angelic armies of Jesus.

As we move toward the end of the age, the sounds of war are being heard across our planet. Dark forces are drawing strength from false religions and are following demonic leadership toward the final conflagration on Earth. All roads lead toward the valley below the mountain of Megiddo, the place called Armageddon!

Islamic militants are receiving visits from the dark side instructing them in acts of terror, preparing for an all-out assault on the Jews and the nation of Israel. America and her allies are at war in the Middle East now and are searching for strategies to obstruct the purposes of darkness. As chaotic as the conflicts are on Earth, above the atmosphere of our planet, larger wars are raging. Here, our authentic allies, the angels, can and must be trusted. Daniel reveals the pattern of angelic operation among the nations.

Above every nation, Satan has assigned a "principality," and under that demon, "hosts of wickedness." Scripture affirms that there are evil demonic spirits over territories. Daniel rips the secrecy off this fact in his prophecy found in Daniel 10. Daniel had been fasting and mourning over captive Israel for three weeks. During that time of intense spiritual focus and physical deprivation Daniel received an angelic visit. That vision gives us some idea of what angels look like.

> On the twenty-fourth day of the first month, as I was by the side
> of the great river which is Tigris, I lifted up my eyes and looked
> and saw a certain man clothed in linen, whose loins were girded
> with the fine gold of Uphaz. His body also was like beryl, and his
> face had the appearance of lightning, and his eyes were like lamps
> of fire, and his arms and his feet were like the gleam of polished
> bronze, and the sound of his words like the sound of a tumult.
> —DANIEL 10:4–6, MEV

This strong angel was brighter than lightning, glistening as fine
jewels, and glowing as polished bronze. His words were as majestic as a
waterfall. Daniel was the only one who saw the vision, however; as this
magnificent scene unfolded, the men who were with him ran and hid
in terror. They could sense the supernatural presence. Daniel was himself slain in the Spirit with his face to the ground as the angel spoke.
The power of this supernatural encounter left him with no power in
his flesh. He tells us that "suddenly, a hand touched me, which made
me tremble on my knees and on the palms of my hands" (Dan. 10:10).

When the angel touched Daniel, he gained strength enough to get
on all fours, in a reverential position, bowing down. His whole body
trembled at the experience.

> He said to me, "O Daniel, man greatly beloved, understand the
> words that I speak to you, and stand upright, for I have been sent
> to you now." And when he had spoken this word to me, I stood
> trembling. Then he said to me, "Do not be afraid, Daniel. For
> from the first day that you set your heart to understand this and
> to humble yourself before your God, your words were heard, and
> I have come because of your words. But the prince of the kingdom
> of Persia withstood me for twenty-one days. So Michael, one of
> the chief princes, came to help me, for I had been left there with
> the kings of Persia. Now I have come to make you understand
> what shall befall your people in the latter days. For the vision is
> yet for many days."
> —DANIEL 10:11–14, MEV

Daniel stood trembling to receive the prophetic word from the angel.
In the middle of this prophecy about "the latter days," the angel spoke
of warring with a territorial spirit called "the prince of the kingdom

of Persia." This demon was so strong that the archangel Michael was summoned by God to rescue and release the message.

Here we get a glimpse of the invisible war in the heavenly dimension. Intense warfare erupted in the heavenlies because one man with a prophetic calling prayed and fasted. However, this demonic opposition resulted in a three-week delay in answer to the prayer of Daniel. Note also that the struggle in this prophecy was about Israel in the latter days! "Now I have come to make you understand what will happen to your people in the latter days, for the vision refers to many days yet to come" (Dan. 10:14, MEV).

It is a fact that we are living witnesses to that struggle. That same demon of Persia is threatening Israel today. Behind every earthly conflict is demonic influence. "The prince of Greece" is also mentioned in this chapter: "Then he said, 'Do you understand why I have come to you? But now I shall return to fight against the prince of Persia, and when I have gone forth, then truly the prince of Greece will come'" (Dan. 10:20, MEV).

This is not simply a reference to the land of Greece. The spirit of Persia is the force behind Islam today, and this is a visible enemy that we battle alongside our angelic allies. The prince of Greece represents Greek philosophy that has captured and governs Western thought. Rationalism that denies the supernatural has taken over our educational system. Churches that deny the Holy Spirit's power have bowed to this "prince of Greece."

This two-pronged enemy is arrayed against the Spirit-filled church today. The prince of Greece bows to the mind of man while the prince of Persia bows to a demon god. Can you see that the world conflict has clandestine operations going on in the spiritual realm? The prince, or spirit, of Greece (which is represented in the architecture of our government buildings in Washington, DC) cannot defeat the Persian spirit. The church must rise to take down these spirits.

EXAMPLES OF ANGELIC INFLUENCE IN GOVERNMENT

There is a remarkable story in the Book of Judges when an angel comes to Manoah during a season of distress for the nation of Israel. God had allowed the Philistines to enslave the nation because they had done wrong. The angel came to prophesy the birth of Samson. Now Manoah's wife had been barren. This angel revealed his name to be "wonderful" (Judg. 13:18). "Wonderful" comes from the Hebrew word *pala*, which means wonder worker or miracle worker. This angel called "wonderful" announced to Manoah and his barren wife that they would have a son named Samson who would deliver his nation from forty years of bondage! On a later occasion angels prophesied the death of Ahaziah through Elijah. Here was a regime-changing action initiated by angels. In this compelling story angels kill two captains of fifty with all their soldiers. The third captain begs for mercy, and a fearless Elijah issues the verdict of death to the wicked king. (See 2 Kings 1:1–17.)

In the New Testament an angel struck and killed King Herod when he tried to take God's glory for himself. Here again a national leader falls at the hand of an angel. In a later chapter you will see the increase of angelic operations among the nations at the end of the age. Angelic agents operate clandestinely among the nations of the earth. In a constant war with their demonic counterparts, angels affect the destiny of national and international governments.

Chuck Ripka, international banker, entrepreneur, marketplace minister, and author of *God Out of the Box*, shares a story about how he and the ministers of Elk River, Minnesota, were assisted by angels when the destiny of their state needed to be changed. As an ambassador of the kingdom, Chuck had received a specific word from God about the plans He had for bringing a revival to Minnesota. However, there were spiritual bondages that needed to be broken within the state legislature, so God sent them right to the source—the state capitol building—to begin the work through prayer. Chuck says:

> When we were ready to step into the capitol, I sensed a strong demonic presence. I prayed, "Lord, would You please send warring angels to go into the capitol before us?"
>
> Incredibly, I immediately saw two angels before me, each twenty feet tall. One had a sword, and the other had a huge hammer or mallet. They walked inside and caught a demon that looked like a Pan god from Greek mythology. It was half man and half animal. The angels bound the demon's hands, laid it on a block of granite, and then crushed its skull with the hammer.
>
> As its head was being crushed, the hand of the demon opened up. A gold key fell to the ground.

The Lord said to me, "Now, with this key, no door will be locked to you."

We stepped inside...[and] the Lord began revealing to me what He wanted done that evening. "My heart grieves because there has been a separation between church and state," He said. "But My heart grieves even more because there has been a separation between church and church."[1]

Chuck and this group of ministers proceeded to pray and repent for the sins the state and its constituents committed between racial groups, young against the old, and more. There was such a spirit of love and repentance in this meeting all because Chuck activated his authority and called on the angels of God to fight back the enemy and his attempts to cancel the movement of God in their state. Chuck reports that their "prayers and confessions had made a difference...The atmosphere had changed. There was a new spirit of cooperation within the walls of the capitol. By following God's leading, we were able to help reconcile church and state *and* church and church."[2]

By understanding how angels interact with government in the spiritual realm, the believer's alliance with the angels becomes more important. The believer's worship, prayer, and witness can turn the tide in national and international struggle as demonstrated in Chuck's story. Had it not been for the release of those warring angels, he and his ministry team would have been up against enormous opposition to carry out God's plan for revival in Minnesota.

In many respects, the church is viewed as a colony of the kingdom of heaven. Our role is to be ambassadors of the kingdom here on Earth. While loyal to our earthly nation and heritage, we must confess that we have a citizenship elsewhere. (See Philippians 3:20.) This concept elevates the gatherings of the people of God to cosmic and eternal importance. Jesus taught us to pray, "Your kingdom come...on earth" (Matt. 6:10, MEV). In alliance with the triune God, His decrees, and the holy angels, we are a part of a destiny-changing enterprise.

Chapter Nine

PROTECTION—ANGELS ON DEFENSE

Psalm 34:7 says, "The angel of the Lord camps around those who fear Him, and delivers them" (MEV). And in Psalm 91:11 we read, "For He shall give His angels charge over you, to guard you in all your ways" (MEV). God's angels guard and rescue all who reverence Him. The truth of this verse was made known in the life of the late Bill Bright, head of Campus Crusade for Christ, several years ago. His travels took him from continent to continent each year. He traveled in all kinds of circumstances and often faced danger. But he says that there was always peace in his heart that the Lord was with him. He knew he was surrounded by His guardian angels to protect him.

In Pakistan, during a time of great political upheaval, he had finished a series of meetings in Lahore and was taken to the train station. Though he was unaware of what was happening, an angry crowd of thousands was marching on the station to destroy it with cocktail bombs.

The director of the railway line rushed everyone onto the train, put each one in his compartment, and told them not to open the doors under any circumstances. The train ride to Karachi would require more than twenty-four hours, which was just the time Bill Bright needed to finish rewriting his book *Come Help Change the World*.

He recounts that he put on pajamas, reclined in the berth, and began to read and write. When the train arrived in Karachi twenty-eight hours later, he discovered how guardian angels had watched over and protected them all. The train in front of them had been burned when rioting students had lain on the track and refused to move. The train ran over the students. In retaliation, the mob burned the train and killed the officials.

Bill Bright was on the next train, and the rioters were prepared to do the same for that train. God miraculously went before the train and its passengers, and there were no mishaps. They arrived in Karachi to discover that martial law had been declared and all was peaceful. A Red Cross van took them to the hotel, and there God continued to protect them. When the violence subsided, Bill Bright was able to catch a plane for Europe. The scripture is true; God does send His guardian angels to guard and rescue those who reverence Him.[1]

There are angels that desire to release the benefits of the Lord to us. These angels do not bestow the gifts and protection of God, but they desire for us to join the Lord by getting into His presence, the secret place of the Most High. Angels worship in God's presence, and there we find their favor.

In biblical times, devout Jewish men worshipping in the temple wore a covering called a *tallith* or prayer shawl. This shawl was a private covering for the intercessors—a shield to symbolize they were spending intimate time alone with God. The tallith is still worn today.

That is what our secret place is like—a covering. King David wrote, "He who dwells in the secret place of the Most High shall abide under the shadow of the Almighty" (Ps. 91:1). We are to "abide" under the shadow of the Almighty. The word *abide* means "to tarry all night." It speaks of the intimacy of a husband and wife who tarry all night loving each other. When we abide in God's presence, the divine glory covers us, loves us, and hovers protectively over us.

Having entered into this close relationship with Jesus by trust, we become the beneficiaries of divine favor and enjoy protection by the angels.

A PLACE OF PROTECTION

Like a young eagle in its mother's nest, you are safe in His presence. His truth covers and protects you. "He shall cover you with His feathers, and under His wings you shall take refuge; His truth shall be your shield and buckler. You shall not be afraid of the terror by night" (Ps. 91:4–5).

Night terrors are a great problem with many today, children and adults alike. Fears of the dark remain with some youngsters well into their adult lives. Yet the unknown night stalkers of hell have no right when you are in that place of protection. No arrow of the wicked can penetrate the shield of faith and trust that guards the entrance to the secret place. In His presence, the old fears leave. While others may become victims of the enemy, you will be safe because of your close relationship to God.

Some years ago, a demented man approached me after a revival service in another city. He was about to hit me in the parking lot when Eddie Adams, my staff assistant, grabbed the man's arm. With his other hand, Eddie pushed me into the car and faced my attacker for me. That night, Eddie stood between my assailant and me. He was literally my shield!

If we abide in this place of protection, then we have Jesus and His angelic hosts present to step in for us to be our shield and our protection. Read this firsthand account by Mary Beth Barnes.

> I was preparing to go through the Seven Steps to Freedom, a deliverance and counseling ministry, and I found myself very afraid of the enemy. The enemy was telling me he wasn't going to leave me alone, nor was he going to allow me to be free. I knew I had to draw close to God and give Him my fears, or else I wouldn't be free from the hold Satan had on me. As I began to pray and tell God about the fear I had inside, I really entered into His presence. This is the scripture that the Holy Spirit gave me: "Because you have made the LORD, who is my refuge, even the Most High, your dwelling place, no evil shall befall you, nor shall any plague come near your dwelling; for He shall give His angels charge over you, to keep you in all your ways" (Ps. 91:9–11).
>
> As soon as the Holy Spirit ministered this scripture to me, I saw what seemed to be a black "glob" come out of the windows and every portal of my home; it then moved across my front yard and crossed to the other side of the road. When it was on the other side of the road it took on the shape of human-like "shadows," several dark figures.
>
> As I continued to watch these dark figures, suddenly I saw huge figures clothed in white standing about six feet apart all the

way around the property line of my home. They seemed to stand at least ten feet tall with a very broad build and held in their right hands massive flaming swords. As they stood at attention, their focus was on guarding my home and nothing more.

The black shadows tried to force themselves in between each angel but were only allowed to come as far as the angels were standing. It was as if they were hitting a piece of Plexiglas. They had absolutely no power against the authority that the angels were standing in. These angels didn't fight with them, nor did they struggle with the black shadows; they simply stood guard with the flaming swords around my "dwelling place."

On a final note, the Lord has "kept me in all my ways" and propelled me into a fearless life of freedom through the power of His Holy Spirit.

There is a place where neither devil nor disease can disturb our walk or destroy our witness for Jesus. You see, we go because of His strength! We actually carry His dwelling with us! Angels watch over our every step.

Here is another story a man named Al shared about how as a young child he was saved by an angel from certain death. He was born at 4:02 a.m. in Jersey City, New Jersey. His mother and father were on their way to the hospital when they were hit head-on by another car.

His father suffered two broken legs, and his mother was far worse. She was severely injured from the waist down and from the sternum up. She was given her last rites at the scene. Miraculously, she survived, but she spent the next seventeen months in the hospital; Al's grandmother took care of him during that time.

Exactly one year to the day later, baby Al was sleeping in his grandmother's house. It was a beautiful fall evening. The windows were open, and his grandmother had a religious candle burning on a dresser.

The wind kicked up just enough to blow the sheer drapes near the candle flame. The house caught fire, and his nursery was engulfed in flames. The fireman who eventually rescued baby Al could not believe his eyes (according to the fireman and conversations years later). The fireman stated that when he entered the nursery through the smoke and heat, two large angels were crouched over the baby's bed. He said he froze for a moment, and all of a sudden one big angel with a trumpet around his body picked up baby Al and handed the baby to the fireman. Not a scratch was on the baby, and there was no lung damage from smoke inhalation either. Both his birth and his escaping the fire were called miracles of God by the local newspapers and television stations. He is living proof that angels exist and come to a child's aid.[2]

Someone had prayed over baby Al to be protected during all the turmoil surrounding his birth and early childhood. They must have known God's heart for children and that children have angels assigned to assist and protect them. Matthew 18:10 says, "See that you do not despise one of these little ones. For I say to you that in heaven their angels always see the face of My Father who is in heaven" (MEV). This verse shows that angels are assigned to children at birth, yet they watch and wait for God's instruction to assist them. Parents and leaders, like those in Al's life, have authority to invoke angelic protection over their children and others. But there is an order to how angels operate and how we are able to have maximum angelic protection.

ANGELIC PROTOCOL

Angels operate, as we have learned, on divine protocol. They are creatures of order and discipline. More often than not, we desire to skip a step and get our miracle or breakthrough instantly. But there are three important levels to climb before God will release increase. Psalm 91 gives the protocol for increase.

1. Intimacy—moving to safer ground

The first key to victory is intimacy with God: "He who dwells in the secret place of the Most High shall abide under the shadow of the Almighty. I will say of the LORD, 'He is my refuge and my fortress; my God, in Him I will trust'" (Ps. 91:1–2).

If you are going to avoid evil, you must have an intimate relationship with Jesus Christ. Likewise, if you desire to obey the commands of Christ, you must abide in Him. In just the first two verses of Psalm 91, we find four different names of God. Our Maker wants us to know His name, to know His very character.

How do you get into God's presence and abide there? Here is the golden gateway into God's presence: "I will say of the LORD, 'He is my refuge and my fortress, my God in whom I will trust'" (Ps. 91:2, MEV).

You see, God inhabits praise! When we begin to audibly confess His Word out of our mouth, when we extol His might and power, then we discover the place of intimacy with Him. You move into what the psalmist David called the secret place of the Most High, an open door to His presence.

When you look at Psalm 91:1–2, you know God desires our love! Everything flows from God when we have a passionate love for Him.

2. Invincibility—the first line of defense

This psalm moves you from intimacy to a new level of protection, I believe, provided by angels.

> Surely He shall deliver you from the snare of the hunter and from the deadly pestilence. He shall cover you with His feathers, and under His wings you shall find protection; His faithfulness shall be your shield and wall. You shall not be afraid of the terror by night, nor of the arrow that flies by day; nor of the pestilence that pursues in darkness, nor of the destruction that strikes at noonday. A thousand may fall at your side and ten thousand at your right hand, but it shall not come near you. Only with your eyes shall you behold and see the reward of the wicked.
>
> —PSALM 91:3–8, MEV

Once you've come to a place of complete oneness, you move on to a place of invincibility. Psalm 91 tells us that in the safety of the shadow of His presence we will escape many traps of the enemy and that God will "deliver you from the snare of the hunter" (v. 3). In biblical times, a snare containing a lure or bait was used to catch birds or animals. The devil sets dangerous traps for believers, but those who are walking, talking, and speaking forth who Jesus is will be delivered from these traps, including traps of deception, doubt, darkness, demonic forces, disease, disasters, and defeat.

If you are hearing from God and walking with Him on a daily basis, it doesn't mean that disasters won't happen. It doesn't mean the disease doesn't come; it simply means that those things cannot deter you from Christ. Here is a guarantee of victory. Your eyes will see as God walks you through the battlefields of life with complete victory!

Let me share with you a story that was reported on the *FOX and Friends* news show on Christmas Day in 2008. Angels and Christmas seem to go together. During Christmas week in 2008, Chelsea was about to die of pneumonia. The fourteen-year-old girl was about to be taken off life support when Dr. Teresa Sunderland saw an angelic image at the door of the pediatric intensive care unit. The bright white image was caught on a security camera. It couldn't have been a strange light as there are no windows in that part of the building. Dr. Ophelia Garmon-Brown of the hospital declares it a Christmas miracle. By the way, Chelsea recovered immediately and came home for Christmas.[3] Angels help in healing.

3. Immunity—the deepest level of protection

There is a difference between invincibility and immunity. Invincibility means you can escape evil's trap. Immunity means that long before it gets to your borders, you'll know and you will be out of the way. Immunity means that instead of a fight, there is a place where demonic forces cannot go. God provides seasons of rest from the struggle. Notice again that the key is intimacy. Everything begins with intimate worship. The psalmist refers back to making the Lord one's dwelling: "Because you have made the LORD, who is my refuge, even the Most High, your dwelling place" (Ps. 91:9).

At the place of immunity there are four things that start happening.

1. *Accidents stop happening!* "No evil shall befall you" (v. 10). All of a sudden tires do not go flat, appliances do not tear up, falls that break bones stop, and other cars do not hit your car. There is a place of immunity.

2. *Sicknesses stop spreading!* "Nor shall any plague come near your dwelling" (v. 10). How would you like to get through winter without colds and flu ravaging your family?

3. *Angels start helping!* Angels operate most effectively when you are intimate with the Lord Jesus. Your house becomes protected when you have made Him your

dwelling! Angels will even keep you from tripping over a rock! "They shall bear you up in their hands, lest you strike your foot against a stone" (v. 12, MEV).

4. *Devils start losing!* What was once over your head is now trampled under your feet! "You shall tread upon the lion and adder; the young lion and the serpent you shall trample underfoot" (v. 13, MEV). Angels will warn you and protect you from all that the enemy may try to bring against you. In many respects, it's just like a warning before a tsunami.

Millions of dollars have been spent placing tsunami-warning systems on the Indian Ocean following the devastation that hit in December 2004. These new devices are ultrasensitive, sending a split-second signal to a satellite if the ocean rises even a foot and warning affected countries within moments of detection. This reminds us of the power of our connection with God, for His warning system gives us notice and reports long before evil can come to hinder our path! His warning agents are the angels!

In the historic home of John Wesley, the great Methodist, there is a very small upstairs room. This space was his prayer room that he used daily at 4:30 a.m. No wonder so many hymns, so much ministry, and so much anointing flowed out of Wesley. He had an appointment with God at 4:30 each morning! As a result, the promise of Psalm 91:9–10 was his.

God's promise is to "set you on high" because you "set your love on Him." To be set on high indicates honor, to be made excellent, to be shown and proclaimed as special! God has made you significant and special because you love Him.

Psalm 91:14–15 reveals clear promises to those who dwell in His presence, love His name, and have no desire but to know Him better.

- *I will deliver him.* This means the enemy will never hold you in sin's spiritual prison!

- *I will set him on high.* God will take care of your reputation. Let promotion come from the Lord.

- *He shall call upon Me, and I will answer.* God will always answer your prayers.

- *I will be with him in trouble.* This promise assures you that you never will face anything alone! In Matthew 28:20, Jesus said, "Remember, I am with you always, even to the end of the age" (MEV).

- *I will honor him.* Only the applause of heaven really matters. His "well done" is enough.

- *With long life I will satisfy him.* God will extend your days so that you will live a satisfied, full, and overflowing life and will leave this life with blazing energy across the finish line!

- *I will show him My salvation.* The word for "salvation" in this passage is *Yeshua*, which is Hebrew for Jesus! Thus, the best promise is saved for last—God will show you Jesus! To see Jesus is the beginning and end of everything.

SOMETHING ABOUT THAT NAME

There is just something about the name Jesus! His name is power, and within the folds of its protection, believers can know a secret place where there is anointing, safety, and blessing—a tower of strength that keeps us from evil! Our planet has become "the killing fields" of hell, yet we can live, at times, immune to all these plagues.

There is such significance in knowing God's name. This "knowing" means much more than head knowledge; it refers to the closest possible intimacy. To know God's name is to be completely broken, having learned all the secrets and nuances of His character. The name of Jesus encompasses so much! Look at a few of the names of God:

- Yahweh—the Great I Am
- Jireh—my Provider
- Tsidkenu—my Righteousness
- Rophe—my Healer
- Rohi—my Shepherd

- Nissi—my Leader and Lover
- Shalom—my Peace
- Shammah—my Companion

Yes, He is also our Christ, the Anointed One, and the Messiah of the world. He is wonderful! He is our Lord! He is before the beginning and after the end! He is the unceasing song of David resounding across time and all of creation! He is the ever-shining star that will never fade. Angels move on behalf of those who know God's names!

Christ Jesus is the One we meet in that secret place. It is His scarred hand that takes us up and His shining face that welcomes us in. There we will whisper the name of Jesus and find ourselves abiding in the Almighty, overwhelmed with the promise and blessing of His presence! And there the angels will cover us.

Chapter Ten

GUIDANCE—ANGELS OUT FRONT

ANGELS MIRACULOUSLY DIRECT AND PROTECT GOD'S PEOPLE. Read Jacob Lepard's record of an angelic direction given to a group from our church while on a mission trip in Brazil.

In June of 2005, the summer before my senior year, a group of thirteen students from our church, two parent chaperones, and our youth minister were given the opportunity to take a mission trip to Castanhal in northern Brazil. We were to be gone for ten days, spending most of our time in the city working and living with a local pastor and his family. The rest of the time we spent traveling on the Moju River, which is an offshoot of the Amazon, helping with their church-planting ministry. After we had been in Castanhal for about five days, we packed our things and boarded a bus that took us out of the city to a dock near the highway, where we met the boat that would take us up the river. We were told the area where we met the boat was considerably dangerous, as several robberies had occurred there recently. However, like nearly all threats in Brazil, it was only dangerous at night, so this time around we were safe.

Our plans for the second day out on the river were to hike from early afternoon till evening several miles into the rain forest to a village where the missionary would speak at the village church. The boat was to drop us off at the trailhead and continue down the river to meet a van that would transport the missionary, the pastor, and their families to the village. The plan was for us all to load up in the van and return to our boat by road after the church service, but we were in for a surprise. We began the hike apprehensively, having been told countless stories about the local wildlife but all the time being reassured that none of the aggressive animals came out until nightfall, long after we would arrive at the village. As the hike continued, our apprehension evolved into extreme desire to not contract a jungle parasite as our trail turned from packed dirt to rotted planks suspended above swampy wetland. Needless to say I spent far more time in the mud than on the eight-inch-wide trail. This occurred for two reasons: (1) I didn't listen to my mother when she told me a foundation in gymnastics would help me later in life, and (2) the rotted planks had a tendency to bend or break under the weight of a healthy American. Regardless, right at sunset, after about two and a half hours of hiking, we emerged muddy and tired from the forest but steeped in a sense of accomplishment and respect for people who made the trip daily.

Shortly after arriving at the village we received news that the missionary, pastor, and their families had not arrived as they were supposed to, and nobody knew when they would arrive with the van. We wouldn't find out until much later that night that they had been late in meeting the van, and as a result the impatient driver had simply left. Consequently, at the exact moment that we arrived at the village, they were hitchhiking their way up the highway in a beer truck with a driver who never said a word, only smiling and giving aid when it was absolutely needed.

In looking back on that night I understand why it was so full of spiritual warfare. There are a lot of details that I could share about the service, but what moved me the most is how powerfully God moved and how unexpectedly He did it. The church was a small 30 x 30 building lit by a single light bulb connected to a car battery, and every believer from the surrounding area, probably two hundred in all, was crammed in.

In the absence of the expected missionary, our youth minister got up and spoke via translator about what was on his heart, consisting mainly of the truth of the cross and the reality of grace. At the end of the short message several people received salvation, after which nearly everyone came forward to be prayed over for healing. This last part caught all of us by surprise. I can say for sure that God was present and that He was fulfilling promises and healing His people when there were no doctors for hundreds of miles. I am astounded by what He did and the way He moved during the service. In looking back, I know that this was the reason that we were supposed to be there and the reason why we were under such heavy attack from the enemy.

By the end of the service it was well past the planned leaving time, and the others had finally been able to reach us, only to inform us that there was no van and we would have to hike back through the rain forest. The prospect of a night hike had been in the back of our minds the entire time, knowing full well that the already low chances of staying out of the mud during the day would be greatly reduced by darkness, not to mention fear of large snakes. But because we had no other option, we trusted that God would make a way. We began quoting Psalm 91 and started walking back toward the trail. Probably no more than fifty feet from the trailhead we heard somebody shouting for us to stop and go to the road instead, that there was someone waiting for us there. Not fully understanding, we walked a quarter of a mile to the deserted highway where we found an air-conditioned city transport bus waiting with the engine idling. God had made a way out, which was undeniably His doing.

We boarded the bus and found the driver sitting in the back. When we asked why he was there, his only reply was that he had been told to wait there until people arrived, never offering any more explanation than that. He drove us all the way back to the dock, where we had originally boarded the day before, in silence. There we would wait on the boat to receive word of where we were and travel downriver to pick us up. We sat together in a circle, waiting by the river and watching clouds gather overhead that signified the Amazon rainy season. All the time that we sat there in the dark, the bus driver stood alone just outside of our circle, in many ways seeming to be standing guard. As I said, we'd been told the place was very dangerous at night.

After a comparatively short wait the boat arrived, and just as the last person had gotten under the shelter of the boat, the storm hit like a tidal wave. I looked back at the riverbank and saw the bus pulling back onto the highway. I had not gotten the chance to say a word to the silent bus driver the entire night, but I've given him much thought since then. To be honest, I can't say whether he or the beer truck driver were man or angel, but I can tell the story, and I know for a fact that there was unseen opposition to the movement of God that night in the rain forest. Despite this, our God was present powerfully, faithful in fulfilling His word to believers, and, even more, was glorified. This tells me there also had to be unseen allies, and in two possible cases ones that took physical form.

The truth is no one knows who sent the bus, who paid for the bus, or why it was there. Did angels direct that bus to them? Was the driver an angel? I know our thirteen young people were protected and delivered out of the Amazon jungle by angels.

Angelic intermediaries are often used by God to get God's people from one place to another. Sometimes they simply give direction, and the believer must, by faith, obey. Such an event took place in the life of Paul when he was making his final journey to Rome. Strangely the angel could not stop the shipwreck because the sailors had already violated the laws of sailing during that season. Despite Paul's warning that the voyage would end with disaster with the loss of the cargo and ship and also their lives, the captain set sail. Still Paul fasted and prayed. Soon the winds arose, the ship was battered, and when impending disaster loomed near, Paul said:

> Men, you should have listened to me and not have set sail from Crete, incurring this injury and loss. But now I advise you to take courage, for there will be no loss of life among you, but only of the ship. For there stood by me this night the angel of God to whom I belong and whom I serve, saying, "Do not be afraid, Paul; you must stand before Caesar. And, look! God has given you all those who sail with you."
> —ACTS 27:21–24, MEV

Because of Paul's fasting and prayer, an angel came and granted Paul the lives of all on board. Even when we make unwise decisions, angels will bring wisdom to deliver. You may be the beneficiary of the angels watching over someone else whom you have led into a mess. If you are in a storm not of your own making, cry out to God! He will send His angels to direct you.

Another notable example is Lot, who, along with his family, was warned of impending judgment. It is interesting to notice the ministry of these angels to Lot. First of all, they were visible: "Now the two angels came to Sodom, and Lot was sitting at the gate of Sodom. When Lot saw them he rose up to meet them, and he bowed himself with his face toward the ground" (Gen. 19:1, MEV).

Most of us have never seen angels with our physical eyes; however, Scripture is filled with angelic appearances. In the case of Lot, not only did he see them, but he also approached them. And if this divine intersect was not dramatic enough, Lot actually invited them to his house and offered to wash their feet: "'Here, my lords, please turn in to your servant's house and spend the night and wash your feet; and then you may rise early and go on your way.' They said, 'No, we will stay in the open square all night'" (v. 2, MEV).

The angels wouldn't let Lot wash their feet, but they did eat the feast that he prepared: "But he insisted strongly, so they turned aside with him and entered his house. Then he made them a feast and baked unleavened bread, and they ate" (v. 3, MEV).

They were physically attractive and looked like men.

> Before they lay down, the men of the city, the men of Sodom, both old and young, all the people from every quarter, surrounded the house. They then called to Lot and said to him, "Where are the men who came to you tonight? Bring them out to us, so that we may have relations with them."
>
> —GENESIS 19:4–5, MEV

Sodom was a corrupt and immoral society. These angels were not only visible but also attractive to the lost men of that city. They did not respect the holy state of these spiritual beings. In fact, they lusted after them. These angels also had supernatural power: "Then they struck the men that were at the door of the house, both small and great, with blindness so that they wore themselves out groping for the door.... 'For we are about to destroy this place, because the outcry against its people has grown great before the presence of the LORD, and the LORD has sent us to destroy it'" (vv. 11, 13, MEV).

These angels were there to exact judgment on the city. However, they were subject to the needs of Lot; they served Lot: "'Hurry, escape there, for I cannot do anything until you arrive there.' Therefore the name of the city was called Zoar" (v. 22, MEV).

In my own life I have received direction from angels. In 1978 I was in my eighteenth day of ministry in the village of Mingading on the island of Mindanao, Philippines, when suddenly during the service an earthquake caused all in attendance to flee the building. Later that evening I could hear gunfire, and in the middle of the night I was awakened by an English-speaking person. It was obvious that my interpreter had fled with all his belongings, and the soldiers assigned to protect me were nowhere to be found. The one who awakened me said, "Get all your things together and be ready to leave." While I packed my belongings, this stranger disappeared. As I stepped out of the bamboo hut, I saw headlights coming up the mountain road. To my relief, it was a Jeep with a female American missionary. The same "English-speaking person" had instructed her in the middle of the night to leave M'lang and come to Mingading to help someone in need. I left with her and went to the Baptist Mission Compound in M'lang. The next morning "Moros," Muslim rebels, came to the village of Mingading looking for the American. I firmly believe an angel intervened.

Chapter Eleven

STRENGTH—ANGELS PLUGGED IN

THREE DAYS AND NIGHTS HAD PASSED WITH NO SLEEP following the birth of our second daughter. Still a seminary student, I served as a full-time pastor and was on my way to church with my head still buzzing from lack of sleep. I had scribbled an outline and a few thoughts on paper but felt exhausted and inadequate.

As I entered my small study and closed the door, a feeling of utter aloneness swept over me. With a knock on the door, Dave Davidson brought in a cup of steaming, hot coffee and a big, fresh doughnut.

"How are you, preacher?" he asked. I fell into his arms in exhaustion. Dave said, "I know you're tired, but God's angels will strengthen you!"

At exactly 11:20 that morning as I rose to preach, a warmth and strength flowed through my body and my spirit. Dave was so right! The angels came and strengthened me.

Angels are here to strengthen believers who have an intimate relationship with Jesus Christ. Angels will not do for us what we have been asked to do. They can, however, strengthen us for our assignments. Because we need the strength given us by angels, it causes us to face our own inadequacies. Often we find ourselves weary and worn out from the daily struggles of life. Fatigue is a first cousin to depression. Satan's goal is to cause us to quit! The Word of God says that in the last days Satan's emissaries will try to "wear out the saints of the most High" (Dan. 7:25, KJV). Life at its best can be a wearisome experience; however, God makes provision for our strength.

ELIJAH STRENGTHENED

The prophet Elijah had won a great victory over the forces of darkness. In the Super Bowl of spiritual warfare, Elijah had called down fire from heaven and exposed the false prophets of Baal. Elijah defeated those prophets and turned the people back to the one true God. With that battle won and the three-and-a-half-year drought broken, revival came to the land. There was no rest for the prophet, however.

Queen Jezebel made Elijah number one on her hit list and pursued him. Elijah fled until exhausted, and he sat under a "broom tree." As depression took over, Elijah wished he could die. Scripture records this marvelous story of angelic assistance as Elijah received a touch and food from an angel. In fact, the angel baked him a cake that gave him forty days of strength. (See 1 Kings 19:6–8.)

DANIEL STRENGTHENED

We find once again in Scripture the story of the prophet Daniel, who also received strength from an angel. Daniel was so overwhelmed by all God had revealed to him, he almost died. But the angel came and touched Daniel. Then the angel gave him a word from the Lord. Both the touch and the word gave Daniel strength for his assignment. (See Daniel 10:17–19.)

THE LORD JESUS STRENGTHENED

On two occasions we find our Lord receiving strength from the angels. At His temptation in the wilderness, Jesus encountered strength-sapping temptation from Satan. Remember, as we discussed earlier, Satan's goal is to "wear out" the believer. In the wilderness, Satan attacked Jesus with a threefold blow, testing His resolve. Jesus defeated Satan by answering every test with the Word of God. When the battle was over, the angels came. "Then the devil left Him, and immediately angels came and ministered to Him" (Matt. 4:11, MEV).

As our Lord faced the dreadful cup of our sins in the Garden of Gethsemane, He looked into that cup and shrank from it in horror. Yet in the end, Jesus drank its awful potion to the last dregs. How was Jesus able to face that horrible assignment? An angel came from glory to help Him: "An angel from heaven appeared to Him, strengthening Him" (Luke 22:43, MEV). Jesus Christ did not avoid the inevitable cup but was strengthened for the task by the angel.

HOW BELIEVERS ARE STRENGTHENED BY ANGELS

Even in contemporary times, God's angels still come to strengthen believers during difficult times. A young man shares a story about when he had trouble recovering from surgery and an angel came to his aid. He recalls:

> I required knee surgery a few years ago; I prayed a lot before surgery asking God to guide the hands of all those in the theatre and to bring me safely out of the anesthetic. I apparently inhaled too deeply the anesthetic and had a hard time coming back into consciousness.
>
> I remember being very frightened, as I did not want to die—I had so much more to live for. Immediately, a white light appeared and a voice encouraged me. It said, "Breathe, breathe, you can do it, you will come out of the anesthetic. Do not fight it."
>
> I know it was an angel of God speaking to me, so I can attest to angels being present all the time and having us always in their care. I have experienced it.
>
> Thank God for His angels![1]

Observing this story and the biblical antecedents presented in the previous section, we see some ways we may receive strength from the angels. Make note and remember the following:

1. Angels strengthen those on serious assignment from God. Angels do not strengthen one simply because he or she is tired; they are available to those on kingdom assignments.

2. The presence of angels releases a measure of strength. The word *appear* means to bring the assistance of one's presence. As a young boy I was threatened by a bully five years older than me. One day the bully beat me. My mother sent her younger brother with me to avenge my beating. My uncle took care of that bully! Even though

I did not strike a blow, I felt strong! I was strong in my uncle's presence! When he appeared, all my weakness left. Likewise, angelic appearance routs demonic strength killers.

3. Angels touch and minister to weak believers. The brush of an angel's wing can strengthen the believer for their journey.

4. Angels speak the Word of God, and believers are strengthened by the word of angels. God will send us a hopeful, faithful message through the angels that will strengthen and prepare us for what lies ahead.

5. Angels can cook and feed believers. With this, we see angels can use tangible items to bring strength to the body and soul of a believer, or many times angels will use people to provide the necessities that strengthen the believer.

6. Angels can transport believers on occasion, as we see the deacon Philip whisked away from Samaria by an angel (Acts 8:26–40). Angels can carry us when we are too tired in our own strength and can lift us up to keep us from tripping over a stone (Ps. 91).

To summarize, angels are available to strengthen us along the way. As we see in Revelation 5:2, which speaks of a "strong angel," the word *strong* translates to mean "force, innate power." In essence, strong angels are with us to strengthen us.

Section Three

HOW ANGELS ARE ACTIVATED

Chapter Twelve

ANGELS OBEY ORDERS

A NGELS ARE ASSIGNED THE RESPONSIBILITY TO SERVE believers. When a believer operates as an heir to the kingdom of God, then angels are sent to serve. Our failure to activate angelic assistance has limited our growth and success in our mission enterprise. There is a powerful word on angels found in Hebrews 1:14. It says, "Are they not all ministering spirits sent forth to minister for those who will inherit salvation?" The phrase "sent forth" is the Greek word *apostello*, which is the same word translated as "apostle." Angels are "sent forth" with those who are willing to "go forth." The phrase "sent forth" means to be sent out with a commission. Angels protect and endorse the message God is speaking today by using their authority. The phrase also speaks of the apostolic, prophetic, and evangelistic work done as they help to spread the good news.

ANGELS GIVE INSTRUCTIONS

I had just turned twenty-one years old and was experiencing one of the most exciting times in my young life. I was newly married, a student at Samford University, and had just begun a new ministry at a church in Wilsonville, Alabama. As I drove to Birmingham for a long day of classes, I noticed a young man hitchhiking. Normally, I never stop for hitchhikers; however, on this day I stopped for the young man.

As I watched him get in my car, he said, "Now worship Jesus Christ."

Then he said, "I must tell you something. You will have an awakening, and you will baptize dozens of people. Do not be dismayed if the old church does not receive all that God releases. You are appointed here for the purpose of touching the people no one wants."

He then asked me to let him out of the car. As he got out of the car, I said, "God bless you."

He looked at me, smiled, and said, "He already has, and He has blessed you!"

Two weeks later we baptized thirty-six new converts; most of them lived in a poor community of small shotgun houses. The church did not receive them, but God put a love in my heart, from that moment until now, for the needy and outcast. I believe I encountered an angel.

Angels go before us on life's journey toward our promised destiny. In Exodus 33:2, God said, "And I will send My Angel before you, and I will drive out the Canaanite and the Amorite and the Hittite and the Perizzite and the Hivite and the Jebusite." It is comforting to know that the Lord is directing our way and that His angels take each step before us. There are angelic "scouts" exploring and preparing the way ahead.

ANGELS WARN BELIEVERS

Remember, the angel warned Joseph of Herod's evil intention: "Now when they departed, the angel of the Lord appeared to Joseph in a dream, saying, 'Arise, take the young Child and His mother, and escape to Egypt, and stay there until I bring you word. For Herod will seek the young Child to kill Him'" (Matt. 2:13, MEV). Throughout history angels have waved red flags in front of believers, and we can count on that same protective intervention in our lives today.

Bart was on his way to Branson, Missouri, for the annual Yamaha motorcycle convention when he had an unbelievable encounter that he will never forget. He was traveling on his motorcycle behind a semi-truck, going seventy to seventy-five miles an hour, when he heard a clear voice inside of him say, "Switch lanes to the left."

As soon as he had completed the lane change, the semitrailer in front of him blew a rear tire and scattered large pieces of tread in the right lane, where he had been just moments before. Bart honestly believes that if it were not for that divine intervention telling him to switch lanes, he would not be alive today. He probably would have crashed into the back of the semi or flipped the bike after hitting the separated tread.

That day Bart is sure that he heard his angel tell him, clear as a bell, to switch lanes because there was trouble ahead.[1]

Angels Are Watching

When we bind the enemy and loose our allies, the angels do the work for us. Many times the church, collectively and as individuals, does not stand on our position in Christ. As a result, we fail to engage the legions of angels standing ready to assist. Matthew 16:19 puts it like this: "I will give you the keys of the kingdom of heaven, and whatever you bind on earth shall be bound in heaven, and whatever you loose on earth shall be loosed in heaven" (MEV). As believers operate, they must understand that angelic assistance is a "key" to kingdom power in the earth. These wonderful beings are the agents of God who operate in opening doors and binding the curses.

The mighty hosts of heaven are called "watchers" in Scripture. I am convinced that angels can reveal international crises and international needs. As "watchers," they are looking out for all believers! Angels are God's scouts on the earth doing reconnaissance. In Zechariah chapter 1 we find the angels walking to and fro, or to put it in more contemporary language, walking back and forth throughout the earth keeping watch over creation. This night they had a good report: "We have walked to and fro throughout the earth, and behold, all the earth is resting quietly" (Zech. 1:11).

The prophet Daniel also calls angels "watchers." They are doing surveillance over all creation. Above our earth are man-made satellites recording global activities; in a greater way, angels are also watching over us. "I saw in the visions of my head upon my bed, and there was a holy watcher coming down from heaven" (Dan. 4:13, MEV).

I was chatting with my recently widowed mother-in-law, a faithful Christian, about living alone. She has opted to stay in the large house where she and my father-in-law, Billy, had lived for so long. She quickly told me she was not afraid. With a shy smile, she said, "I know that angels are watching over me."

When Billy was in his last living moments, there in their home with all the family gathered around, he opened his blue eyes and looked heavenward as a glory filled the room. Billy then closed his eyes and went to heaven. Though not visible, an angel had come to transport him home to glory, and I firmly believe angels have stayed with my mother-in-law, Polly, ever since.

Angels are always on guard, covering the earth. They report on all that they observe on the earth. If we are on the right channel, we too can have wisdom on what God is doing in the earth.

Chapter Thirteen

ANGELS RESPOND TO SCRIPTURE

F
OR THIRTY YEARS I HAVE SERVED AS PASTOR OF ABBA'S HOUSE. During that time I have prepared and delivered over five thousand messages, which totals over sixty-five thousand written pages. I have written seventeen books and have taught daily radio for over ten of those years, which equal more than three thousand messages. During all this time, I can honestly say that most people who heard these scriptural messages didn't respond. However, it is encouraging to know that not a single angel disobeyed the Word of God that came forth from my mouth.

Angels are activated by the Word of God and move accordingly. They don't do as we humans sometimes do—respond to God's commands reluctantly or depending on how we feel about what He is asking. When God speaks, they act. Angels reverence, respect, and respond to the Word of God. They have a special interest in presenting, protecting, proclaiming, and performing the Word of God. Angels will not violate the written Word of God; they are committed to its dictates. In most cases when angelic involvement occurs, a message from heaven is being delivered. Angels know that the messages they deliver change the destiny of nations and are of life-and-death importance.

ANGELS AND THE ORIGIN OF SCRIPTURE

Scripture speaks of their heavenly origin. Scripture is the God-breathed writings of men giving witness to the mighty acts of God: "All Scripture is inspired by God and is profitable for teaching, for reproof, for correction, and for instruction in righteousness" (2 Tim. 3:16, MEV).

In this verse Paul declares the writings of the Bible to be God breathed. The Holy Spirit actively superintended the writing of Scripture. Simon Peter affirmed that Scripture came from God to humanity: "And we have a more reliable word of prophecy, which you would do well to follow, as to a light that shines in a dark place, until the day dawns and the morning star arises in your hearts. But know this first of all, that no prophecy of the Scripture is a matter of one's own interpretation. For no prophecy at any time was produced by the will of man, but holy men moved by the Holy Spirit spoke from God" (2 Pet. 1:19–21, MEV).

Beyond the connection between God and man, we find an ally in the formation of Scripture, the holy angels. The angels were deeply involved in the giving of the Word. When Moses ascended Mount Sinai, he was met by an innumerable company of angels, who participated in the revelation of the Law: "And he said: 'The LORD came from Sinai, and dawned on them from Seir; He shone forth from Mount Paran, and He came with ten thousands of saints; from His right hand came a fiery law for them'" (Deut. 33:2). The word *saints* is "holy ones," and scholars agree that it is a reference to angels.[1]

Psalm 68:17 affirms the angelic covering at Mount Sinai when Moses conferred with God about the Law that would become the bedrock of human civilization: "The chariots of God are twice ten thousand, even thousands of thousands; the Lord is among them as in Sinai, in the holy place" (MEV).

When you turn to the pages of the New Testament, you find a clear affirmation of angelic assistance with the Scriptures, especially the Law. The deacon Stephen, in his sermon that resulted in his martyrdom, declared the same truth: "…who have received the law by the direction of angels and have not kept it" (Acts 7:53).

The Law came "by the direction of angels." The apostle Paul, in writing to the Galatian church, said the Law was "appointed" by angels: "What purpose then does the law serve? It was added because of transgressions, till the Seed should come to whom the promise was made; and it was appointed through angels by the hand of a mediator" (Gal. 3:19).

Furthermore, the writer of Hebrews declares the absolute integrity of the "word spoken through angels": "For if the word spoken through angels proved steadfast, and every transgression and disobedience received a just reward..." (Heb. 2:2).

Angels participated in the giving of the Law, and they also carried out the sentences of the Law.

ANGELS ENFORCE THE WORD

Look again at Hebrews 2:2: "For if the word spoken through angels proved steadfast, and every transgression and disobedience received a just reward..." The word *transgression* means "to trespass, to go beyond the ordinary boundary"; indeed, "to break the rules." *Disobedience* means simply "to act against what has been commanded." Angels punish lawbreakers! This is why you must never assign angelic protection in your life if you are violating the law and disobeying authority. It is abundantly clear that angels respect, respond, and release the Word of God. As we have observed, the angels were present at the giving of the Law (Ps. 68:17), the Law came by angelic direction (Acts 7:53), the Law was "appointed through angels" (Gal. 3:19), and the Word was "spoken" in some cases by the angels (Heb. 2:2). We conclude from these scriptures that obedience to the Word of God is vital to release angelic activity. Also, could it be possible that angels are grieved by humans who transgress God's laws? As we witnessed earlier, both angels and demons are arranged in military hierarchy; therefore, rebellion would be considered grievous. Could it be that angelic help is stifled by rebellious activity?

ANGELS AND THE CONFESSED WORD

Moving from the negative to the positive, we see that angels are activated and released when we confess, by faith, the Word of God: "Bless the LORD, you His angels, who excel in strength, who do His word, heeding the voice of His word. Bless the LORD, all you His hosts, you ministers of His, who do His pleasure" (Ps. 103:20–21). Here this scripture gives us clear direction on how angels are moved by God's Word. Notice that the Word is powerfully embraced by the hosts of heaven in an atmosphere of worship. When a believer worships, angels gather.

Secondly, angels "do His word." This is their vocation and purpose. Angels will cause the Word of God to come to pass in the lives of believers.

Third, notice that when the Word is voiced, angels are activated. When a faithful Christian says aloud the Word God has released in him or her, that Word is carried forth on the wings of angels to be answered. Angels do God's Word and respond to the Word spoken aloud! Angels cannot read your mind. When you confess the Word of God by faith out of your mouth, angels move instantly. It is their joy to speedily bring your confession to pass! As we obey, heed, and confess the Word of God, we bring our angelic allies into full partnership. They will bring to pass what God has promised.

At a staff meeting in our church some years ago, there was a report of a financial need. I prayed and dispatched harvest angels to go get what God's Word had promised us. Before the meeting ended, a local businessman brought in a five-figure check that met the need. God's angels moved when the promise of God's Word was embraced and spoken.

Chapter Fourteen

ANGELS ANSWER PRAYER

NGELIC ACTIVITY SWIRLS AROUND AND MINGLES WITH things of the Spirit. We have already observed how angels are connected to the glory of worship and to the needs of believers. Angels are especially attuned to the spiritual discipline of prayer. Angels are activated by a sincere heart seeking God in prayer. It appears in Scripture that angelic worship includes watching over the prayers of believers. On two occasions angels are viewed as attending the prayers of believers.

First, in the dramatic worship scene found in Revelation 5, the Lamb takes the scroll from the strong angel. This scroll recounts all of the trials of humanity across the ages. Only our Lord Jesus, by His sacrifice, can restore what has been lost. In this powerful vision, the Lamb bears the visible signs of having been slain. (See Revelation 5:6–7.)

When the Lion/Lamb seizes the scroll, triumphant worship breaks out among those redeemed and among the heavenly hosts. As the praise begins, there is a mysterious mention of angels and our prayers: "When He had taken the scroll, the four living creatures and the twenty-four elders fell down before the Lamb, each one having a harp, and golden bowls full of incense, which are the prayers of saints" (Rev. 5:8, MEV).

It appears the prayers of all believers across all time are being watched over by angels. Prayers are viewed as "golden bowls" of "incense." This image takes us back to temple worship where the incense burned before the cloud of glory, God's presence. Angels keep our prayers as a sweet smell before the throne of God. Prayers are cherished in heaven and are in the care of the worshipping hosts. In the Scripture reference above, the angel hosts play their harps (*kithara* in the Greek, from which we get the English word *guitar*). As they play and lead worship, the prayers ascend as incense before the throne of God: "The smoke of the incense, with the prayers of the saints, ascended before God from the angel's hand. Then the angel took the censer, filled it with fire from the altar, and threw it to the earth. And there were noises, thundering, lightning, and an earthquake" (Rev. 8:4–5, MEV).

As this scene unfolds, the prayers of believers loose the seven trumpets of judgment on the earth. Notice our prayers "ascended before God from the angel's hand." Then our prayers are hurled back to the earth as fire! This powerful image of prayer is confirmed in Psalm 141:1–2: "LORD, I cry unto You; make haste to me; give ear to my voice, when I cry unto You. Let my prayer be set forth before You as incense, and the lifting up of my hands as the evening sacrifice" (MEV). Notice the image of incense and prayer. Angels of worship attend to the sincere cries of God's people.

NO PRAYER GOES UNNOTICED

Angels collect all of our prayers, and they are offered as a sacrifice to God. Until the answer is ready, they burn before the throne of God as a sweet sacrifice. Angels tend our prayers and are agents used to answer our prayers. In due season the Holy Spirit and the angels of fire move to answer the righteous prayers of believers. A clear example of how this works is recorded in Luke 1:8–12.

Zacharias was serving as the high priest and ministering by burning incense as all the people were in the outer court of the temple praying at the hour of incense. The people knew that prayer mixed with sacrifice and worship was powerful and effective. In that moment the invisible works of God became visible. Astonishingly, the angel of the Lord stood at the right side of the altar of incense. What was this angel doing? He was gathering the prayers of believers as he always did, but on that day he manifested himself to Zacharias. Why did the angel show himself? Because Zacharias and Elizabeth had been praying earnestly all their lives for a child. At the hour of incense, the hour of prayer, the angel who watches over prayer showed up. This scene ends with a fearful Zacharias doubting the word from Gabriel and being struck mute so he could not confess unbelief and contradict the word of faith claimed by his wife, Elizabeth. Angels respond to "the voice of His word" (Ps. 103:20); therefore, Gabriel would not allow a single word of unbelief to be voiced during Elizabeth's pregnancy.

A MOTHER'S ANSWERED PRAYER

My husband and oldest son work at the same place in Colusa, California. We live in Colusa, and our son lives thirty miles away. They work early hours. One morning after my husband left for work I could not sleep. I looked at the clock and it was 4:45 a.m. Our son was on my mind and heavy on my heart. I just thought I was being overprotective and tried to close my eyes to go back to sleep.

The weight got so heavy I could not lie down anymore. I called my husband at work and asked him if our son had gotten to work yet. He said no. By this time it was 5:20 a.m. and he was to start at 5:30. I started praying and asking God to please put His angels around my son and get him safely to work.

I was still praying for God's angels when, about twenty minutes later, I heard a car outside. As I opened the front door, my son was walking up to the door. His car was still running, driver's door open, and his head in his hands. He was crying, and he said, "Mom, I almost died."

He had fallen asleep at the wheel as he was crossing a two-mile bridge. As the road curved, his car went straight into the other lane and hit the cement wall. The car then lifted about one inch from the top of the wall. He woke up and struggled to back the car off the wall, scraping it for at least ten feet.

I hugged my son, and I told him what happened to me earlier and that I had prayed for God's angels to protect him. We both cried and thanked God for giving him a guardian angel.[1]

AN ANGEL TO THE RESCUE

There are angels among us. You never know if it's that person standing next to you in an elevator, behind you in line at the market, or even the pizza delivery guy!

One of my dearest friends worked as a full-time nanny for a

very nice family of five that lived way out in the Indiana country-side. Being a mother-to-be herself, she certainly had her hands full with taking care of their children, and she did an amazing job!

I'd gone over there one weekend to spend some time with her and the kids while the parents were out of town. It was a won-derful December day and had started to get late. It was time for me to leave. It *really* snowed that day, so everything was com-pletely covered. After I'd warmed my car, I was trying to back out and had somehow found myself no longer on their driveway but on their yard. That's when I got stuck. I tried rocking the car back and forth in my attempt to get the car out, but all that did was give them a pretty decent yard job! Feeling just awful about it, I went back inside and announced to my friend, "I'm stuck!" My friend was looking for shovels, salt, two-by-fours, anything that might help. "Surely these folks have tools; they live in the country!" No luck.

I'd gone back out to the car to have another go at it and was getting really frustrated. It was around 11:00 p.m. and very cold, and although the snowing has slowed to almost nothing coming down, it was difficult to get around since the snow from the day was so deep. Back in the car, I sat there thinking that I didn't want to worsen the near ditch I'd already dug into their front yard. I couldn't believe this. "How could I have done this?" I asked myself. I didn't even have anyone to call for help. I started to pray. After a few minutes, for some reason I glanced at my trip odometer. To my horror, it read the numbers 666. I became angry and yelled, "I rebuke this!" and quickly pushed the button, changing the odometer back to zero.

Just then, a small car with a Domino's Pizza delivery sign on top pulled up to the house. I thought, "Way out here? That's odd." A man got out of the car. With a big smile, he walked over and chuckled. "Looks like you could use a little help."

I was giddy with thankfulness and replied, "Oh, yes! Thank you! Thank you so much!"

He laughed and said that he'd give it a push while I gave it a little gas.

I sat in the car and looked behind me through the rear window. The man stood behind my car, and for a few moments, he looked at it in what appeared to be a very thoughtful way. It was like he was gathering information with his smiling eyes.

"OK, then!" he called out. So I pressed gently on the gas pedal. I certainly didn't want to fling slush and mud on him.

He placed his hands on the trunk of my car and forward, up, and back onto the driveway I went. I thought, "Oh my! He didn't even lean!"

I got out of the car and was so surprised, all I could get out of my mouth was a barrage of thank-yous and a "Wow, you're strong!"

He laughed and asked that I be very careful out there on the road.

I went to reach for my purse in the car to give him some cash for helping me out, and when I looked up, he'd already gone all the way back to where his car was on the road. He stood by his car and waved before getting in and pulling away.

I quickly jumped into my car and backed out to the road. He was gone. No taillights. No tire tracks in the snow.[2]

WHAT DOES ALL THIS SAY TO US?

1. Angels abide in the secret place of prayer.

2. Angels are stirred and motivated by both individual and corporate prayer.

3. Prayer is best offered in a context of intense worship.

4. Angels watch over prayers yet to be answered.

5. Prayers are a pleasant and sweet aroma to God our Father.

6. Prayers rise to God from the hands of our angel allies.

7. Angels respond negatively to wrong words; negative confessions, curses, and unbelief hinder the miracle-working Word.

8. Prayers offered in passionate faith and trust in God will be answered by God and delivered by angels.

Your prayers matter to our Father and activate angelic assistance. Remember, no prayer goes unnoticed or unanswered. I realize to some of you that doesn't make sense, when you have prayed for healing and the healing hasn't come, or when you have suffered greatly and there seemed to be no relief. However, this passage shows us that our prayers have been entrusted to angels until their appointed time. As allies with the angels, we must be reassured by the power of prayer and spend time regularly with God.

Chapter Fifteen

ANGELS MOVE ON MIRACLE GROUND

NGELIC ACTIVITY IS ON THE INCREASE IN THESE LAST DAYS. The reason for supernatural operations is twofold.

First, as we move toward the end, human options begin to dwindle. Human ingenuity creates a world that rushes toward ruin and chaos. As this time approaches, God releases more angelic intervention to protect His people and to promote His kingdom. Furthermore, for the past century, the church has been experiencing the renewal and restoration of the Pentecostal gifts. Beginning at Azusa Street in the early twentieth century and continuing to this very day, a mighty outpouring of the Holy Spirit is sweeping across our world. Historians tell us that we are actually in the third wave of this worldwide move of the Spirit. Conversions to Christianity in the third world are reaching record numbers. Even the Islamic world is being powerfully impacted by the supernatural. Visions, dreams, and angels are appearing even where there is no missionary presence.

As churches and ministries embrace charismatic ministry, old divisions are falling away and kingdom unity is spreading worldwide. The last days' church must be kingdom oriented in order to release the supernatural, including miraculous angelic assistance.

KINGDOM MINISTRY

As we discuss the miracle ground that angels operate from, it is essential for us to know how to place ourselves in prime position to receive and activate their supernatural influence in our world. One of the main things to understand is how the kingdom of God works in relationship to us and the earth realm. As I have already pointed out, there are certain kingdom laws in the Word of God that angels abide by, and if we are to benefit from them as our allies, we need to abide by those laws as well. Our understanding of God's kingdom will help us understand the connection between the laws of the kingdom and our angelic allies.

According to Luke 17:21, the kingdom of God dwells within us. So if Jesus is Lord in our lives, then His kingdom has come through us. Yet we will only have full access to it and its resources once we are born again by the Spirit of God. (See John 3:5.) This access to kingdom resources requires a willingness to change (repent) and a submissive, broken spirit. (See Matthew 3:2; 6:33.) With the kingdom of God being present all around us through angelic miracles, old divisions between churches being broken down, and even conversions in the Islamic countries, it is clear that we are living in a time of kingdom breakthrough.

But not only is the kingdom of God here now, it is also yet to come. Hebrews 2:8–9 says, "Yet now we do not see all things subject to him. But we see Jesus" (MEV). We do not yet see all of the aspects and inner workings of God's kingdom, but its fullness is yet to come because we are still waiting for Jesus to return to the earth a second time. In John 18:36 Jesus confirms this by saying that the kingdom of God is "not of this world."

The kingdom breaks through into the "now" by the Holy Spirit. In the letters of Paul, he calls the baptism of the Holy Spirit a guarantee of the powers of the world to come in the here and now! Furthermore, the powers of the kingdom are released at our sealing and anointing. (See 2 Corinthians 1:21–22; Ephesians 1:14.) I am convinced that many Christians are children of the kingdom but are not sons! All who are saved are children, yet the rights of sonship, which include angels, miracles, signs, and wonders, belong to those who have been baptized in the Holy Spirit.

The Holy Spirit releases the power of the kingdom now! Angels are a part of that realm we call "the kingdom of heaven." When a church or a believer is willing to sell out to all God has, the angelic activity will increase exponentially! In a hurting, sad, and dirty world, we need this kingdom that is "righteousness and peace and joy in the Holy Spirit" (Rom. 14:17, MEV) to be activated.

Now that we have explored how we can place ourselves in position to receive and/or activate the kingdom of heaven with angelic ministry, let's look at some of the grounds upon which angels tread in order to impact the earth with kingdom power.

ANGELIC MINISTRY IN THE CHURCH

At Abba's House (Central Baptist Church, Chattanooga, Tennessee), where I have served for thirty years, we have moved from a traditional ministry to what some call charismatic. The transition began in 1989 and continues until this day. Since 1993 angel sightings, angelic singing, orbs of light, and bursts of fire have taken place. All of these manifestations occurred after I was baptized in the Holy Spirit and as the church moved into that realm. It is my belief that angelic ministry in today's kingdom church is similar to what took place in the New Testament church.

When we read the New Testament, we find its pages filled with angelic activity. When the church brings those who are lost to a saving knowledge of Jesus Christ, the angels join in the celebration and praise for their conversion. Scripture says that when the lost are found, "there is joy in the presence of the angels" (Luke 15:10, MEV). When the church gathers for worship, angels gather with us (Heb. 12:22). Angels exhibit a strong curiosity about believers' spiritual lives (1 Pet. 1:12). Undoubtedly because of their large number, their activity in the spiritual realm, and their presence among the members of the kingdom church, we are warned not to make the angels objects of our worship (Col. 2:18).

In his book *The Truth About Angels*, Terry Law illustrates how angels are moved by our worship. He shares several stories that tell of angelic activity in churches.[1]

> Sharon Abrams, a physician's wife who attends Agape Church, told of seeing two angels during a church service. The angels were hovering over the congregation with their arms outstretched. They were light-skinned and had light-colored hair, and they stood seven or eight feet tall. Abrams wrote: "Their faces were broad with high cheekbones and beautiful smiles. They looked like men except they did not have beards. There was an innocence to their faces, and the joy of their expressions was wonderful. They did not wear shoes, but wore long white gowns with gold braid. I cannot remember exactly where the braid was

located on the gowns. I knew they were in the service because of our praise and worship...because Jesus was being lifted up and adored. I sensed there were many more beings present in the auditorium, but I was only able to see those two."[2]

Marilyn Cappo of Louisville Covenant Church in Kentucky says she has seen angels on a number of occasions. She reported seeing three angels dancing on the roof of a house where a home group was meeting. One of them was playing something like a small harp, perhaps a lyre. Later, during a church morning worship service, she saw a nine-foot angel standing behind the worship leader. Most recently, she said she has seen two angels standing on the front platform of her church during several different services. She described them this way:

"They are a little over six feet tall and dressed in white. They do not speak but raise their wings when songs are sung of direct praise to the Father.

"They stand to the left of the pulpit, watching the congregation, and look at us expectantly. I have seen them off and on over a period of months and have prayed often to understand their purpose and mission at our church. One morning one of them walked over behind the pastor and spread his wings as our pastor was making declarative statements about God to us. The angels appear to be waiting for us to do something and always watch intently."

Patsy Burton of Wethersfield, Essex, in England, wrote of hearing angels singing during a church service. She said the "clarity, pitch and harmony was absolutely incredible. In fact, there are no words to describe how they sounded."

In *Somewhere Angels,* one of the best books that I have found on angels, author Larry Libby wrote about a worship meeting in Alaska: "Outside, the winter wind moaned and hissed against the frosted church windows. But inside the little church, people were warm and happy and singing song after song of praise to God...something mysterious and wonderful happened that icy, starlit night. After one last praise song...people stopped singing. The musicians put down their instruments. But somehow, the singing kept going. Everyone heard it. The beautiful praise music kept rolling on and on for a little while, like a long, silvery echo."[3]

ANGELS AND KINGDOM LEADERSHIP

Furthermore, angels accompany those who serve in the fivefold ministry. Let's look carefully at this often-quoted but misunderstood scripture on angels: "Do not forget to entertain strangers, for thereby some have entertained angels unknowingly" (Heb. 13:2, MEV).

This verse, when viewed in context, concerns church authority and order. Believers are called to "remember those who rule over you, who have proclaimed to you the word of God" (Heb. 13:7, MEV). Note again the following mandate: "Obey your leaders and submit to them, for they watch over your souls....Let them do this with joy and not complaining, for that would not be profitable to you" (Heb. 13:17, MEV). The point is quite clear: angels accompany those who lead, speak the Word of God, teach faith, and watch for our souls, and they release profit or prosperity. When a believer refuses to submit to apostles, prophets, evangelists, pastors, and teachers, then the angels that accompany them are insulted and will not release blessing. Those who mock and make fun of men and women of God are blocking the ministry of angels.

Let's take a look at a couple of stories that illustrate God's care for His chosen leaders through the intervention of angels. The first story tells how a whole mission headquarters was kept from certain calamity because a man of God was there to serve.

> The Reverend John G. Paton, pioneer missionary in the New Hebrides Islands, told a thrilling story involving the protective care of angels. Hostile natives surrounded his mission headquarters one night, intent on burning the Patons out and killing them. John Paton and his wife prayed all during that terror-filled night that God would deliver them. When daylight came they were amazed to see that, unaccountably, the attackers had left. They thanked God for delivering them.
>
> A year later, the chief of the tribe was converted to Jesus Christ, and Mr. Paton, remembering what had happened, asked the chief what had kept him and his men from burning down the house and killing them. The chief replied in surprise, "Who were all those men you had with you there?" The missionary answered, "There were no men there; just my wife and I." The chief argued that they had seen many men standing guard—hundreds of big

men in shining garments with drawn swords in their hands. They seemed to circle the mission station so that the natives were afraid to attack. Only then did Mr. Paton realize that God had sent His angels to protect them. The chief agreed that there was no other explanation.[4]

A missionary who came home for a short break shared this story at his home church in Michigan:

> While serving at a small field hospital in Africa, every two weeks I traveled by bicycle through the jungle to a nearby city for supplies. This was a journey of two days and required camping overnight at the halfway point. On one of these journeys, I arrived in the city where I planned to collect money from a bank, purchase medicine and supplies, and then begin my two-day journey back to the field hospital.
>
> Upon arrival in the city, I observed two men fighting, one of whom had been seriously injured. I treated him for his injuries and at the same time talked to him about the Lord. I then traveled two days, camping overnight, and arrived home without incident.
>
> Two weeks later I repeated my journey. Upon arriving in the city, I was approached by the young man I had treated. He told me that he had known I carried money and medicines. He said, "Some friends and I followed you into the jungle, knowing you would camp overnight. We planned to kill you and take your money and the drugs. But just as we were about to move into your camp, we saw that twenty-six armed guards surrounded you." At this, I laughed and said that I was certainly all alone in that jungle campsite.
>
> The young man pressed the point, however, and said, "No, sir, I was not the only person to see the guards; my friends also saw them and we all counted them. It was because of those guards that we were afraid and left you alone."
>
> At this point in the sermon, one of the men in the congregation jumped to his feet and interrupted the missionary and asked if he could tell him the exact day this happened. The missionary told the congregation the date, and the man who interrupted told him this story.
>
> "On the night of your incident in Africa, it was morning here and I was preparing to go play golf. I was about to putt when I

felt the urge to pray for you. In fact, the urging of the Lord was so strong; I called some men in this church to meet with me here in the sanctuary to pray for you. Would all of those men who met with me on that day stand up?"

The men who had met together to pray that day stood up. The missionary wasn't concerned with who they were; he was too busy counting how many men he saw. There were twenty-six men.[5]

These stories make it clear that when we welcome the ministries of godly men and women, we entertain the angels who are assigned to them. Those accompanying angels are released in the community being visited by the guest; there they battle the ruling powers of the enemy and release the miracles of God. Only as we receive those whom God sets over us can we have the full ministry of the hosts at their disposal.

Even the business community can turn from loss to profit by welcoming God's servants and their angelic helpers. In the election of 2008, it is interesting that the financial downturn and loss of profit in America happened when the media and the Left mocked the faith of Sarah Palin. *Newsweek* mocked her charismatic expressions, and the media laughed. Angels of profit were insulted as this woman of God was not respected. You can mark the loss of profit in the stock market from the mocking of her charismatic faith. Angels were insulted and businesses failed. (See Hebrews 13:2, 17.)

ANGELS AND AWAKENING

The hosts of heaven can move on behalf of our Western nations again only if we respect the spiritual leaders God sends. When this happens, angels will come with fire to cleanse and to rekindle our spiritual lives. This will result in a release of supernatural power and resources. Hebrews 1:7 declares that angels are flames of fire. Pentecostal fire includes angelic fire released to do its powerful work in the earth. (Even our speaking in tongues is called by the Scriptures "tongues of angels," as we see in 1 Corinthians 13:1.) As faith increases and the church operates in kingdom power, our angelic allies will help us take dominion in our communities and our nations. Let us activate our angels by making the kingdom of God our priority. God will order the angels into our dimension as we move in the power of the Holy Spirit.

Chapter Sixteen

ANGELS EXECUTE GOD'S WRATH

A NGELIC ACTIVITY ERUPTS AT THE MIGHTY EPOCHS OF GOD'S kingdom. As we have observed, angels sang and shouted as God called the creation out of nothing. Angels conveyed the glory of God with a backslidden Judah to Babylonian captivity. Angels covered God's ancient people during their captivity. Angels welcomed the Messiah above Bethlehem's fields with a sound and light show not seen since Creation. Sadly, the same angels who raised the curtain on our planet and have guarded its destiny will also release the judgments that are yet to come.

GOD'S WRATH FULLY RELEASED

The last book in the Bible records two phenomena intensifying at the same time. Worship intensifies in a powerful crescendo that shakes all of creation. Conversely, wars and catastrophes intensify. God will judge every failed human system and then every human being outside of Christ. Angelic activity in judging nations and in times of war is evident in Scripture and history. In 1 Chronicles 21 one angel stretched his sword over Jerusalem, and 70,000 men of Israel died in a plague. Angels announced the judgment of Sodom and Gomorrah in Genesis 19. In 2 Kings 19 Hezekiah prayed, and one warring angel killed 185,000 Assyrians, thwarting their occupation of Israel. In Acts 12 an angel struck down King Herod because of his pride. Only in the next life will we understand how many dictators, presidents, kings, sheikhs, and prime ministers have had their careers affected by angels. Furthermore, we will know then how many battles were won or lost at the hand of the angel allies. Perhaps then we will understand the angelic involvement that has swayed the nations.

All of these judgments pale in comparison to the end-time scenario of Revelation. Angels are the enforcers of God's wrath on the cursed earth. When we turn the pages of Revelation, there is an explosion of angelic activity like never before witnessed on planet Earth. In the opening three chapters, angels are assigned to the church and are active in communicating God's will. In Revelation chapters 4 and 5 angels join all of creation in the most majestic worship service ever assembled.

After that phenomenal worship, angels begin to blow trumpets that summon horrific judgments on the planet. As we continue to read in Revelation 6, we see the horror of wars, famines, plagues, and natural disasters claim one-third of the human population of the earth. Interestingly, at the sixth trumpet, angels of judgment bound in the river Euphrates are released to kill that one-third of humanity mentioned earlier. Yes, from Iraq, ancient Babylon will issue horrific bloodshed on Earth.

As we continue to turn the pages of Revelation we see an extreme intensification occur. Chapters 15 through 16 of Revelation record the pouring out of seven bowls of wrath on the earth. Images such as the river of blood brought on by angelic actions are terrifying. Angels will bring down false religions, and it is angels who judge the great religious harlot in Revelation 17:1–2: "Then one of the seven angels who had the seven bowls came and talked with me, saying to me, 'Come, I will show you the judgment of the great harlot who sits on many waters, with whom the kings of the earth committed fornication, and the inhabitants of the earth were made drunk with the wine of her fornication.'"

Angels announce the collapse of Wall Street and all other world markets. The fear that gripped our nation in these current seasons of recession and depression is nothing in comparison to that final hour.

> After this I saw another angel coming down from heaven, having great authority, and the earth was illuminated with his glory. He cried out mightily with a loud voice, saying: "'Fallen! Fallen is Babylon the Great!' She has become a dwelling place of demons, a

haunt for every unclean spirit, and a haunt for every unclean and hateful bird. For all the nations have drunk of the wine of the wrath of her sexual immorality, the kings of the earth have committed adultery with her, and the merchants of the earth have become rich through the abundance of her luxury." Then I heard another voice from heaven saying: "'Come out of her, my people, lest you partake in her sins, and lest you receive her plagues.'"

—REVELATION 18:1–4, MEV

All of the greed, thievery, and luxury will be brought down by the angels of God.

On the final pages of Revelation, angels accompany our Lord Jesus at His Second Coming. The mighty hosts of heaven who are His palace guards come to "mop up" the remaining foes on Earth. Paul describes that scene vividly: "And to give you who are troubled rest with us when the Lord Jesus is revealed from heaven with His mighty angels, in flaming fire taking vengeance on those who do not know God and do not obey the gospel of our Lord Jesus Christ" (2 Thess. 1:7–8, MEV). The Lord will come with mighty angels to finish off the enemy. Angels will implement the death of the wicked.

God will avenge His people at the revelation of Jesus Christ. Our Lord will be revealed with His "mighty angels." The word *mighty* translates *dunamis*, which means "explosive power." These angels will come in *phlox pur*, or "flaming fire," to purify the universe and punish the wicked! Second Thessalonians 1:9 says this punishment will be "everlasting destruction from the presence of the Lord."

Then Satan will be captured and contained by one mighty angel.

And I saw an angel coming down out of heaven, having the key to the bottomless pit and a great chain in his hand. He seized the dragon, that ancient serpent, who is the Devil and Satan, and bound him for a thousand years. He cast him into the bottomless pit, and shut him up, and set a seal on him, that he should deceive the nations no more, until the thousand years were ended. After that he must be set free for a little while.

... The devil, who deceived them, was cast into the lake of fire and brimstone where the beast and the false prophet were. They will be tormented day and night forever and ever.

—REVELATION 20:1–3, 10, MEV

All of the unsaved will be cast into hell by angels! Let the idea that angels are small effervescent creatures fluttering around leave you forever. Angels are mighty warriors and, in the last days, will execute God's wrath without mercy!

Finally, angels will announce the Rapture of the church. Our glorious translation will remove the final restraint, and God will unleash the final judgment: "For the Lord Himself will descend from heaven with a shout, with the voice of the archangel, and with the trumpet call of God. And the dead in Christ will rise first" (1 Thess. 4:16, MEV).

ANGELS SING A SONG OF END-TIMES DISASTERS

Further proof of angelic activity in the last days is a story a missionary to China tells about angels warning of end-times disaster through rural Chinese churchgoers who were singing in the Spirit during a 1995 worship service. The account reads as follows:

> The whole province of Shandong, in eastern China (population: 57 million), is in the midst of a sweeping revival. For fear of arrest, believers meet secretly in house churches, often by candlelight. At a 1995 meeting in Shandong, everyone was singing "in the Spirit" together (1 Corinthians 14:15), not in their own language, but "as the Spirit gave them utterance," all in harmony but all singing different words.
>
> Someone audiotaped the meeting. Later, when they played back the cassette, they were shocked! What they heard was not what had happened there at all—but the sound of angels singing in Mandarin—a song they had never heard before, and with a musical accompaniment that had not been there!!! When my friend first heard the tape, before anyone told him what it was, he exclaimed, "Those are angels!!" Actually, there was no other explanation. A Chinese Christian co-worker translated the tape. Below are the actual words sung by the angels! Note that the words express ideas with which these rural Chinese peasants were not familiar.

The End Is Near: Rescue Souls

The famine is becoming more and more critical. There are more and more earthquakes. The situation is becoming more and more sinister. People are fighting against each other, nation against nation. Disasters are more and more severe.

The whole environment is deteriorating. Disasters are more and more severe. People's hearts are wicked, and they do not worship the true God. Disasters are more and more severe.

Floods and droughts are more and more frequent. There is more and more homosexuality and incurable diseases. Disasters are more and more severe.

The climates are becoming more and more abnormal. The earth is more and more restless. The skies have been broken. The atmosphere is distorted. Disasters are more and more severe.

Chorus

The end is near. The revelation of love has been manifested. Rise up, rise up, rescue souls. The end is near. Rise up, rise up, rescue souls.[1]

GOD'S WRATH ON SATAN RELEASED AT THE CROSS

While I have shown through Scripture and real-life events that wars and catastrophes increase toward the close of time, let me make it clear that all demonic spirits are already defeated. At the cross and empty tomb, Christ won a transdimensional, cosmic victory over all the forces of darkness. The Bible affirms this truth. At Jesus's ascension, He laid claim to full authority in heaven and earth: "Then Jesus came and spoke to them, saying, 'All authority has been given to Me in heaven and on earth'" (Matt. 28:18, MEV).

In a cosmic display of power Jesus stripped the forces of darkness of their rights and authority: "…having wiped out the handwriting of requirements that was against us, which was contrary to us. And He has taken it out of the way, having nailed it to the cross. Having disarmed principalities and powers, He made a public spectacle of them, triumphing over them in it" (Col. 2:14–15).

He destroyed the devil's threat of death and his right to hold captive those who come to Christ: "So then, as the children share in flesh and blood, He likewise took part in these, so that through death He might destroy him who has the power of death, that is, the devil, and deliver those who through fear of death were throughout their lives subject to bondage" (Heb. 2:14–15, MEV).

All of the forces of darkness are subject to Jesus. As we have seen, Jesus has defeated them all in the eternal realms; we are here to enforce the victory already won: "…who has gone into heaven and is at the right hand of God, with angels and authorities and powers being made subject to Him" (1 Pet. 3:22, MEV).

The enemy is subject to Jesus but not subject to those who are not Christ's followers.

Though the war is won, we must enforce the victory of Christ. One of the reasons the enemy is here is to train followers for the future world. More significantly, the enemy is here for you to defeat him and display God's wisdom in saving you. (See chapter 6.)

History has an example that might help you understand this concept. The War of 1812 was over, and peace agreements had been reached when the Battle of New Orleans was fought. Andrew Jackson led the army to a great victory in New Orleans; however, one of the greatest battles of that century served no purpose beyond that of making Andrew Jackson president.

Likewise, our victory was won by Jesus Christ at the cross and the empty tomb. Yet, like the War of 1812 and the Battle of New Orleans, we are still in a battle, even though the war has been won. However, in this battle, we have the privilege to fight alongside our angel allies who enforce the victory already won!

The war is won, but we are in the final countdown to its finish. The Scriptures are very clear on the angelic actions at the end of the age, especially in the Book of Revelation where angelic activity is recorded on almost every page. We can be confident in our God who has already announced the victory and set His war plan in writing in Scripture.

PART TWO

DEMONS

INTRODUCTION

MONG THE MOST POPULAR TELEVISION PROGRAMS IN RECENT years is the reality show *Survivor*. A group of people are left in a desolate location and must survive on what is at hand. As a part of the intrigue, only one can win the large cash prize at the end of the contest. As the show progresses, the contestants never know who are their friends or who are their enemies!

Major Nidal Hasan was a psychiatrist in the United States Army. His education was paid for by the taxpayers. At thirty-nine years of age, the major had never served in a combat zone. In November of 2009 he shouted "Allahu Akbar" at a troop enlistment center in Fort Hood, Texas, and began to fire two weapons, killing thirteen and wounding more than thirty-five individuals, both civilian and military.[1] As his background was investigated, it was discovered that he had connections with Islamic terrorists.[2] Pretending to be a friend of the American soldiers, he was a plant of the enemy. The US Army did not know an enemy was among them.

We live in a beautiful world, yet to survive we must know our real enemies. Our strong enemies are not people but invisible forces of darkness. These forces from the dark side carry out the orders of a former ally who turned against our God. Satan, along with the forces of evil demons, is very near and ready to take out God's soldiers. Yet God has given us the resources to survive and thrive. But to do so we must know our enemy and be fully aware of the resources and weapons at our disposal.

This thought is captured beautifully by the psalmist in Psalm 126. This passage is a song of freedom, celebrating the return of captive Israelis from Babylon to Zion. Their emotion and confession picture for us freedom from Satan's snares and chains! Keeping us captive to wrong living, wrong thinking, wrong decisions, and wrong relation-ships is Satan's strategy to hold us down. His plan is to keep us from ever discovering our true selves and our way home.

In this psalm we observe the five legacies of liberty. These facets of freedom will be clearly seen in the life of the individual or in the life of the liberated church.

1. FREEDOM IN CHRIST IS LIKE A DREAM COME TRUE

When the LORD restored the captives of Zion, we were like those who dream.

—PSALM 126:1, MEV

The Christian life experienced to its fullest is also a dream come true. Most believers are living far beneath their privileges. Jesus promised, "I came that they may have life, and that they may have it more abun-dantly" (John 10:10, MEV). Are you living with an abundance of power, resources, and joy? The supernatural power of God is our heritage. The fruit of the Spirit is our promise.

Having led hundreds of people to freedom in Christ, I can say hon-estly that for many of them life becomes new, fresh, and exhilarating. One young lady was suffering from anorexia nervosa—self-destructive starvation. Although she had seen some counselors, her problem was not physical but spiritual. After extended counseling she rejected the enemy and his deception. The truth set her free. She is now active for Christ and especially enjoys singing in the choir.

People who have been set free from the enemy's strongholds invari-ably experience an amazing awakening to the spiritual life. Suddenly their eyes are open to all that they have in Christ.

In the early 1950s, before cruises became vogue, a poor man booked a passage from London to the United States in order to see his family. On board he stuck to himself and never entered the dining room. Toward the end of the journey passengers asked him why he did not eat in the dining room. "Oh, I could afford only a ticket for the trip. But I brought along cheese and crackers to sustain me," he assured them.

"Sir, the food is included in the price of the ticket!" a fellow passenger said.

It is possible to live the Christian life this way. We must realize that our commitment to Christ has brought us all that we need for this life and the life to come.

2. CHRISTIAN FREEDOM IS A SOURCE OF JOY

> Then our mouth was filled with laughter, and our tongue with singing.
> —PSALM 126:2, MEV

Never have I seen more joyless people than in the average church or religious gathering. People seem restrained and bound by tradition, denomination, or religious pride. Where are the exuberance, the wholehearted singing, the joyful shout, and the sounds of laughter?

No wonder so many believers and churches are insipid and weak. Nehemiah 8:10 says, "The joy of the LORD is your strength" (MEV). Shortly before the cross, Jesus prayed these words: "I say these things in the world, that they may have My joy fulfilled in themselves" (John 17:13, MEV). You may protest and say that Jesus was talking about our future joy in heaven. Yet Jesus went on to say, "I do not pray that You should take them out of the world, but that You should keep them from the evil one" (v. 15, MEV). It is "the evil one" who hinders our joy in the Christian life. Joy is the birthright and privilege of every Christian.

Once I was preaching the truths of spiritual freedom in an east Tennessee church. I was focusing on freedom from the spirit of heaviness or depression. (See chapter 17.) After teaching, I led the people through a prayer, repudiating the spirit of heaviness and releasing the fruit of the Spirit, which includes joy. I began reading Isaiah 61:3: "[I will] give them...the garment of praise for the spirit of heaviness." I then turned to Romans 14:17: "For the kingdom of God is not eating and drinking, but righteousness and peace and joy in the Holy Spirit." Suddenly a young woman, normally extremely shy, began to laugh, weep, and shout, "Praise the Lord! I am free! I'm free!" The truth of her freedom exploded in joy and poured out of her. Joy is the birthright of every Christian.

3. FREEDOM IN CHRIST IS EVIDENT
TO THE UNCHURCHED

> Then they said among the nations, "The LORD has done great
> things for them." The LORD has done great things for us; we
> are glad.
> —PSALM 126:2–3, MEV

The joy of ended captivity is convincing evidence to the unreached
around us. Seeing people delivered who have been in bondage is per-
suasive proof for witnessing. Christians who cannot handle the vicissi-
tudes of life faithfully and joyfully have no effective witness for Christ.
Yet when the unreached see the believer coping with anger, bitterness,
pride, depression, and other problems in a victorious manner, then the
message of Christ gets through. You see, friend, being a witness means
that your lifestyle is a part of the evidence.

A young married woman began to experience real freedom in
Christ from the assaults of depression by Satan. Though her problems
and pressures were unchanged, her perspective changed as she began
to see herself in Christ. Soon her children and husband came to Christ.
Since that time, others in her family have come to the Lord.

When our lives are lived in Christ, it is evident to the unchurched.

4. FREEDOM IN CHRIST RELEASES
THE FLOW OF REVIVAL

> Bring back our captivity, O LORD, as the streams in the South.
> —PSALM 126:4

Not long ago I was in Israel, and we were scheduled to travel into
normally dry southern Israel. Our Masada trip was postponed a day
because of rains in Jerusalem. Southern Israel by the Dead Sea is the
lowest point on the earth, so rains in upper Israel fill the streambeds
in the south. These flowing streams give life to the land.

What a beautiful picture of revival! When believers are set free from
the bondage of captivity, it releases the flow of the life of God into
the church. The dry places are where demons live, according to Luke
11:24. When revival comes, God's enemies are scattered (Ps. 68:1). Real

revival cannot come until the church knows her identity in Christ and begins to walk in the heritage of freedom.

Spiritual warfare is not destruction to revival; it is an impetus to revival. When believers experience the liberating power of the truth of the good news of Christ, then the power of God is released through them. Only when the church is released from carnal captivity will the Spirit of God be released in heaven-sent revival.

5. Freedom in Christ Inspires Witness

Those who sow in tears shall reap in joy. He who goes forth and weeps, bearing precious seed to sow, shall come home again with rejoicing, bringing his grain sheaves with him.

—Psalm 126:5–6, MEV

These familiar verses are usually preached alone, calling the church to passionate soul winning. Yet the sowing and reaping can only take place if the people have come home from spiritual bondage to the promised land of the Spirit-filled life.

How futile to call on people to sow and reap in the rocky and infertile soil of a spiritual wasteland. It is in the fertile land of the will of God that believers find the Bible to be a rich bag of precious, life-giving seeds. Only when one is free can he or she effectively sow in tears and reap in joy.

God promises revival and a harvest to those who come home from bondage. Believers can experience freedom that leads to a new effectiveness in their witness.

What you hold in your hand is the result of this decade of frontline combat against the forces of darkness. I have done hand-to-hand combat with demonic forces and rejoiced as they fled, terrified and defeated, from their victims.

Author Jack Taylor reminds us that Satan and the demons are decisive forces but defeated foes. The victory has been won at the cross and the empty tomb, yet the battle rages on Earth. You do not have to live in bondage and defeat. You can know the joy of victory and release.

While by no means all-encompassing, this manual can assist the church and individual believers in moving to the next level of spiritual warfare. Unless we restore unity and move together in the body of Christ, we shall live in defeat. Revival awaits us if we will move into battle against Satan together.

I summon all who are following Christ to train themselves for war. We will not see a moral revolution, nor can we stop the erosion of our own Western culture, without a spiritual fight. An increasingly militant Islam will not stop its advance unless the church takes the truth, empowered by the Spirit, into battle.

The victory is ours, but we must enforce it.

Section One

Tracing the History of Your Enemy

Chapter One

BATTLE BEYOND THE STARS

S OMETHING IS TERRIBLY WRONG IN OUR WORLD THAT CANNOT be explained by human reason. Unfortunately, most of the world, especially Western society, has rejected the idea of supernatural evil.

Our own Western culture is the only society both historical and contemporary that has largely rejected the idea of evil spirits. Since the Age of Enlightenment the Western scholar has sought to understand the world through verifiable, rationalistic, and explainable terms. There is no place for good or evil spirit beings in this "scientific" era. While there is much good that has come from the scientific method, there is a large blind spot when it comes to the spiritual side of man.

Christians have no choice but to face the scriptural, historical, and even contemporary fact that there is a supernatural enemy. Because of ludicrous literature and movies, the idea of a supreme evil being is viewed by many as a joke. Satan is caricatured as a red-suited villain with a tail, horns, and a pitchfork. This is a serious underestimation of the enemy.

Sun Tzu, the ancient Chinese philosopher, wrote the now classic *The Art of War* nearly twenty-five hundred years ago. This book has become the classic on how to achieve victory in the battlefield. He said this about the enemy: "If you know the enemy and know yourself, you need not fear the result of a hundred battles. If you know yourself but not the enemy, for every victory gained you will also suffer a defeat. If you know neither the enemy nor yourself, you will succumb in every battle."[1]

This is true of our spiritual warfare. We must have a healthy recognition and knowledge of our enemy combined with a thorough knowledge of our own identity.

The Christian must balance the fierceness of the enemy with powerful resources on our side of this spiritual battle. When this is done, we will exclaim with the prophet Elisha of old, "Do not be afraid, for there are more with us than with them" (2 Kings 6:16, MEV).

THE FORMATION OF SATAN

The name *Satan* appears less than twenty times in the Old Testament. The full revelation of our ancient foe comes in the New Testament. We find Satan already present in the Garden of Eden at the dawn of man's appearance on Earth. The war we are engaged in is the battle beyond the stars, the battle before history begins, indeed, the battle beyond time! We are a part of an intense war that began in the timeless realm we call eternity.

Our universe, with all its galaxies, solar systems, and vast expanses of space, size, and mystery, was created by God before time. There are other realms and dimensions beyond even our created universe. In spite of its beauty, there is something wrong in creation! The presence of evil, death, and struggle are evident on our planet. The human race has an enemy who hates us and wants to destroy us.

- We find Satan described as a serpent in Genesis 3 tempting our ancient parents and destroying their home.

- We find him testing Job and losing.

- We find Satan provoking David to trust in numbers instead of God: "Now Satan stood against Israel and incited David to number Israel" (1 Chron. 21:1, MEV).

- We find Satan resisting the ministry of worship in Zechariah's time: "Then he showed me Joshua, the high priest, standing before the angel of the LORD, and Satan standing at his right hand to accuse him. And the LORD said to Satan, 'The LORD rebuke you, Satan! The LORD who has chosen Jerusalem rebuke you! Is this not a burning brand taken out of the fire?'" (Zech. 3:1–2, MEV).

Where did this enemy come from? What is the mystery of prehistory called evil? We must piece together several passages from both the Old and New Testaments to understand evil and its origins. In Isaiah 14:12–15, we see a picture of the fall of Satan. We discover that Satan was once known as Lucifer, which means "light" or "daystar."

LUCIFER'S SINS AND FAILURES

Pride brought Lucifer down.

1. He fell from the dimension of glory—the heaven of heavens (Isa. 14:12).

2. He weakens nations (Isa. 14:12).

3. He sought God's place of supremacy. He wanted to be worshipped by the congregation and rise above the Shekinah glory—the cloud of God's presence (Isa. 14:13–15).

WHAT WAS HE LIKE BEFORE HIS FALL?

Far more informative is the passage beginning in Ezekiel 28:11. Like Isaiah, Ezekiel is predicting the fall of earthly kings. Ezekiel's proclamation is against the kings of Tyre and Sidon. Ezekiel also moves beyond an earthly king's description in this prophecy.

There are several reasons why many have viewed him as talking about Satan in this passage. First, there is no historical reference that has been discovered that Tyre ever had a king of this description. During this period there was a prince who ruled over Tyre. He was overthrown. The king of Tyre would be the father of this prince. Second, verse 13 says, "You were in Eden, the garden of God" (MEV). According to Genesis 3, the only persons in the Garden of Eden were God, Adam, Eve, and the serpent. Since it is obvious that none of these other personages here are being described, we feel confident, along with many other interpreters, that this is a symbolic reference to Satan.

Ezekiel 28:13 says that Satan was created. This reference gives us the opportunity to answer one of the often-asked questions, "Did God create evil?" If this is indeed a description of the formation of Satan, then we can answer resoundingly no! Verse 15 of Ezekiel 28 again refers to his creation: "You were perfect in your ways from the day that you were created, until iniquity was found in you" (mev).

According to this verse, our present-day enemy was created perfect but with a choice that one day he exercised toward evil. God gave the angelic host a will to choose just like man. This gives us a picture of the formation of Satan, but we must turn to the earlier description we find of him in the Scriptures.

THE CHARACTERISTICS AND FUNCTION OF SATAN

Let us look at these ancient texts and imagine what Satan was like before the fall!

He was beautiful!

Look again at Ezekiel's description: "Son of man, take up a lamentation for the king of Tyre and say to him, Thus says the LORD GOD: You had the seal of perfection, full of wisdom and perfect in beauty" (Ezek. 28:12, mev).

He gave off a rainbow of iridescent colors. He was the combined brilliance of every precious stone. He was as valuable as the most costly stones and as beautiful as the colors of the rainbow. The problem was that stones do not give off light of themselves; they only reflect light. He evidently forgot this most important truth as he was puffed up with pride.

He was assigned to cover the angels and the land of Eden.

Eden was part of ancient earth: "You were in Eden, the garden of God; every precious stone was your covering: the sardius, topaz, and the diamond, the beryl, the onyx, and the jasper, the sapphire, the emerald, and the carbuncle, and gold. The workmanship of your settings and sockets was in you; on the day that you were created" (Ezek. 28:13, mev).

The stones indicate that he was a part of a worshipping host. These stones are similar to the stones an Israelite high priest wore. He was musical.

He was also a created being; he was called a cherub.

You were the anointed cherub that covers....
—Ezekiel 28:14, mev

Lucifer's assignment was established by God as guardian over the earth and all its life forms. Also, he was set over the land we now know as Israel.

He knew the secrets of creation and life.

> You were upon the holy mountain of God; you walked up and down in the midst of the stones of fire.
> —Ezekiel 28:14, mev

The stones of fire seem to be God's ancient source of creative power. Satan's fall and ultimate judgment are also described by the prophet: "And you sinned; therefore I have cast you as profane out of the mountain of God; and I have destroyed you, O covering cherub, from the midst of the stones of fire...I cast you to the ground" (Ezek. 28:16–17, mev).

The Fall of Satan

When did he fall?

Many see the time of his fall as coming between Genesis 1:1 and 1:2. While the scope of this chapter will not allow a lengthy defense of this cosmological view, several key points need to be given as they bear upon our understanding of the origin and function of the enemy. First, there is scriptural warrant that God did not create this earth "without form and void" originally. This designation found in Genesis 1:2 consists of the Hebrew words *tohuw*, which means "without form," and *bohuw*, which means "void."

We find the same Hebrew word *tohuw* in Isaiah 45:18, but it is translated as "vain": "For thus says the Lord, who created the heavens, who is God who formed the earth and made it...who *did not create it in vain*, who formed it to be inhabited" (emphasis added).

If God did not create the earth this way, then a catastrophe of cataclysmic proportions must have happened between these two verses. Genesis 1:3 and the verses following would indicate a "re-creation" after an undesignated period of time. This is textually possible because the word *created* in Genesis 1:1 is the Hebrew word *bara*. This word stands out as a word meaning "to create something from nothing." The rest of the Hebrew words for "create" (excluding animal life) mean "to create out of existing materials."

Secondly, this would give us an understanding of many other scriptures. Jesus said in Luke 10:18, "I saw Satan as lightning fall from heaven" (MEV). While many interpret this verse in light of the work of the seventy disciples Jesus had sent out (Luke 10:1–17), there is also strong merit to understand Jesus's statement in light of His preincarnate existence. This would help explain why the enemy in the form of the serpent was already present in the Garden of Eden. The whole idea of Satan as a created angel that rebelled and fell, along with other rebellious angels, fits with this understanding of Bible cosmogony.

Why did Satan fall?

A discussion of why the enemy fell from heaven must follow. Look again at Isaiah 14. It gives insight into the steps that led to the enemy's downfall. Five times in this passage he says, "I will…" Isaiah records them: "For you have said in your heart: '*I will* ascend into heaven, *I will* exalt my throne above the stars of God; *I will* also sit on the mount of the congregation on the farthest sides of the north; *I will* ascend above the heights of the clouds, *I will* be like the Most High'" (Isa. 14:13–14, emphasis added).

When the enemy purposed in his heart to carry out his sin, a terrible thing came to God's domain. There were now two wills in existence. Up until this time there had only been God's will, and everything moved in harmony and peace. God cannot allow any being to oppose His will and continue without punishment. The very essence of sin is to choose our will rather than God's.

What happened? There was an old earth, pristine and beautiful—God was preparing it for human beings so it would have all the resources necessary for us.

Satan was jealous of God's plan to set man into the earth. He and certain angels "covered" the earth. His rebellion was exposed, and he fell to Earth!

This fall was a catastrophe of monumental proportions. Much of the ancient earth and its prehistoric life were destroyed. The earth became void and empty!

God returned to the land of Eden, which stretches from the Mediterranean all the way across the Middle East. This area is the cradle of civilization. He planted a garden in Eden to take back this planet for humanity. This battle began beyond the stars!

In this war one-third of the angels went with the rebel leader, Satan, and are now what we call demons or evil spirits.

God was not surprised, and from fallen humanity He would bring His Son into the world. The battle would rage against Jesus at the cross. And at the cross Jesus would defeat Satan.

Satan is a defeated foe because of the work of Christ on the cross, but he is also a formidable foe. Our struggle with him is likened to the famous battle of New Orleans during the War of 1812. General Andrew Jackson commanded this greatest battle of the war after the papers of treaty had already been signed! Word had not reached them of these events.

We too fight in a battle that has already been decided. Jesus forever sealed the fate of the host of demonic forces and Satan himself when He died on the cross. Yet Satan still "walks around as a roaring lion, seeking whom he may devour" (1 Pet. 5:8, MEV).

Thank God Jesus has overthrown Satan. We must put away our pride and bow at Jesus's feet as our Lord and Savior. According to Scripture, one day Satan will be cast down at our feet (Ezek. 28:17). One day he shall be gone forever. "Yet thou shall be brought down to hell, to the sides of the pit" (Isa. 14:15, KJV). Satan is defeated, and you will learn in this study that the victory is already ours.

In January of 1994 the Dallas Cowboys professional football team was preparing to play the San Francisco 49ers for the NFC championship. The coach of the Cowboys, Jimmy Johnson, caused a media uproar when he called in to a local radio show the Thursday before the game and boldly asserted, "The Dallas Cowboys will win the game!" When questioned why he would make such a bold statement before playing such a talented opponent, he stated that it didn't matter what team they were playing. He had seen the Cowboys in preparation that week, and they had fire in them. He didn't have to measure their opponent—they were ready.[2] (And by the way, the Cowboys won!) Are we ready?

Chapter Two

THE CONTINUOUS WAR IN EDEN

AFTER LUCIFER'S FALL THE EARTH BECAME WITHOUT FORM and void. (See Genesis 1:1–2.) The Hebrew word translated "was" is often translated "became." Since Genesis 1:1–2 can be read, "...*became* without form, and void," it seems obvious that something happened between Genesis 1:1 and 1:2—an earth-shaking, world-destroying catastrophe.

THE OLD CREATION

Lucifer had reigned over the earth from a land called Eden, whose place of worship was located on the "Mountain of God" in the place the ancients called Salem ("peace") and that we now call Jerusalem. The world was a wonder of animate life. It was God's zoo, with strange creatures we call dinosaurs. From Jerusalem Lucifer led worship and walked in the stones of fire, which represent healing power. (See Ezekiel 28.)

Lucifer's fall was like the impact of an asteroid. Suddenly all animal life on the terra firma vanished. It was sudden and catastrophic. When I visited the Dinosaur National Park in eastern Utah, I was amazed by two things. First, dinosaurs died with food in their mouths, eggs in the process of hatching, and they were frozen in terror! Second, the river bored through a solid rock hill like a drill. Under normal circumstances that river would have gone around the hill. A force not known in geology drilled through that rock!

I believe this ancient tragedy is the result of Satan's fall to ruin. What scientists call the Cambrian age was caused by the impact of God's judgment on Satan. Here we find the fossils of multitudes of ancient life forms. Though scientists call this time "an explosion of life," it was really an "explosion of death." The aftermath of the death of all these living creatures is the vast deposits of oil and gas that drive the world system and economy even now.

EDEN, A VAST LAND

When we look at the original Eden, we see a vast and beautiful land! In Genesis 2:10–14, we discover that out of the northern part of the land of Eden flowed four large rivers—Pishon, Gihon, Hiddekel (Tigris), and Euphrates. Two of the four rivers are easily recognizable—the Tigris and Euphrates.

The river Pishon is no longer flowing, but its rift has been discovered by land-penetrating satellite technology. Its rift runs through Saudi Arabia all the way to what is now the Red Sea. Some believe that before the continental shifts, it flowed all the way to India, to what is now the Ganges River.

The river Gihon is a different matter; it flowed through Israel and Jordan all the way through what is now the Red Sea into Egypt and into the Nile! The Flood made changes in the direction of the rivers.

ANOTHER CATASTROPHE

The big change came in a massive earthquake that was caused when the continental plates of Africa, Europe, and Asia collided. This event is recorded in the Bible during the days of Peleg (101 years after the Flood).

> To Eber were born two sons: the name of one was Peleg, for in his days the earth was divided; and his brother's name was Joktan.
> —GENESIS 10:25; SEE ALSO 1 CHRONICLES 1:18–19

This great division created what is called the Africa rift where the Jordan Valley is located today. Before that, the river Gihon ran through Jerusalem. Its remnant is still called the spring of Gihon to this day.

Knowing then that Eden was a huge landmass before the destruction of the old creation, we see that God determined to reclaim the planet and His ancient holy mountain. Many believe that the garden planted as Eden was located in Jerusalem! Genesis 2:8 says that Yahweh planted it in the east of Eden.

In the same place where Lucifer led worship and had been the covering cherub of the old earth, God placed human beings to restore the ruined earth.

As proof of this, a closer examination of Ezekiel 28 will clear up the mystery. Ezekiel 28:13 declares that Lucifer was in Eden when it was still pristine. The same verse declares that Lucifer was beautiful and musical, giving glory to the Lord. As one of the cherubim, Lucifer was close to the Lord, serving as a traveling throne for God. Psalm 18:10 says, "He rode on a cherub, and flew; He flew swiftly on the wings of the wind" (MEV).

After the fall Lucifer became Satan, a serpent. Fallen from his former glory, Satan lurked in Eden. His desire was to thwart God's plan and dethrone the new king of Eden and of the earth, Adam.

SATAN'S EARLY SUCCESS

The Lord set Adam and Eve in a perfect environment. Made in God's image, they were given a mind to think, a heart to love, and a will to choose. To test the mind, God gave Adam the assignment to name all of the animal life. To prove his heart, God gave Adam his counterpart—the female, Eve. To test his will there were two trees planted—the tree of life and the tree of the knowledge of good and evil. God planted the tree of life, and I believe Satan planted the tree of the knowledge of good and evil! I believe this because God had already given Adam and Eve permission to eat everything except that tree. They could eat of the tree of life, but not of the tree of the knowledge of good and evil. Every day they could choose life or death. God allowed that tree to be there to test the will of Adam. It is this free will that makes us like God. This would be precisely Satan's tactic to tempt our ancient parents. Genesis 3:5 says, "For God knows that on the day you eat of it your eyes will be opened and you will be like God, knowing good and evil" (MEV).

This resulted in man being driven out of the garden east of Eden near what came to be Jericho, Earth's oldest city. Joshua 3:16 speaks of the city of Adam when describing the miraculous parting of the

Jordan River. To this day there is a place identified seventeen miles north of Jericho, exactly east of Jerusalem, called the Village of Adam.

It is also interesting that Abel, who was murdered by Cain, is said to have lived in the same region. In fact, "the stone of Abel" mentioned in 1 Samuel 6:18 is cited as the place of Abel's death. There are also four villages named to this day east of Jerusalem connected to Abel (Abel Maim, Abel Meholah, Abel Shittim, and Abel Keramim). All of this indicates that the Garden of Eden could have been in Jerusalem.

Perhaps the most telling evidence is the Spring of Gihon. The river of Eden that flowed through the garden was named Gihon. It remains an underground water source until this day. Satellite photography shows riverbeds all the way through the Dead Sea into Africa from Syria to the Nile. As we said earlier, the continental shift changed the riverbeds. This shut off the Gihon and created the Dead Sea.

EAST OF EDEN

Adam and Eve continued to worship by returning to the gateway to Eden. There they offered sacrifice and taught their children to do the same.

It is interesting that the presence of God was guarded by other cherubim, Lucifer's replacements! "He drove the man out, and at the east of the garden of Eden He placed the cherubim and a flaming sword which turned in every direction, to guard the way to the tree of life" (Gen. 3:24, MEV). In man's fallen condition, had he eaten of the tree of life, he would have been condemned to live in an aging body that could never die.

It is interesting that when the tabernacle and later the temple were built, they placed golden images of two cherubim to cover and protect God's throne on Earth, the ark of the covenant! The cherubim still attend and cover the presence of God.

When Genesis 3:8 speaks of the cool of the day when God appeared to Adam and Eve, the word *cool* is *ruwach*, or "spirit." Perhaps when Adam's fallen family approached the gate of the garden to worship, they could see the glory cloud or Shekinah and feel its cooling breezes.

After Adam and Eve were driven out of Eden, two sons were born to them. The elder one, Cain, killed his brother, Abel, and was driven away to the land of Nod. This is the land of Iran!

RETURN TO THE GARDEN

The Flood would come, and catastrophe would again touch the whole earth. The land of Eden would disappear, as would the garden. Yet God had chosen Jerusalem to be His point of contact with the earth and mankind! Because of God's love for that land, He called Abraham to leave everything and go there to plant a new nation. Why did God choose that land? I believe it was His mountain! In Psalm 135:21 God is said to dwell in Jerusalem. Jerusalem is mentioned in Scripture more than eight hundred times. The traveling city, which will house the bride of Christ, the church, is called the New Jerusalem. Many believe it will sit in stationary orbit over old Jerusalem.

Abraham returned to Jerusalem, also called Salem, to pay tithes to Melchizedek (Gen. 14). According to the Book of Jasher, which gives us the historical perspective of the Old Testament, Melchizedek was Shem, the son of Noah. Shem lived one hundred years after this visit and talked with Isaac and Jacob.[1] (See Joshua 10:13; 2 Samuel 1:18.) Abraham offered Isaac on the mountain of the Lord.

Later David would take Jerusalem from the Jebusites. From that day until now Satan has hated the Jews and Jerusalem, and he hates the plan of God to save the world through a Jewish Messiah.

SATAN'S ULTIMATE PLAN

Satan's war against humanity still targets Jerusalem. Here he was humiliated. Here Christ died on the cross and was raised from the dead. Here, in the Middle East, Satan has stirred up war and hatred until this day. Satan hates the Jews, hates Israel, and hates the church.

Adam fell in the Garden of Eden. It is my firm belief that the Garden of Gethsemane is the old Eden. Here the Second Adam refused the voice of Satan and took our cup of death. At the cross Jesus opened the gates of a new paradise and a new Eden.

It is important for you to understand that Satan, through the Muslims, is still trying to conquer Jerusalem. It is also important for you to understand that your personal struggles are rooted in an ancient conflict. But you must rejoice in the victory given to us at Calvary; though two thousand years old, this victory is available to you today.

THE TREE OF LIFE

Adam forfeited eternal life by choosing Satan's tree of the knowledge of good and evil over God's tree of life. Because of Jesus we can again taste the tree of life.

> In the middle of its street, and on either side of the river, was the tree of life, which bore twelve fruits, each tree yielding its fruit every month. The leaves of the tree were for the healing of the nations.
> —REVELATION 22:2

And Revelation 22:14 tells us, "Blessed are those who do His commandments, that they may have the right to the tree of life, and may enter through the gates into the city" (MEV).

Chapter Three

WAR ON HUMANITY

IN GENESIS 3:1–15 WE READ THE HORRIFIC RECORD OF THE FALL AND ruin of humanity. The enemy was present in this most pristine garden.

> Now the serpent was more cunning than any beast of the field which the LORD God had made. And he said to the woman, "Has God indeed said, 'You shall not eat of every tree of the garden'?"
> —GENESIS 3:1

Here our enemy questions God's integrity and love. Eve responds to the serpent by repeating God's warning.

> And the woman said to the serpent, "We may eat the fruit of the trees of the garden; but of the fruit of the tree which is in the midst of the garden, God has said, 'You shall not eat it, nor shall you touch it, lest you die.'"
> —GENESIS 3:2–3

Clearly she added to the word of God with the phrase "neither shall you touch it."

In verse 4 Satan targets her soul by calling God a liar and then issuing a false promise:

> Then the serpent said to the woman, "You will not surely die. For God knows that in the day you eat of it your eyes will be opened, and you will be like God, knowing good and evil."

Lured by the temptation, Eve bites the poisoned fruit, and Adam does the same.

> When the woman saw that the tree was good for food, that it was pleasing to the eyes and a tree desirable to make one wise, she took of its fruit and ate; and she gave to her husband with her, and he ate.
>
> —Genesis 3:6, MEV

They had been clothed in God's glory, and now they are stripped naked by their sin. "Then the eyes of both were opened, and they knew that they were naked. So they sewed fig leaves together and made coverings for themselves" (Gen. 3:7, MEV).

They could not cover themselves, so they hid from God.

> Then they heard the sound of the LORD God walking in the garden in the cool of the day, and the man and his wife hid themselves from the presence of the LORD God among the trees of the garden.
>
> —Genesis 3:8, MEV

Again, the word *cool* is *ruwach* in Hebrew, which means "spirit." God came for communion, and Adam and Eve hid from what they had once enjoyed.

In verse 9, "The LORD God called to the man and said to him, 'Where are you?'" (MEV). Here is the call of justice and love to fallen humanity. "He said, 'I heard Your voice in the garden and was afraid because I was naked, so I hid myself'" (v. 10, MEV). Fear has replaced favor and faith, and God exposes their failure.

> And He said, "Who told you that you were naked? Have you eaten from the tree of which I commanded you not to eat?" The man said, "The woman whom You gave to be with me, she gave me fruit of the tree, and I ate."
>
> —Genesis 3:11–12, MEV

Adam blamed Eve, and she blamed Satan; yet ultimately they both made the fatal choice.

"Then the LORD God said to the woman, 'What have you done?' And the woman said, 'The serpent deceived me, and I ate'" (v. 13, MEV). God pronounced judgment on Satan and issued the great promise of a Seed that would come to be bruised yet would ultimately crush Satan's head.

> So the LORD God said to the serpent: "Because you have done this, you are cursed more than all cattle, and more than every beast of the field; on your belly you shall go, and you shall eat dust all the days of your life. And I will put enmity between you and the woman, and between your seed and her Seed; He shall bruise your head, and you shall bruise His heel."
>
> —GENESIS 3:14–15

Now, having read the story, let's look at the implications for our lives today. As we have seen, there is a basis for the belief that before his fall Lucifer was the principality God had appointed over our created order. At his fall the primeval creation was ruined and enshrouded in darkness. Lucifer, the light bearer, became Satan, the adversary or enemy. The shining cherub became the stalking dragon. Satan thought that he was the source of his beauty, wisdom, and music. He is described as a jewel whose glory can only be seen in pure light. In his pride Lucifer refused to see that his glory was the reflected glory of the Most High God. A diamond in total darkness is no more than a sharp pebble.

Consequently Satan receives the verdict of heaven and is cast out in devastating judgment, losing his position and authority. Creation lies under devastating judgment and darkness. Here are several Scripture verses that confirm his ruin: Job 9:3–10; 38:4–13; Psalm 18:7–15.

The earth bears the scars of two ancient catastrophes: the ancient ruin and the Flood. Our planet has been shaken, its continents torn apart with an age of ice and glaciers having left deep canyons, unstable underground faults, unpredictable volcanoes, and devastating earthquakes testifying to the original ruin.

The preincarnate Christ was the divine creator. John 1:3 tells us, "All things were made by him" (KJV), and in Colossians 1:16–17 we read, "For by him were all things created...and by him all things consist [hold together]" (KJV). Satan's fall from heaven led to the devastation of the ancient creation. It was an attack on Christ before He became incarnate, God in the flesh.

Here the earth remained for an unknown period as a wreck and a ruin. Then God instituted His plan for the ruined creation. He recaptured it through a creature to be known as man.

The state of creation is reset in Genesis 1 and 2; from existing matter God remade the earth and placed in it a paradise called Eden. Out of the chaos God assembled order. In the six-day account of Creation we read that God made, divided, formed, set, and so on. The word *create* is only used in reference to the "breath" of God. He created moving life out of existing materials, but He made it live by His breath. Even man was formed of "dust of the earth" and given life by God's creative Spirit.

So God made man in His own image. This means man was given a spirit, a spirit that has the three qualities of God. Man was given a mind to think, a heart to love, and a will to choose. He was placed in an environment to test all three capacities. He could use his mind to name the animals and govern the earth. He could use his heart to love both Eve and God. He could use his will to choose right or wrong.

In the midst of the garden stood the tree of life and the tree of death. God instructed Adam and Eve to eat of all the trees, including the tree of life. The only one forbidden was the tree of the knowledge of good and evil.

At this point Satan embodied himself in a fiery creature called a serpent, or *nachash* in the Hebrew, which speaks of beauty and brilliance. Please note, only three times in Scripture does Satan take over a body: the serpent, Judas Iscariot, and the Antichrist. Also notice that Satan is already present on the earth!

THE COMMENCEMENT OF THE WAR

With the stage set, Satan launched his attack on mankind. There are two important things to notice about Satan's attack in the verses we read in Genesis: his motive and his method of attack.

First, the motive of the enemy can be seen. Why did he attack man? Because he viewed the creation of man as a mistake. He was jealous of the future glory God promised man. Psalm 8:5 says, "You have made him a little lower than the angels, and crowned him with glory and honor" (MEV). Satan and his hosts of heavenly beings desired the earth and its glory. They hated man and his position. Hebrews 2:7 states, "You...set him over the works of Your hands" (MEV). Satan's motive remains the same—to thwart God's plan on the earth.

Secondly, the method of the enemy's attack is clear. Satan attacked the first human beings in an attempt to get to God through mankind. Satan has a method. Ephesians 6:11 warns us of the "wiles" of the devil.

The word *wiles* is the Greek word *methodeia*, from which we get our word *methods*. Satan is deceptive but predictable; he used deception and temptation, methods often repeated since his fall.

THE CASUALTIES OF THE WAR

Satan launched his attack through the woman. The Bible calls woman the weaker sex (1 Pet. 3:7). That does not mean weaker in mind, body, endurance, or worth. It means more susceptible. While some commentaries may argue this point, Matthew Henry says in his commentary that Satan approached Eve while she was away from her husband. She was completely deceived and thought that she was doing what was best for her husband. First Timothy 2:14 states, "Adam was not deceived..." He knew exactly what he was doing. He chose by his own free will to disobey.

Through this act mankind became lost. (See Romans 5:12, 17, 19; 1 Corinthians 15:21–22.) At one point there had been only two wills: God's and Satan's. Now every man has a will to choose for God or against God. Man is, by fact of nature and by choice of will, a sinner. Man is utterly lost.

THE CONTINUATION OF THE WAR

God announced the continual enmity between man and Satan, our adversary. It would seem as though Satan had won. He had deceived woman. He had succeeded in getting man to doubt the veracity of God's words. He had succeeded in bringing doubt about the goodness of God. But Satan failed at one decisive point. He could not govern the will of man. Isaiah 53:6 states, "We have turned, every one, to his own way." Man now asserts his fallen will. Satan cannot take the chaos of humanity and weld it together for long for his evil purpose.

This explains the terrible tragedies and difficulties of our world. It is a fallen world under the curse of sin. Satan is a rebel against God, and so is every person who chooses his own way. There is a war going on. The very nature of war is to leave tragedy in its wake. Human history is one vast parade of man and Satan trying to do something for man without God. God has permitted the horror of tragedy to convince an unbelieving world it is utterly helpless without Him.

THE CLIMAX OF THE WAR

As we observed in Genesis 3:15, God announced ultimate triumph right from the beginning: "And I will put enmity between you and the woman, and between your seed and her Seed; He shall bruise your head, and you shall bruise His heel." There will be a bruised seed and a crushed serpent. Satan's defeat is to come through man. This is the first prophecy of the decisive battle that took place on Calvary's cross. Satan would vent his anger on the Son of God. Christ died for our sins and destroyed Satan's demand for our souls. Satan held the power of death according to Hebrews 2:14: "So then, as the children share in flesh and blood, He likewise took part in these, so that through death He might destroy him who has the power of death, that is, the devil" (MEV).

When we are saved into the family of God, according to Colossians 2:13–15 we rest in the victory of Christ. Christ stripped demonic forces of their authority as well as robbed them of their powers. Satan has already been defeated.

It is our task, then, to enforce the victory of the cross until Jesus returns for us. We do not belong to Satan. He has no authority over us. We are God's property. All we need to do is simply affirm the fact that now all the kingdoms of this world are already overthrown. They are defeated even if they don't know it.

Ultimately all of Satan's invisible forces will be forever confined to the lake of fire. Until that day it is the purpose of God to display His glory in His new people, the church. Ephesians 3:9–11 (NIV) states this ultimate purpose:

> To make plain to everyone the administration of this mystery, which for ages past was kept hidden in God, who created all things. His intent was that now, through the church, the manifold wisdom of God should be made known to the rulers and authorities in the heavenly realms, according to his eternal purpose that he accomplished in Christ Jesus our Lord.

God was not surprised by the fall of man. His plan is right on schedule. Everyone who surrenders to Him and lays down the weapons of rebellion becomes a part of His new kingdom. We become soldiers as well as saints and servants until that day.

Chapter Four

WAR AGAINST THE PROMISED
SEED OF ISRAEL

ONE OF THE KEY WORDS IN REVELATION IS THE WORD *NIKAO*, which means "conqueror." The Nike corporation chose *overcome*, from this Greek word, to describe their athletic shoes and apparel, implying that the wearers can be conquerors or, better said, "overcomers."

Revelation 12:11 speaks of such a conquest over Satan when it says, "And they overcame him [Satan] by the blood of the Lamb." Satan must be overcome!

That particular word of victory follows some strange battle imagery. In Revelation 12:4–5 Satan is described as a dragon standing before a pregnant woman ready to devour her child as soon as it is born. The next verses describe a war in the spiritual realm between Michael, the prince of the host of righteous angels, and Satan, the fallen prince. This colossal struggle ensues over God's purposes on Earth and culminates in the Incarnation, God coming to Earth in human flesh through "the seed of a woman." This ancient prophecy is found in Genesis 3:15, which declares this seed of woman will crush the head of the serpent while being bruised in the process.

When we look at the prophetic promises of the Messiah, we discover that the Messiah had to be a male descendant of Abraham and Isaac (Gen. 22:18), a Jewish man born from the lineage of Jacob (Num. 24:17). Not only was the Messiah to be Jewish, but He was also to be a descendant of the royal line of David (Matt. 1:6). This prophesied seed had to be born in Bethlehem (Mic. 5:2). This child must be born of a virgin (Isa. 7:14). His arrival must take place 450 years after Cyrus's decree and Daniel's seventy weeks of years prophecy (Dan. 9:24). This coming One could only be Jesus Christ, born unto the Virgin Mary.

Satan declared war on the promised seed. He would try to stop the coming of God's Son into the world.

> His tail drew a third of the stars of heaven, and threw them to the earth. The dragon stood before the woman who was ready to give birth, to devour her Child as soon as He was born. She gave birth to a male Child, "who was to rule all nations with an iron scepter." And her Child was caught up to God and to His throne.
> —REVELATION 12:4–5, MEV

SATAN'S HATRED OF ISRAEL

As we turn the pages of Scripture, the struggle unfolds. Satan provoked Cain to murder righteous Abel, yet God sent Seth! Satan corrupted the people of the earth so the judgment of the Flood came. However, Noah and his family were saved, and Noah's son, Shem, became a cousin of the seed. Abraham almost lost Sarah to Pharaoh. Esau sought to kill Jacob (Israel) and destroy the Jewish nation before it could be birthed.

During the Egyptian captivity, Satan stirred wicked Pharaoh to kill the firstborn of Israel and destroy the prophetic line, but Moses was appointed to save the Jewish people once again.

David had to face the giant Goliath and the threats of a demonized King Saul. Furthermore, David's family experienced intrigue, division, and murder.

Later, when King Jehoshaphat died, his son Jehoram murdered all of the royal offspring. Then an Arab enemy attacked Israel while Jehoram was king and killed all of his children except for one, Ahaziah. When Jehu slew Ahaziah, Jezebel's daughter Athaliah saw her chance to become queen. In a bloodthirsty rage, she murdered all the children of Ahaziah, again except for one!

A MIRACULOUS PRESERVATION

The wife of Jehoiada, the high priest of Israel, rescued the one remaining child in the royal line of David, Joash, and had him taken away. For a period of six years the entire prophetic promise of the Messiah resided in that one child.

FOR SUCH A TIME AS THIS

The little Book of Esther never mentions God. However, the book's sole purpose is to declare God's victory over another satanic effort to exterminate Israel and stop the advent of the Messiah. The courage of Esther and a king's insomnia exposed the plot of wicked Haman to destroy the Jewish nation.

God's preservation of Israel through the Babylonian captivity and through the murderous scheme of Antiochus Epiphanes is miraculous.

BETHLEHEM BLOODBATH

Finally, the moment came for the promised seed to be born in Bethlehem. Mary and Joseph made the long, arduous journey, and Jesus was born in a cave, swaddled in rags, and laid in a feed trough!

Satan stirred the Edomite Herod, an evil king, to destroy all the babies in the vicinity of Bethlehem. His wish was to destroy any rival for the throne. God sent wise men from Persia (Iran) to bring finances to Mary and Joseph. Once supernaturally warned, Mary, Joseph, and the baby were able to spend seven years in Egypt because of the wealth given them by the wise men.

GOD INCARNATE IN JESUS

When Jesus began His ministry, Satan showed up and tried to get Jesus to kill Himself by jumping from the pinnacle of the temple. Jesus's old friends in Nazareth turned on Him and tried to push Him off a cliff. Satan thought he had finally won when Christ was nailed to a cross and died.

For three days, Jesus faced Satan in the realms of death. Peter declared that Jesus made a proclamation to "the spirits in prison" (1 Pet. 3:18–20). Jesus seized death, Satan's most formidable weapon, and took the keys!

> So then, as the children share in flesh and blood, He likewise took part in these, so that through death He might destroy him who has the power of death, that is, the devil, and deliver those

who through fear of death were throughout their lives subject to
bondage.

—HEBREWS 2:14–15, MEV

On the Day of Pentecost Peter, who had been tempted by Satan,
declared that death could not hold Jesus: "Whom God raised up by
loosening the pull of death, because it was not possible that He should
be held by it" (Acts 2:24, MEV).

Satan made the mistake of the ages. In seeking to destroy the seed
by killing Jesus, Satan's act of retaliation resulted in the salvation of
humanity.

A NEW RACE OF MEN

Jesus was raised from the dead and became the Second Adam, the
head of a new race of men not subject to the old division of color and
culture.

Romans 5:12–14 declares that a Second Adam has come. A new king
has come in Jesus of Nazareth. Jesus has broken the tyranny of Satan,
exposed the darkness, and shattered the empire of evil. Jesus has
crushed the headship of Satan and rendered sin's dominion powerless.
Now grace reigns through Jesus Christ. (See Romans 5:21.)

This "one new man" is the church for whom the Messiah, Jesus,
is the head. The reign of grace has resulted in millions becoming
Christians. (See Ephesians 2:8–9.) New possibilities appear and are
attainable for every obedient believer. God has made a new race of
people in the church. We are part of God's new order called "one new
man" (Eph. 2:14–15).

THE BATTLE CONTINUES

In the next chapter we will trace the battle lines throughout the history
of the church. It is important to note that anti-Semitism is on the rise.
The continuing struggles in the Middle East are over Jerusalem. Hitler
sought to exterminate the Jewish people. His purposes, if achieved,
would have stopped God's chosen people from returning to their
homeland and would have thwarted Bible prophecy. Israel survived,
and so does the church in spite of two millennia of struggle and strife.

Chapter Five

SATAN'S WAR ON THE CHURCH

THE BOOK OF REVELATION IS STUDIED AND CITED FOR ITS striking prophecies and thrilling pictures of the coming of the Lord. However, at the beginning of this important book is a collection of letters directed to seven churches. Within these letters is a remarkably complete treatment of problems that face the church in the twenty-first century. Under the inspiration of the Holy Spirit, John penned warnings about the dangers of losing their first love (Rev. 2:4), of being afraid of suffering (v. 10), of doctrinal defection (vv. 14–15), of moral departure (v. 20), of spiritual deadness (Rev. 3), of not holding fast (v. 11), and of straddling the fence (vv. 15–16). These problems are just as prevalent in today's church as they were in the first century.

I believe that the use of the word *overcome* (*nikao* in Greek) (Rev. 2:7, 11, 17, 26; 3:5, 12, 21) used here in the context of Revelation is related to spiritual warfare. The besetting sins or failures of each of the churches were caused, influenced, and encouraged by demonic forces that Satan assigned to attack these churches. Each church had to repent and overcome by recognizing and exposing the demonic force.

If you doubt the operation of Satan in the local church, take a look at the straightforward references to him in these chapters of Revelation!

> I know your works and tribulation and poverty (but you are rich). And I know the blasphemy of those who say they are Jews and are not, but are a synagogue of Satan. Do not fear any of those things which you are about to suffer. Look, the devil is about to throw some of you into prison, that you may be tried,

and you will have tribulation for ten days. Be faithful unto death, and I will give you the crown of life.
—REVELATION 2:9–10

I know your works, and where you dwell, where Satan's throne is. And you hold fast to My name, and did not deny My faith even in the days in which Antipas was My faithful martyr, who was killed among you, where Satan dwells.
—REVELATION 2:13–14

Now to you I say, and to the rest in Thyatira, as many as do not have this doctrine, who have not known the depths of Satan, as they say, I will put on you no other burden.
—REVELATION 2:24, MEV

Listen! I will make them of the synagogue of Satan, who say they are Jews and are not, but lie. Listen! I will make them come and worship before your feet and to know that I have loved you.
—REVELATION 3:9, MEV

Although more than one demonic spirit can operate in a single church, each church in these chapters of Revelation manifested one primary satanic influence.

SATAN'S PLAN IN THE CHURCH

The enemy loves to attend church! Satan has shown his hand clearly through the following methods. These same methods are his *modus operandi*, or mode of operation, in the lives of individual believers as well!

- **He attempts to distract your worship.** In the Book of Matthew we find recorded the temptation of Christ by Satan. The devil tried unsuccessfully to pull our Savior's attention and worship away from God the Father. Jesus told him, "Get away from here, Satan! For it is written, 'You shall worship the Lord your God, and Him only shall you serve'" (Matt. 4:10, MEV). If the enemy can get your focus off Jesus and onto yourself, your surroundings, your circumstances, or the people around you, he will gain a foothold. The devil desires to control your worship, knowing that will open the door for his attacks.

- **His goal is to subvert workers.** "Then the Lord said, 'Simon, Simon, listen! Satan has demanded to have you to sift you as wheat. But I have prayed for you that your faith may not fail. And when you have repented, strengthen your brothers'" (Luke 22:31–32, MEV). Here the Lord Jesus clearly warns His disciples that Satan attacks those who work for God. To "sift as wheat" refers to the ancient process of separating the wheat kernel from the chaff. The wheat was cast into the air and the kernels were caught in baskets. The heaviest seed would fall, but the lighter and useless chaff would be blown away. Satan wants Christians to be blown off course and find themselves useless for service to the Lord. Yet the prayers of Jesus keep us.

  1. He is still praying for us, as we see in Hebrews 7:25: "Therefore He is also able to save to the uttermost those who come to God through Him, because He at all times lives to make intercession for them" (MEV).

  2. Satan also tries to take the offerings of God's workers and stop the work of God from going forward. Acts tells the story of Ananias, who decided to keep back some of his tithe to God: "Then Peter said, 'Ananias, why has Satan filled your heart to deceive the Holy Spirit and keep back part of the proceeds of the land?'" (Acts 5:3, MEV). Satan is always looking for ways to hinder our witness. We must be on the lookout for his traps "lest Satan should take advantage of us. For we are not ignorant of his devices" (2 Cor. 2:11, MEV).

- **Satan tries tirelessly to steal the Word.** "These are those beside the path, where the word is sown. But when they hear, Satan comes immediately and takes away the word which is sown in their hearts" (Mark 4:15, MEV). Satan goes to church, and when the Word of God is being preached, he works hard to take away the seed. Satan will do whatever it takes to rob you and hide the truth of God from you. He knows the truth is the only way for you to walk in freedom, so he comes to steal the liberating, life-giving Word.

- **Another one of his goals is to inflict wrath.** Scripture tells us that the enemy attacked Paul with blow after blow. Paul himself wrote, "And lest I should be exalted above measure by the abundance of the revelations, a thorn in the flesh was given to me, a messenger of Satan to buffet me, lest I be exalted above measure" (2 Cor. 12:7). God even used the enemy's wrath to bring forth a humble, more powerful servant in Paul. It is clear from the example of Paul's life that Satan can and will buffet even the most upright saints. However, God will also turn sinning Christians over to Satan, removing His protective hedge, in order to bring them toward repentance: "Among these are Hymenaeus and Alexander, whom I have delivered to Satan that they may learn not to blaspheme" (1 Tim. 1:20, MEV).

- **Satan will incite wickedness and immorality.** Scripture gives a special warning to married Christians: "Do not deprive one another except with consent for a time, that you may give yourselves to fasting and prayer. Then come together again, so that Satan does not tempt you for lack of self-control" (1 Cor. 7:5, MEV). We see here that sexual relations in marriage are approved and encouraged by the Lord. When a married couple refuses to sleep with each other, it can open the door for the enemy to attack the marriage.

- **Ultimately Satan wants nothing more than to hinder God's work on Earth through the church.** Obviously, the enemy will throw up every roadblock he can to stop believers from pursuing the will of God. The apostle Paul faced these roadblocks, as he explained in one of his letters: "Therefore we wished to come to you—even I, Paul, once and again—but Satan hindered us" (1 Thess. 2:18, MEV). Remember, Satan is not asleep; he is on the prowl to destroy the work of God's children. We must be watchful and ready!

Chapter Six

SEVEN DEMONS THAT ATTACK THE CHURCH

WE HAVE EXPLORED MANY OF THE WAYS SATAN ORGANIZES the demonic forces. We have also exposed many of the demonic strategies against individual believers. When we begin to look at the seven churches described in the Book of Revelation, we discover specific demonic strongholds that can be found at church. Let's take a look at these spirits.

SPIRIT OF RELIGION (REVELATION 2:4–5, 7)

The church at Ephesus had "left their first love" (Rev. 2:4). They were doctrinally sound and had everything in order, but they had lost their passion for God. When you turn to Acts 19 to look at "first works" and "first love," you discover an astounding truth.

At the birth of the Ephesian church they were baptizing in water, laying hands on the people for the baptism of the Holy Spirit, magnifying God in tongues, casting out demons, healing with prayer cloths, and being evicted from the old order.

The church at Ephesus had every element of church life in order, and they were a hardworking congregation. Yet the fire, the passion, the love had gone out of it. We see now that religion had taken over with its dull duty and tired traditionalism. The power of God was missing; demons were no longer leaving, tongues were absent, and miracles were simply a memory. A loveless routine of religious works had replaced the power and passion of the Holy Spirit.

Who can deny the present reality of this destructive demon of religion? Many churches, like Samson, have been shorn of their power by the Delilahs of religion! Now blind to spiritual things, we grind out our religious activities and traditions with no transforming power. This demon must be exposed and expelled.

SPIRIT OF INTIMIDATION (REVELATION 2:10–11)

The church at Smyrna endured persecution, and many members suffered martyrdom. With this threat Satan tries to strike fear in the hearts of believers by sending intimidation to frighten us away from faithfulness to God and His Word. Remember Simon Peter warming himself by the enemy's fire on the night of Jesus's arrest? This faithful disciple was intimidated by his surroundings and the questioning voice of a little servant girl. Today the church is silent and cowed down before the world and its governments. This demon must be cast down!

SPIRIT OF COMPROMISE (REVELATION 2:12, 14–17)

Pergamos was the capital city of the province of Asia and is mentioned in Revelation as the seat of one of the seven churches of Asia. It was a celebrated city of Mysia in the Caicus Valley, fifteen miles from the Aegean Sea and about sixty miles north of Smyrna. The river Selinus flowed through it, and the river Caicus ran just south of it. This city was rich in historical and literary heritage with a library that boasted well over two hundred thousand volumes, topped only by the library in Alexandria.

The city had a "pet" god in Asklepion, an idol symbolized by a snake who called himself a savior. They believed that their god incarnated himself into the area snakes, so serpents were allowed to slither freely around the temple. Those who desired healing spent the night in the darkness of the temple, hoping a snake would crawl over them. The city was an outpost to Greek civilization and was home to the temples of many other deities.

Can you see the parallels of the secular plight in America and its churches? Most churches operate in a community or environment that is controlled by Satan rather than God. What can a church do when ministry becomes difficult? Can we allow the snakes of secular humanism to slither through our congregations? Compromise is not the answer. We cannot become comfortable with the sin around us!

The church of Jesus must take active steps to stand strong in our lost and dying world!

- **We must recognize the conflict**. Jesus pointed out that the city was the church's dwelling place or permanent residence. To flee was not an option. Instead, He advised them to settle into service and draw the battle lines. Paul recognized the need for battle readiness when he penned Ephesians 6. The armor of God is needed in the middle of war. Most of all, the church must go forward under the name and banner of Jesus, never operating in their own strength, for in the flesh the enemy could find weakness.

- **We must repent of compromise.** The church at Pergamos had some weaknesses to be dealt with. There were doctrinal problems, along with problems with some of their deacons and leadership. One in particular is mentioned, Nicholas, who began teaching heresy and leading others into sin. How sad when a leader goes bad and quits truly serving the Lord! Oftentimes they lead others astray and take others with them.

  1. Yet another conflict in the Pergamos church was a discipline problem. They tolerated the mess they were in by overlooking the sin in their own camp. Jesus called them to repentance.

  2. Another problem that arose was the spirit of Balaam. To give you some history of this, the pagan king Balak literally bought the prophet Balaam's ministry. Balak eventually sent women to seduce the men of Israel, thus bringing judgment upon them. It was Balaam who sold out the people of God. In keeping the spirit of Balaam, too often today money

has become the goal and prize of many in the church. Popular preaching has replaced prophetic preaching. Image has replaced anointing, and the church is reduced to no more than a place where pop psychology tickles the ears of its parishioners on Sundays. The image-makers and the politically correct have dulled the sword of the churches and its men of God.

- **We must rely on Christ**. The Pergamos church needed to rely on their Savior, who provided the weapon of the sword of the Spirit, His own Word. This is the weapon we claim as Christians. The popular *Star Wars* phenomenon has had two generations of children captured in imaginative play with light sabers, defending the galaxy as Jedi knights! The movies show the young Jedi apprentice was carefully taught to use his weapon, to guard it, to perfect its use. In the same way, we must cling to the Word of God as our weapon—it has a power that is supernatural and effective against the onslaughts of Satan. Our weapons are not carnal but mighty in God (2 Cor. 10:4), and Satan can be defeated by the power of the Word.

- **Overcomers are promised gifts.** Jesus promised this church that those who didn't succumb to the sins around them—not eating things offered to idols and partaking in sin—would eat hidden manna, the blessing of Jesus Himself. They are promised the presence of Jesus in the barren wasteland of the world's wilderness. He also promised this church that He would set among them a white stone, promising acquittal, acceptance, and acclaim. The new name upon this stone was Jesus!

Spirit of Jezebel (Control) (Revelation 2:18–20, 26)

A war goes on in today's church, and the battle lines are drawn. One of the most powerful spirits at work in this ongoing battle is the spirit of Jezebel, or control. First Kings tells the story of the woman for whom this spirit is named.

Jezebel was known as the wife of King Ahab and a follower of the false god Baal, and Scripture regarded Ahab's marriage to this woman as a horrible sin: "He not only considered it trivial to commit the sins of Jeroboam son of Nebat, but he also married Jezebel daughter of Ethbaal king of the Sidonians, and began to serve Baal and worship him" (1 Kings 16:31, NIV).

Jezebel ordered a "hit" on the innocent man Naboth so that she could obtain his prize vineyard. Not only was this murder, but it also broke God's land covenant with His people. In addition to her disrespect for ordinary people and their property, she hated the prophets of God. Scripture says, "While Jezebel was killing off the LORD's prophets, Obadiah had taken a hundred prophets and hidden them in two caves, fifty in each, and had supplied them with food and water" (1 Kings 18:4, NIV).

Later, Jezebel pursued the prophet Elijah following the great contest where God sent fire from heaven and defeated the prophets of Baal. Her relentless pursuit drove the prophet into depression and suicidal thoughts.

Jezebel's character was wicked, controlling, sexually immoral, murderous, and demonic! It is astounding that the same strong spirit was still operating in Revelation 2:20 and still operates in today's church. In every congregation we find those who want to control, manipulate, and subvert the men and women of God.

Recognizing the spirit

This spirit is basically the spirit of domination or an unwillingness to cohabit peacefully. This is not about women or liberation, for this spirit can attach itself to either a man or a woman. Many may think that this spirit is identified with sexuality, believing that a woman who looks a certain way is a "Jezebel" in her character. But this is not so. A wolf can easily hide in sheep's clothing.

When you find a spirit of Jezebel operating, you will also find an "Ahab" nearby, or someone in leadership who is allowing the spirit access and control.

The strategy of Jezebel

The tool this spirit uses is manipulation. In 1 Kings 21, we learn that King Ahab would pout when he did not get his own way. He had seen a vineyard that he greatly desired, but the owner would not give up his precious property, even to the king. As King Ahab lay on his bed sulking, Jezebel assured him she would get him what he wanted. This powerful woman had introduced pagan worship into her kingdom, and now she was not above killing to obtain the things she needed to gain more power.

The seat of Jezebel

> But I have a few things against you: You permit that woman Jezebel, who calls herself a prophetess, to teach and seduce My servants to commit sexual immorality and eat food sacrificed to idols.
>   —REVELATION 2:20, MEV

When the spirit of Jezebel begins to manifest in the church, it seeks a high seat in the church or a place of dominance. Usually it will manifest in someone who wants to teach or lead, usually leading them astray! To find that place of leadership, Jezebel must look and act in a spiritual manner.

One of these spirits operated in Moses's and Aaron's day. The Book of Numbers tells us:

> Now Korah the son of Izhar, the son of Kohath, the son of Levi, with Dathan and Abiram the sons of Eliab, and On the son of Peleth, sons of Reuben, took men; and they rose up before Moses with some of the children of Israel, two hundred and fifty leaders of the congregation, representatives of the congregation, men of renown. They gathered together against Moses and Aaron, and said to them, "You take too much upon yourselves, for all the congregation is holy, every one of them, and the LORD is among

them. Why then do you exalt yourselves above the congregation of the LORD?"

—NUMBERS 16:1–3

Korah was operating in the spirit of Jezebel, with Dathan and Abiram operating as his power core and two hundred fifty other princes as a structure under them. Moses took immediate action—he fell on his face before God and prayed. Following his prayer, he confronted the spirit, saying, "Is it a small thing to you that the God of Israel has separated you from the congregation of Israel, to bring you near to Himself, to do the work of the tabernacle of the LORD, and to stand before the congregation to serve them; and that He has brought you near to Himself, you and all your brethren, the sons of Levi, with you? And are you seeking the priesthood also?" (Num. 16:9–10).

Judgment came to this Jezebel spirit—an earthquake came and took the three evil leaders, and fire consumed all the rest.

Jezebel's targets

The controlling spirit wiggles into the church, bent on destroying and undermining the very things that we hold dear as believers. Through manipulation, domination, and control, the spirit begins its battle against the body of Christ.

First, this spirit hates the prophets, the true leaders of God. She cannot control them, and when she tries to win their approval and fails, she will stop at nothing to try to kill them.

In addition, the spirit of Jezebel hates the preaching of the Word. She can't cope with its message. She will try to either reduce the messenger or the message.

The controlling spirit also hates the praise of the church. During times of true, powerful worship, her carnality is exposed. In 1 Kings when the prophet Elijah prayed fire down from heaven against the prophets of Baal and Jezebel's schemes, praise broke out (1 Kings 18:39). Jezebel had lost, and the praises of God filled the air.

A Jezebel spirit also hates the preeminence of Christ. There is no way to compete against it. The first time *preeminence* is mentioned is in Colossians 1:18: "And he is the head of the body, the church: who is the beginning, the firstborn from the dead; that in all things he might have the preeminence" (KJV). However, the second time we find the word, a Jezebel spirit is attempting to control a body of believers: "I wrote unto the church: but Diotrephes, who loveth to have the preeminence among them, receiveth us not" (3 John 9, KJV).

Banish the spirit

If you sense this spirit is at work in your church, it is important to see the enemy as spiritual, not fleshly. Don't hate the person being controlled by the spirit of Jezebel; recognize that it is a spiritual power—one that God must fight. Let your prayer be, "O our God, will You not render judgment on them? For we have not strength enough to stand before this great army that is coming against us. And we do not know what we should do, but our eyes are on You" (2 Chron. 20:12, MEV).

SPIRIT OF TRADITIONALISM (REVELATION 3:1–6)

For centuries the church has been the victim of rumors, hostility, and, what we call in this day and age, negative press. Churches often have to survive this hostile environment; however, outward hostility is not the greatest threat to a local church! Very often the greatest danger comes from within!

The Sardis church lived in a favorable environment with a great reputation. However, in Christ's letter to this church, He ignored their human reputation and told this church they were listed in the obituary!

Environment of death

The city of Sardis was a city of wealth. History tells us that in 550 BC King Croesus found gold in the city's river and issued the first gold coins in history. Even in New Testament times gold could be found all along its rivers.

In addition to its wealth, the city was known for its paganism. The favored idol was Cybele, and worshippers of this pagan god participated in wild, frenzied worship that included sexual immorality.

Remarkably, the community was at peace, for the inhabitants were comfortable in their self-sufficiency. This peaceful self-sufficiency had also invaded the church in Sardis; it became the peace of death. A peaceful coexistence with the city and its wickedness had settled into the church, and all they had left was their reputation.

Evidence of a church's death

Viewers of our television broadcast often write and ask, "How can I find a good church in my area? How can I tell if a church is alive and healthy?" A dead church has some basic characteristics that are spotted easily.

- **It ignores the Holy Spirit.** When the complete work of God's Spirit isn't embraced in a church, that body is already headed for the grave. Jesus told the church at Sardis that they had a spirit of religion and didn't have the Spirit of God. The Holy Spirit will not be managed or controlled by religious tradition or preferences! John 3:8 says, "The wind blows where it wishes....So it is with everyone who is born of the Spirit" (MEV).

- **There is a lack of godly leadership.** The "seven stars" mentioned in Revelation 3 stand for the messengers or pastors of the seven churches addressed in the letters. What the church in Sardis needed was a leader who was called by God and who served Him wholeheartedly. Too many churches today fail to get God's man. Several times a month our church offices receive requests from pastorless churches that have been searching for a replacement. If these churches choose a pastor by his reputation, résumé, physical appearance, or even recommendation, they may find later that they've made a big mistake. As important as background information is, the fruit issued in a pastor's life and his walk with the Spirit of God is what should be investigated. The superficial doesn't matter as much as the supernatural. Hiring solely on superficial facts may result in a short-tenured, flash-in-the-pan, or morally bankrupt leader.

- **It values reputation over reality.** Sardis was a busy, working church with a good name—but it had death upon it. They were an organization but not a living

organism. Sadly, they were so caught up in their reputation they didn't even realize that they had died.

One winter night I noticed our house becoming
colder and colder, even though I had turned our heat
on full power. I called upon our faithful church grounds
supervisor to take a look at the gas-heating unit, and he
discovered the pilot light had gone out. The blower was
blowing, but the fire was out. Going to church is good
if you meet God. Worship is good if it brings on God's
presence. Giving is good if we have first given ourselves.
Prayer is good, but "if [we] regard iniquity in [our] heart,
the Lord will not hear" (Ps. 66:18). Form without force is
death to a church. It is like a store window containing lots
of fluff and finery but hiding an empty stockroom.

- **There is growth in numbers without growth in people.**
  The letter to Sardis indicated that even Christians who
  had life in the Sardis church were dying in the cold
  environment. Churches must offer ministry that encour-
  ages its members to grow in the Lord.

- **Ministry and work were incomplete.** Beginning a new
  program or outreach is easy; seeing it to completion is
  much more difficult! A dead church is a graveyard of
  partially fulfilled goals and half-baked programs. These
  skeletons are evidence that they went "partway" with the
  Lord and then backed up and sat down. A church that
  goes backward is doomed to death.

Escape from death!

To eliminate the spirit of religion from your church, the leadership should gather and repent of religious death. Together they should
acknowledge that Jesus's kingdom is coming and there will be an
accounting for what they accomplish in His name. In almost any dead
church there remain a handful of believers who do live in triumph
and desire to be alive in God. This team of people should be lifted
up and encouraged. Stay with the winning crowd! Finally, rebuke the
religious pride that strangles your church. Reject the love of religion

and its rules and reputation, and fall in love with Jesus. Determine to listen to the voice of the Holy Spirit in all decision-making regarding the church. Let His Word edify, rule, and reign from the pulpit.

SPIRIT OF INFERIORITY (REVELATION 3:7–8, 12)

Many times a pastor will contact me about a speaking engagement at a church, and he will begin by saying almost apologetically, "We are just a small church…" His tone implies a sense of weakness or inability. But there is nothing little or insignificant in the kingdom of God!

At the other end of the spectrum is the church that thinks they have all the answers, that loves to proclaim their statistics and numbers but are satisfied with mediocre efforts as long as they bring the church notoriety and recognition.

God deals strongly with the church in Revelation 3:

> Because you have kept My command to persevere, I also will keep you from the hour of trial which shall come upon the whole world, to test those who dwell on the earth. Behold, I am coming quickly! Hold fast what you have, that no one may take your crown. He who overcomes, I will make him a pillar in the temple of My God, and he shall go out no more. And I will write on him the name of My God and the name of the city of My God, the New Jerusalem, which comes down out of heaven from My God. And I will write on him My new name.
> —REVELATION 3:10–12

Too many churches and individuals use their supposed weakness as an excuse for failing to advance the cause of Christ. Such notions and statements are foreign to the New Testament portrait of the church. I am convinced that such an attitude is not only false and hurtful but also demonic in its origin. There is a stronghold of inferiority, self-pity, and weakness. The enemy deceives those manifesting this spirit by making them think their attitudes are actually meekness and humility. This counterfeit humility is debilitating to the kingdom of God, crippling the advance of the gospel, and insulting to the Holy Spirit.

The church at Philadelphia was at risk to be overtaken by such a spirit. If they were ever to become a pillar in the kingdom, they would have to overcome the spirit.

Scripture sets forth the church as a victorious company. Matthew 16:18 declares, "The gates of hell shall not prevail against it" (KJV). In his great prayer for the church in Ephesians 3:14–21 Paul ends with this benediction: "Now to Him who is able to do exceedingly abundantly beyond all that we ask or imagine, according to the power that works in us, to Him be the glory in the church and in Christ Jesus throughout all generations, forever and ever. Amen" (vv. 20–21, MEV).

It is in the church that Jesus looses His divine ability, energy, and glory. The answer to our inferiority is His superiority! It is not in trying harder but in trusting wholly that His work is accomplished.

The church at Philadelphia had "a little strength" (Rev. 3:8). Greek culture, international commerce, and religious diversity dominated them. The pagan god Dionysus was worshipped. This ancient Greek god of wine was credited with inspiring ritual madness and ecstasy. Worship of Dionysus was thought to bring an end to care and worry. The city of Philadelphia was also a center of orthodox Jewish worship.

This small church could have surrendered to the pressures around them. Yet they did not! They received the wonderful encouragement in Revelation, and history tells us that for nearly fourteen hundred years this city stood as a Christian city in the face of Muslim pressure. It was only after centuries of courageous resistance that the city was overthrown by an unholy military alliance of Byzantine and Muslim forces.

How did this church overcome inferiority and have a ministry that would last for fourteen hundred years? They came to know the Lord of opportunity (Rev. 3:7–8). Obedience always leads to opportunity! God promised this church the "key of David." With God's favor and their dependence upon His superiority, nothing could stop this body of believers!

SPIRIT OF PRIDE (REVELATION 3:14–17, 21)

Revelation 3 also issues a charge to the church at Laodicea. This city was a wealthy and prosperous one. So vast was their wealth that when an earthquake destroyed the city, they required no outside help to recover! The Roman historian Tacitus recorded that Laodicea "was…overthrown by an earthquake, and, without any relief from us, recovered itself by its own resources."[1]

The city was famous for the dark, black wool they produced and was known as the center for fine wool in the ancient world. Laodicea also boasted a famous medical school, having produced two of the most popular medicines for the treatment of eye and ear maladies. In short, this city was pompous and full of pride.

But here in Revelation 3, years have passed, and now the church in Laodicea has fallen into a rut of mediocrity. The Lord Jesus Himself renders the verdict on this church. What was His appraisal? This lukewarm church was nauseating Him! What had happened to this church to make it slide into a state of mediocrity?

Lost fervency

Sadly, this church reflects the state of many American churches today. Not too cold...not too hot. Not too bad...not too good. Not too faithful...not too unfaithful. The Laodicea church was an ordinary church that had warmth but no fire. If asked about their work, they would say, "We are holding our own."

Jesus is sickened by the mediocre. He would rather a church be as cold as the Arctic or as hot as the Sahara. In God's work, there should be no place for "just getting by."

Elijah recognized this need for commitment when he challenged Israel at the contest of the prophets of Baal in 1 Kings 18. He shouted to the congregation, "If Baal be God, serve him, but if the Lord be God, serve Him!" Standing in the middle was not an option.

A complacent church is a disappointment to Jesus! Laodicea had lost the fire of love for Jesus and for lost souls. The altar fires of prayer were in need of rekindling. It was business as usual week after week. They needed to pray!

The following prayer of Amy Carmichael should be the earnest prayer of the church needing a fresh fervency:

> O for a passion for souls, dear Lord!
> O for a pity that yearns!
> O for a love that loves unto death!
> O for a fire that burns![2]

Lost faith

The Laodicean church had tried to become self-sufficient. They boasted of wealth, increase of goods, and that they needed nothing, not even the Lord. They were cursed by their wealth.

When the great Thomas Aquinas visited the Vatican, an officer of Pope Innocent the Fourth brought in a bag of money. The pope said to Aquinas, "You see, young man, the age of the church is past, in which she said, 'Silver and gold have I none.'" To which Aquinas replied, "True, holy father, but the age is also past, in which she could say to a paralytic, 'Rise up and walk.'"[3]

A church's reach must exceed its grasp. An ever-enlarging vision must be forged. The challenges we take should be beyond our resources so that our reliance and faith remain upon God. Our dreams and our plans should be God-sized.

When God blesses financially, the church should give more to missions, build a needed building, add another staff member, and have the faith to stretch those resources to their limit.

Unfortunately, the Laodicean church did not really see their true condition. God said they were "wretched, poor, blind, naked"—they were pitiful in the sight of God. They were without riches and spiritually blind in God's eyes. He looked at them and saw them as they really were: spiritually bankrupt.

Lost fear

This church no longer trembled in the presence of a righteous God. There was no remorse recorded for their failures. Jesus warns them by giving three motives to repent: His love, His rebuke, and His chastening rod. These three things could provide the motivation to set this church on the right track.

Lost fellowship

Jesus was standing and knocking outside the door of this church. At one point, He had been shut out; He was no longer the center of things. The church had no basis for fellowship with other churches because Jesus Christ was the only common ground among the fellowship of churches. Without Him, a church can have a "get-together" without really being together in unity! "That which we have seen and heard we declare to you, that you also may have fellowship with us; and truly our fellowship is with the Father and with His Son Jesus Christ.... But if we walk in the light as He is in the light, we have fellowship with one another, and the blood of Jesus Christ His Son cleanses us from all sin" (1 John 1:3, 7).

The presence of Jesus Christ is the ground of all true fellowship, but too many churches have shut Him out.

God's promise and plea

Jesus keeps on knocking, hoping that someone in the church will open the door. When that happens, it sets the stage for revival, and fellowship can be restored. A seat at the Lord's table is promised when we welcome Him at ours. We can share in His glorious reign! So, let us blaze and burn for Him until He comes in the blaze of His glory.

Section Two

UNDERSTANDING THE DYNASTY OF YOUR ENEMY

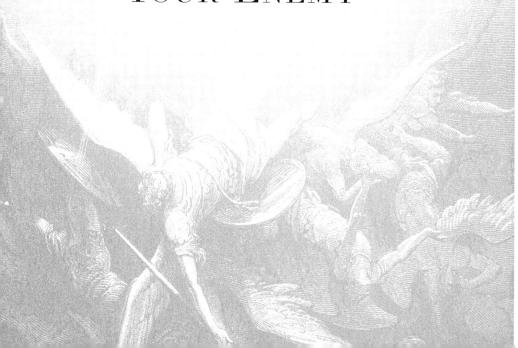

Chapter Seven

HOW SATAN OPPRESSES

OW DOES SATAN OPERATE? WE CAN TRACE HIS CAREER throughout the pages of Scripture. Let's focus on the times in Scripture when *diabolos* is used in reference to Satan.

The first mention of Satan in biblical history is found in Job 1 and 2 when he attacks and accuses Job. Job's response and subsequent victory silenced Satan for centuries.

Satan then provokes David to number Israel, putting his strength in numbers and not the living God. Satan is a provocateur that will try to move us to actions that do not demonstrate faith (1 Chron. 21:1).

Satan comes to a worship service and opposes the high priest of Israel. He further opposes Jerusalem and Israel (Zech. 3). His next move is to tempt Jesus, the Second Adam, with the same threefold temptation with which he had tempted our ancient father, Adam (Matt. 4). His approach has not changed. Satan still throws before us the lust of the flesh, the lust of the eyes, and the pride of life.

Satan influenced Peter to hinder Jesus's commitment to the cross in Matthew 16:22.

In Luke 10:18, Jesus tells us that He saw Satan fall. He warns us in Mark 4:15 that Satan will try to steal the word of faith from our hearts. Satan crippled a woman for eighteen years (Luke 13:16). Satan entered the heart of Judas to deny Jesus (Luke 22:3), and he sifted and shook the disciple Peter like wheat (v. 31)!

In the early church we see Satan fill the hearts of Ananias and Sapphira, causing them to lie to the Holy Spirit (Acts 5:3). Lost people who come to Christ are said to be delivered "from the power of Satan" (Acts 26:18).

Satan can kill disciplined Christians who embarrass the testimony of Christ and the church by continuous immoral behavior (1 Cor. 5:5). Satan attacks marital fidelity and sexual enjoyment (1 Cor. 7:5). Satan desires to gain an advantage over every believer (2 Cor. 2:11) and can come disguised as a heavenly messenger (2 Cor. 11:14). Satan tries to hinder the work of the church (1 Thess. 2:18). Satan can operate through charismatic miracle-working ministries (2 Thess. 2:9). Satan attacks with idleness, gossip, and busybody activity (1 Tim. 5:13). Satan blasphemes, kills, attacks synagogues, and deceives (Rev. 2:9, 13).

Although Satan's methods of oppression are many, do not be discouraged or overwhelmed. Satan can be crushed under the feet of every faithful believer (Rom. 16:20). Remember, Jesus's victory at Calvary assures our victory today. Then one day Satan will be confined to hell, which was prepared for him and all his demons (Rev. 20:10).

THE DEVIL

As the enemy, we find him sowing tares in the good field to deceive (Matt. 13:24–29). He is called the father of those who are not believers in Jesus (John 8:44). The devil causes illness (Acts 10:38). The devil can take over a physical location (Eph. 4:27). The devil has methods and schemes with which to attack believers (Eph. 6:11). The devil instills pride, sets traps, and takes captives (1 Tim. 3:6–7; 2 Tim. 2:26). He has the power of death only with Jesus's permission. The devil desires to devour like a lion and put believers in a prison of spiritual chains (1 Pet. 5:8; Rev. 2:10). As you can see, the enemy is a decisive force on the earth. The devil can be resisted and will flee from believers: "Therefore submit yourselves to God. Resist the devil, and he will flee from you" (James 4:7, MEV). Hallelujah!

Chapter Eight

THE HIERARCHY OF HELL

I N THE EPIC STAR WARS MOVIE SERIES, BOTH EVIL AND GOOD
practiced the Force. The Force was an invisible power that had
a good side and a dark side. The Force called the dark side was per-
sonified in an evil character called Darth Vader. Vader had once been
Anakin Skywalker, but he had turned to evil.

Strangely enough, this scenario mimics what happened before time.
In an earlier chapter we learned that Lucifer, an angel of God and a
messenger of light, had turned to the dark side and become Satan. In
Holy Scripture evil is never an indefinable force but rather has indi-
viduality and personality.

Satan leads the forces of darkness. His former name, Lucifer, means
"bearer of light," "daystar," or "right light." His light was a reflection of
God's light. He became Satan, which means "accuser" or "adversary."
The Hebrew *Ha-Satan* means "the chief adversary." *Satanas* in Greek
means "the accuser" (Rev. 20:2). Satan is called a dragon. "Dragon"
comes from the Greek word *derkomai*, which means "fearful to look
upon." It came to mean a fearful, monstrous creature. In the same
verse Satan is called an "old serpent," which in Greek is *archaios ophis*
and means "old snake eyes." This is the serpent that has been watching
to wound for ages. Finally, Satan is called "the devil," which is *diabolos* in Greek. This means "one who hurls through." The idea is of one
throwing a spear or, in our day, shooting a bullet through another body.

Clearly Satan can appear as an angel of light (2 Cor. 11:14), a monstrous creature, a hidden viper, a prosecutor, an assassin, and a deadly
enemy. Jesus describes our adversary and his mission when He said,

"The thief does not come, except to steal and kill and destroy" (John 10:10, MEV).

THE ARMY OF HELL

I believe that Satan is a great imitator, so he patterned his army like that of the holy angels. The letter to the Ephesians identifies these dark forces in the following flow of authority: "For our fight is not against flesh and blood, but against principalities, against powers, against the rulers of the darkness of this world, and against spiritual forces of evil in the heavenly places" (Eph. 6:12, MEV).

Principalities

Top-ranking demonic beings are called principalities. The word *principalities* is translated from the Greek word *arche*, which means "chief." These are the chief demons, which correspond to the archangels among the holy angels. These princes hold sway over the souls of people (Eph. 2:1–3). A principality is what assigns demonic spirits to operate in the disobedient. Also, these princes rule over continents and nations. In Daniel 10:12–13, the prophet is informed by Gabriel that a principality of Persia had hindered his arrival to Daniel for three weeks. Gabriel had to summon the archangel Michael to take on the archdevil of Persia. These demons are subject to Christ (Eph. 1:20–22). They are also subject to Spirit-filled believers, as we read in Ephesians 2:6; this scripture explains that Christ has "raised us up and seated us together in the heavenly places in Christ Jesus" (MEV).

Powers

The next rank of evil officers of darkness is called "powers." The word *powers* come from the Greek word *exousia*, which means "delegated authority," like that of a policeman. These demons seem to operate invisibly in governmental centers such as national governments. These powers cannot separate us from the love of God (Rom. 8:38). These powers will be shaken at the end of the age (Matt. 24:29). These powers, like the principalities, are subject to Christ (1 Pet. 3:22).

Rulers of the darkness

This next level of demonic leaders touches the created order. "Rulers of the darkness" is translated from the Greek word *kosmokrator*, which means "to seize and take hold of governments for the sake of darkness and evil." *Kosmas* has to do with "an arrangement or order." These rulers want to take over the offices of government, the legislatures, and the courts.

Spiritual forces of wickedness

Spiritual forces of wickedness literally means in the Greek "spiritual fakes." The word *wicked* is *poneria*, from which we get *fornication* and *pornography*. These are the unclean spirits we deal with on a daily basis.

Some of these spirits are named for us. *Beelzebub* means "lord of the flies." *Abaddon*, or Apollyon, means "destroyer." *Demon* means "tormentor of the mind." These lower-level spirits are the ones we deal with daily.

Satan's army is well organized, and his legions employ an array of methods and schemes. We must be prepared to face down this infernal enemy and expose his tactics.

Chapter Nine

UNMASKING THE ENEMY

AKE NO MISTAKE, THERE IS A REAL WAR GOING ON AGAINST a real enemy! Once you assume your position in Christ, the next step is to know the enemy so you can be properly equipped. Let us examine the dangerous infernal army at Satan's disposal. Revelation 12:9 reaches back before time, saying, "The great dragon was cast out, that ancient serpent called the Devil and Satan, who deceives the whole world. He was cast down to the earth, and his angels were cast down with him" (MEV). As we explained earlier, these fallen angels are given many different names in Scripture: demons, principalities, powers, ruler of darkness, wicked spirits, unclean spirits, as well as other descriptions. Also remember that, according to Revelation 12:4, one-third of the innumerable hosts of angels fell: "His [Satan's] tail drew a third of the stars of heaven" (MEV). "The stars of heaven" refers symbolically to the angels.

THE INFERNAL ARMY ARRAYED AGAINST US

Jesus Christ regularly confronted demons as an integral part of His ministry. Luke records that when Jesus launched His public ministry, He quoted Isaiah 61:1–2: "The Spirit of the Lord is upon Me, because He has anointed me to preach the gospel to the poor; He has sent me to heal the brokenhearted, to proclaim liberty to the captives . . . to set at liberty those who are oppressed" (Luke 4:18). Obviously Jesus knew His purpose was to rescue humanity from the bondage and oppression of the enemy.

At least nine times in the New Testament Jesus Christ confronts demons. I will give greater detail about demonic operation in later chapters, but let me briefly describe what we learn about demons from one such incident in the life of Jesus. In Luke 8:26–39 we have the beloved physician's version of the demoniac of the Gadarenes's encounter with Jesus.

> Then they sailed to the country of the Gadarenes, which is opposite Galilee. And when He stepped out on the land, there met Him a certain man from the city who had demons for a long time. And he wore no clothes, nor did he live in a house but in the tombs. When he saw Jesus, he cried out, fell down before Him, and with a loud voice said, "What have I to do with You, Jesus, Son of the Most High God? I beg You, do not torment me!" For He had commanded the unclean spirit to come out of the man. For it had often seized him, and he was kept under guard, bound with chains and shackles; and he broke the bonds and was driven by the demon into the wilderness. Jesus asked him, saying, "What is your name?" And he said, "Legion," because many demons had entered him. And they begged Him that He would not command them to go out into the abyss. Now a herd of many swine was feeding there on the mountain. And they begged Him that He would permit them to enter them. And He permitted them. Then the demons went out of the man and entered the swine, and the herd ran violently down the steep place into the lake and drowned. When those who fed them saw what had happened, they fled and told it in the city and in the country. Then they went out to see what had happened, and came to Jesus, and found the man from whom the demons had departed, sitting at the feet of Jesus, clothed and in his right mind. And they were afraid. They also who had seen it told them by what means he who had been demon-possessed was healed. Then the whole multitude of the surrounding region of the Gadarenes asked Him to depart from them, for they were seized with great fear. And He got into the boat and returned. Now the man from whom the demons had departed begged Him that he might be with Him. But Jesus sent him away, saying, "Return to your own house, and tell what great things God has done for you." And he went his way and proclaimed throughout the whole city what great things Jesus had done for him.

Now let's look at the demons and their characteristics in these verses. Demons have personalities, use speed, seem to express the emotion of fear, promote uncleanness, torment, and create mental disorders. Yet the glorious truth is that demons must obey the commands of Jesus Christ!

CAN A PERSON BE DEMON POSSESSED?

The Greek word describing the condition of a person affected by a demon is *daimonizomai*, which was translated as "possessed with devils" in the King James Version of the Bible. According to William Arndt and F. Wilber Gingrich it is a present-tense word with an active voice and a passive ending.[1] A person in this condition can be described as in "a demon-controlled passivity." In other words, the person is controlled to a point of passivity by a demon. C. Fred Dickason rightly points out that the term *possession* never actually appears in the New Testament.[2] A demon can possess an unbeliever. A believer can be demonized by the enemy, which means he or she is controlled but not owned! The degree of demonization is limited in believers.

Demons can use people's voices, confuse, give imaginations, create insanity, appear as multiple personalities, and cause passivity of speech, hearing, and physical movement.

In Luke 8:26–39, which I cited earlier, we observe such feats as unusual physical strength, fits of rage, multiple and disintegrating personalities, resistance to Jesus, clairvoyance (knowing who Jesus was), and occult transference (entering the swine). Some of these will be discussed in greater detail later.

Prominent German pastor Kurt Koch and German psychiatrist Alfred Lechler researched demonization in Germany. They noted in their findings the following about demonized individuals: resistance to the Bible, falling into a trancelike state, opposition to prayer, and a negative reaction to Jesus's name.[3]

DO DEMONS AFFECT CHRISTIANS?

One of Satan's great strategies is to get believers to believe that they are immune to demonic influence. A Spirit-filled believer walking in obedience to Christ is absolutely protected from the enemy. However, while a disobedient Christian's spirit is protected from the enemy, the mind and body of this unfaithful believer can be subject to attack.

A Christian can "give place to the devil" (Eph. 4:27, mev). When a Christian lives with unconfessed, habitual sin, the enemy moves into that place in the believer's life. The enemy constructs a thought pattern around that sin or attitude. Second Corinthians 10:4–5 describes that house of thoughts as a stronghold. Demons can take up residence in that stronghold in the believer's life.

These demons do not possess the Christian any more than a cockroach can possess a house. Cockroaches are dirty, can make a mess, and cause you trouble, but they cannot own your house. In the same way, demons can harass, oppress, depress, and suppress the believer. Demons cannot destroy the Christian, but they can distract the Christian. In the next section we will expose their operation so that as a believer you can be alert.

UNMASKING DEMONIC OPERATION

Having exposed the demonic dynasty in the last section, let us look more deeply into demonic personality and operation. Remember that Satan's kingdom is in direct conflict with the kingdom of God. Though defeated, Satan still has a controlling influence in this world. In Matthew 4:8–9 Satan offers the world, its power, and its glory to Jesus. Let's take a look at this temptation.

> Again, the devil took Him up on a very high mountain and showed Him all the kingdoms of the world and their grandeur, and he said to Him, "All these things I will give You if You will fall down and worship me."
> —MATTHEW 4:8–9, mev

Satan has innumerable demonic forces at his disposal: "The whole world lies under the sway of the wicked one" (1 John 5:19).

In Luke Jesus spoke of the operation of these demonic entities in a strange passage: "When an unclean spirit goes out of a man, he goes through dry places, seeking rest; and finding none, he says, 'I will return to my house from which I came.' And when he comes, he finds it swept and put in order. Then he goes and takes with him seven other spirits more wicked than himself, and they enter and dwell there; and the last state of that man is worse than the first" (Luke 11:24–26).

I believe this is the clearest picture of demonic thinking and process in all of Scripture. Look carefully at these verses, and you will note the following disturbing facts about demonic operation.

First, demons can exist both inside and outside human beings.

Second, demons travel at will. The verse says that they go "through dry places, seeking rest" (v. 24). They seem to prefer traveling over land rather than water. In Mark 5 Jesus dispatched the demons into a herd of swine and sent them into the Sea of Galilee. Demons can move through the atmosphere of this planet.

Third, demons need a human host in order to rest: " . . . goes through dry places, seeking rest." It seems that demons are weary until they find a human to embody.

Fourth, demons can communicate using the vocal apparatus of their host. On many occasions in Scripture demons spoke from the body of their host. Luke 11:24 makes it clear that demons can speak. In Mark 5:7 they speak to Jesus through the human host, saying, "Do not torment me."

Fifth, demons have individual personalities and identities. Notice in Luke 11:24 when the demon says, "I will…" Demons are not impersonal forces, but like the angels, they have names and personalities.

Sixth, demons consider the body they live in to be their home! In Luke 11:24 the demon says of his former human host, "I will return to my house from which I came." Demons are possessive and seek to take ownership of the human life they invade. Think of it—a demon bragging to his cohorts that your body is his house. That is why Paul warns us in Ephesians 4:27, "Do not give place to the devil" (MEV). If you give the enemy a foothold, he will put up a mailbox and declare your body his address.

In the movie *Pacific Heights* a young couple purchases a large home and remodels it. In order to meet the mortgage, they rent out part of it to a man. He refuses to pay rent, harasses the couple, sues them, and makes their life a living hell. The house was possessed by a madman who took over their lives.

That story graphically illustrates the strategy of demons. A demon will come in quietly to live in that little area of your life you refuse to surrender to Jesus. From that stronghold he will try to rule and ruin your life.

Seventh, demons can plant thoughts and influence mental health. In Luke 11:25 we find a reference to the human mind: "And when he comes, he finds it swept and put in order." The demon returns to the person who has been set free. He finds the mind clean and in order. Yet this person has no spiritual fullness. The Holy Spirit is either not present in the life or is in the spirit of the person and not filling the mind and controlling the body. This person has gone back to the same sin. Perhaps anger was the stronghold from which they had been delivered, and instead of growing in the Lord, filling the mind with Scripture, and living in praise, this individual falls into the same pattern as before. The demon can see the emptiness in that individual and will attack the mind that is devoid of the Holy Spirit.

Eighth, demons can remember, think, and plan. Notice in all these verses the strategies employed by these entities. They are not stupid and must not be regarded lightly.

Ninth, demons can communicate with each other. In Luke 11:26 this demon communicates with seven others. When one gives place to a demonic entity, that entity will often bring compatible demons. The Bible speaks of the "spirit of fear" (2 Tim. 1:7), and in 1 John 4:18 Scripture speaks of love as a weapon that "casts out fear." Then it adds, "Fear hath torment" (kjv). Jesus speaks of "tormentors" in regard to those who will not forgive: "And his master was angry, and delivered him to the torturers until he should pay all that was due to him. So My heavenly Father also will do to you if each of you, from his heart, does not forgive his brother his trespasses" (Matt. 18:34–35).

So a demon of fear can bring demons of torment. Unforgiveness can invite tormentors into a person's life. Demons are like cockroaches, as we said before; they tend to increase in number if not evicted by the power of God.

Tenth, levels of evil exist within the demonic hierarchy. Luke 11:26 says that the demon "takes with him seven other spirits more wicked than himself." Demonic entities live in various levels of wickedness. Here a demon enlists seven more to occupy his host. If a person tolerates a little evil, then more evil comes.

Eleventh, demons are a problem to Christians today. Ephesians 6:12

says that we are in a hand-to-hand wrestling match "against princi-palities, against powers, against the rulers of the darkness of this age, against spiritual hosts of wickedness." Though these spirits cannot possess a Christian in his spirit, they can afflict the body and oppress the mind. We must be very vigilant to enforce the victory of the cross on these evil forces.

Twelfth, demons are involved in deceiving believers by teaching false doctrine. First Timothy 4:1 says, "Now the Spirit expressly says that in the latter times some will depart from the faith, giving heed to deceiving spirits and doctrines of demons." In these last days demons are seducing and deceiving many through false teaching. Just because a person waves a Bible and acts spiritually does not mean that their ministry is anointed by God. Religious deception is the worst of all demonic control.

In concluding this chapter, let it be clear that ignoring the truth about demonic forces is frivolous and perilous. By not facing the truth about our enemy, we leave ourselves and the church ill prepared for the battle that rages. How many spiritual casualties will it take before the church wakes up to the reality of spiritual warfare?

Chapter Ten

DEMONIC PROTOCOLS

IN THE GOVERNMENTS OF THE WORLD, THERE ARE THE VISIBLE armies and strategies of war. A more hidden and subtle form of warfare is called covert operations. These are undercover strategies executed by every branch of the military; plus, special operations and agencies such as the FBI and CIA have covert operatives.

Satan uses covert operations as well. Much of what he does is masked and hidden from view.

SATAN'S WILES

The word *wiles* comes from the Greek word *methodeia*. Our English word *method* comes from this word also. It is derived from two Greek words: *meta*, which means "in the midst," and *hodos*, which means "to travel a road or to journey." Satan wants to interrupt your journey, kill your vision, change your route, and move you off center! How does he do that?

Satan uses temptation to lure people away from God's best. *Temptation* is *peirasmos*, which means to "solicit" or "lure to action." Satan uses this tool to draw us away from God and cause us to do evil. Satan may tempt us, but the human will must participate and agree.

> Let no man say when he is tempted, "I am tempted by God," for God cannot be tempted by evil; neither does He tempt anyone. But each man is tempted when he is drawn away by his own lust and enticed. Then, when lust has conceived, it brings forth sin; and when sin is finished, it brings forth death.
>
> —JAMES 1:13–15, MEV

Jesus Christ was tempted, yet He did not sin. We must never confuse temptation with sin. All of us must resist temptation by not allowing wrong desires to take over our thinking and move us away from God. The Bible teaches us that temptation is our common lot as human beings (1 Cor. 10:13). It also teaches that wealth affords a greater problem of temptation (1 Tim. 6:9). We are to pray, "Do not lead us into temptation, but deliver us from the evil one" (Matt. 6:13).

It is interesting that our English word *piracy* comes from the Greek word *peirasmos*. Temptation is Satan's way of stealing your precious life.

Satan uses perversion to destroy that which is good. The word *perverse* (used in Isaiah 19:14) comes from the Hebrew *avah*, which means "to make crooked." It is sometimes translated "iniquity." The Greek word is *diastrepho*, which means "to twist through" or "to distort." Satan takes good things and makes them ugly. For instance, sex in a heterosexual marriage is a gift from God. But Satan can twist it into homosexuality, pornography, and abuse.

Satan uses imitation to draw people away from the true God. Most religions are bad copies of God's teachings. Satan's greatest imitation will be the Antichrist, who will imitate the miracles of Christ. He will even be raised from a deadly wound and will be worshipped as God. (See 2 Thessalonians 2:9; Revelation 13:13–18.)

Satan can still counterfeit worship and ministry (2 Cor. 11:14). That is why we must test those who claim to have the Holy Ghost and not be led away by what is false (1 John 4:1–3).

DEMONS USE DECEPTION

Revelation 12:9 declares that Satan has deceived the whole world. The word *deceive* pictures a person who believes a lie to be the truth. A deceived person is one who is utterly convinced that right is wrong and wrong is right. Satan is a deceiver. He practices his deception in many realms. Basically, deception is practiced in the area of the Word of God. If Satan can convince a person that God is a liar, then he can get that person to violate God's principles of living. The other area of deception is on the person and work of Christ.

Demons use perversion to distort the plan of God. Satan is a perverter of all the physical appetites that God has given us. The appetite for food may be perverted into gluttony. Alcohol given by God as a medicine has been perverted into the worst social problem in America. (See Proverbs 20:1; 23:1–3, 20–21, 29–35.) Sex is God's gift to a man and woman in the bond of marriage. Now this gift has been perverted into every wickedness imaginable. Scripture forbids premarital sex and homosexual acts; Satan says they are acceptable. The world calls it "sexual preference."

Satan perverts the plan of God. Satan produces imitators who misuse the plan of God and lead people astray. When Moses stood before Pharaoh and his rod became a serpent, Pharaoh's magicians did the same thing (Exod. 7:11–22). There have been and will be many wolves in sheep's clothing until the return of Christ. Satan will ultimately produce the Antichrist, who will be an imitation of Jesus.

Therefore it is necessary to test the spirit that speaks out of a man. Test it by the Word of God. "Beloved, do not believe every spirit, but test the spirits, to see whether they are from God, because many false prophets have gone out into the world" (1 John 4:1, MEV).

Satan's greatest device against Christians is that which he used against Job: namely, accusation. Satan will accuse us of sin that God has forgiven. He is a slanderer and a liar. He accused Job of serving God for material blessings. Job was vindicated, and God was victorious. Satan used the weather, death, family, disease, and false friends. Through it all, Job neither cursed God nor charged God wrongly.

Satan will tell you that God is to blame for your troubles. He will tell you sin is to blame. He will accuse you and try to defeat and destroy your faith. Our defense is confession of our sin according to 1 John 1:9. We are not condemned; we are forgiven.

Perhaps one of the greatest ways Satan operates in the world is through rebellion against authority. Human government was permitted in order to thwart Satan's purpose of lawlessness. When rebellion and anarchy overthrow a government, it always brings a more repressive regime. The breakdown of authority in the nation, home, and church will bring a harsher government or total destruction. The bombing of New York City's World Trade Center in 1993 and the tragic bombing of the federal building in Oklahoma City in 1995 are clear examples of demonically inspired rebellion.

The Bible warns us of the sin of rebellion. Saul's rebellion is described as witchcraft and his stubbornness as iniquity and idolatry (1 Sam. 15:23). Satan destroyed Saul by rebellion. Living out from under authority is dangerous! God-given authority must be established and honored in our churches.

Other methods Satan uses include temptations of the flesh, occult involvement, religious charlatans, fear, and intimidation.

The victory is won by the believer who will utilize the weapons provided by God. Only the unarmed will know defeat! When Eliot Ness and the Treasury Department first began fighting the Capone Mob in Chicago, the FBI was not allowed to carry weapons. Only after a number of agents were killed did the government finally agree to arm them.

Our King has permitted us to bear arms! Let us clothe ourselves with God's armor and live in victory!

Chapter Eleven

SYMPTOMS OF DEMONIC OPERATION

T HE SUBJECT OF MENTAL ILLNESS IS VERY CONTROVERSIAL in Christian circles. Inside the extreme schools of thought we must find balance and a scriptural viewpoint. First, let me say clearly, all mental illness is not the result of demonic attack. Further, good psychological care from Christian professionals is vital and in order when an individual is struggling. Also, professionally administered medication may be necessary when chemical imbalances occur. When normal medicine and therapy do not result in a cure, then it is possible that these symptoms could point to demonic operation.

Let me list for you fourteen symptoms of demonic operation. As these symptoms are listed, realize that some of them could also be caused by something other than demonic oppression. The first six symptoms on this list are extreme and are drawn from the account of the demoniac of Gadara in Mark 5. This man had been chained in a cemetery because of his erratic and violent behavior. When you look at Mark 5:1–15, you can see clear symptoms of demonic activity.

Symptom 1: Incapacity for normal living (Mark 5:1–5)
Just as the actions of Legion made him unsuitable for normal social interaction with friends and family, an unusual desire for solitude, accompanied by a deep loneliness, will often set in. The person will often become very passive with no desire to change.

Symptom 2: Extreme behavior (Mark 5:4)
Violence will often be evident in the victim's life. An explosive temper and extreme, uncontrollable anger are dangerous behaviors that control the individual and the people who love him or her.

Symptom 3: Personality changes (Mark 5:9, 12)

Multiple personalities exist in some of the most serious cases of demonic control. This man had a "legion" of spirits within his life. All cases of multiple personality may not be demonic, but in most cases demon activity is involved. Changes in personality, extreme or mild, may be evidence of demonic activity.

Symptom 4: Restlessness and insomnia (Mark 5:5)

In verse 5 we see this man crying in the tombs "night and day." He could not sleep. Insomnia can be a sign of a physical problem or a sign of a spiritual problem. God has gifted His children with sleep (Ps. 127:2). So when you cannot sleep night after night and there is no medical reason for this disturbance, the devil maybe tormenting you. Don't forget; you have the right to rest in Jesus!

In Psalm 3 we see a picture of warfare. Here David was hounded by his enemies. In verses 3 and 4, he cried to the Lord, "You...are a shield for me." In verses 5 and 6, he cried, "I lay down and slept; I awoke, for the LORD sustained me. I will not be afraid of ten thousands of people who have set themselves against me all around." He also said in Psalm 4:8, "I will both lie down in peace and sleep; for You, LORD, make me dwell safely and securely" (MEV). Sleep is God's gift to all who trust in Him.

Symptom 5: A terrible inner anguish (Mark 5:5)

This man was deeply tormented in mind and heart. Various levels of anguish are evident in those who are afflicted by demons. Grief and anguish are normal emotions for us all. Yet, persistent, unresolved anguish that will not leave after normal therapies of counseling, encouragement, and prayer could well be demonic.

Symptom 6: Self-inflicted injury and suicide (Mark 5:5)

Here we see the demonic man was cutting himself. If you read Mark 9:14–29, you will see the story of the man whose son was both deaf and mute because of a demon: "Wherever he [the evil spirit] seizes him, he throws him down....Often he [the demon] has thrown him [the boy] both into the fire and into the water to destroy him" (vv. 18, 22). Jesus cast out the demon. "The spirit cried out, convulsed him greatly, and came out of him. And he became as one dead....But Jesus took him by the hand and lifted him up, and he arose" (vv. 26–27). Demons can cause people to injure themselves. They even incite suicide.

Symptom 7: Unexplained illness with no obvious medical cause

When medical testing produces no physical cause for an illness, then we should look to the mind and spirit for answers. Sometimes illnesses are psychological, and good counseling can result in a cure. Other times the battle is with demons.

A scriptural example of this is found in Luke 13:11–16, the story of a woman afflicted by a "spirit of infirmity" (v. 11). Jesus called her "a daughter of Abraham, whom Satan has bound" (v. 16). Obviously she was a child of God and faithful to her synagogue, with a desire to know more about the Lord. "Jesus…said to her, 'Woman, you are loosed from your infirmity.' And He laid hands on her, and immediately she was made straight, and glorified God" (vv. 12–13). There are physical illnesses caused by a class of demons known as "spirits of infirmity."

Symptom 8: Addictive behavior

Addiction to alcohol, drugs, sex, food, gambling, and other things opens the door to demonic influence and control. I am not saying demons cause all of these problems; certainly people are responsible for their own wrong choices. But anything that causes one to be out of control opens that person to infernal control.

Symptom 9: Abnormal sexual behavior

When Jezebel's son inquired about peace, Jehu responded, "What peace, so long as the harlotries of your mother Jezebel and her sorceries are so many?" (2 Kings 9:22, MEV).

In Ezekiel 16:20–51 the spirit of harlotry is mentioned several times. This spirit infected the nation of Israel with the sins of Sodom (vv. 49–50). They even sacrificed their own children (vv. 20–21).

Homosexuality, adultery, fornication, and even infanticide are all inspired by the spirit of harlotry. Hosea 4:12 says, "The spirit of harlotry has caused them to stray, and they have played the harlot against their God." Look at Hosea 5:4: "They do not direct their deeds toward turning to their God, for the spirit of harlotry is in their midst, and they do not know the LORD."

A nation and a people given over to sexual sins and abominations are governed by this spirit of harlotry. Look at Nahum 3:4: "Because of the multitude of harlotries of the seductive harlot, the mistress of sorceries, who sells nations through her harlotries, and families through her sorceries."

Nations and families are sold into spiritual bondage by the witchcraft of the spirit of harlotry. When we play around with sexual sin, we open ourselves to this demonic spirit. We must battle this principality that dominates our nation.

Symptom 10: Defeat, failure, and depression in the Christian life

Paul wrote in 2 Corinthians 2:14, "Now thanks be to God who always causes us to triumph in Christ" (MEV). Notice this verse is preceded by an exhortation from Paul to forgive others "lest Satan should take advantage of us. For we are not ignorant of his devices" (vv. 10–11, MEV). It is Satan's purpose to take advantage of our situations and to rob us of the victorious life that is ours in Christ. The psalmist cried out, "By this I know that You favor me, because my enemy does not triumph over me" (Ps. 41:11, MEV).

This symptom is often manifested by an inability to praise and worship. Psalm 92:1–4 is a testimony to the power of praise. It culminates in verse 4, where David said, "For you, O LORD, have made me glad through Your work; I will sing joyfully at the works of Your hands." Again he said, "Save us, O LORD our God…to give thanks…and to boast in Your praise" (Ps. 106:47, MEV).

Symptom 11: Occult involvement and behavior

Deuteronomy 18:9–12 catalogs the works of the occult and witchcraft, including child sacrifice; fortune-telling; soothsaying; interpreting omens; sorcery; and the work of those who conjure spells, mediums, spiritists, and those who call up the dead. Then verse 15 instructs the people to hear the word of God from the prophet of God and order their lives accordingly. Occult involvement is clearly a symptom of demonic control.

Symptom 12: Speech difficulties

In Matthew 9:32–33 Jesus rebuked a demon, and the mute man was able to speak. Speech difficulties may be physical, emotional, mental, and, in some cases, demonic. Extreme language and cursing may be prompted by the enemy.

Symptom 13: Doctrinal error

In 1 Timothy 4:1 we receive a warning that in the last days deceiving spirits will teach the doctrines of demons. Today, religious cults and charlatans abound. The reason these deceivers draw many people is the power of the demonic that teaches them.

Symptom 14: Religious legalism

Galatians 3:1 says to the believer who is in danger of going back under the Law, "Who has bewitched you that you should not obey the truth?" (MEV). The church at Galatia had forsaken a faith ministry that resulted in the miraculous (v. 5) for a law ministry of rules and regulations. Paul classified this error as witchcraft.

Some deeply religious people are under the bondage of tradition, man-made rules, and outward appearances. Demons thrive in this kind of environment, especially demons of control. It is a lot easier to keep a ritual or list of rules than it is to walk by faith. Wherever there is any substitute for faith in the finished work of Christ, it is a doctrine of demons.

ENFORCING THE VICTORY OVER YOUR ENEMY

Chapter Twelve

THE VICTORY AT CALVARY

A BIBLICAL UNDERSTANDING OF SPIRITUAL WARFARE BEGINS at the end and not at the beginning. This is correct because it is ever important to keep our focus on Christ and not on the power of the enemy. Satan has no rightful authority over any believer. He is a usurper and a trespasser on God's earth. We cannot even acquiesce to his proud claim to the kingdom of this world. This would be treason to Christ, who refused to avoid the cross by bowing to the enemy at the wilderness temptation.

We must go right to the heart of spiritual warfare: the battle has already been won! Satan has lain under judgment since Eden. We must never forget that judgment was announced in Eden and implemented on Calvary! We must proclaim that the sentence handed down upon Satan in Eden has been executed: "And I will put enmity between you and the woman, and between your seed and her Seed; He shall bruise your head, and you shall bruise His heel" (Gen. 3:15). Strong man that he is, he has been dispossessed by one stronger.

In John Bunyan's classic *The Pilgrim's Progress*, Timorous and Mistrust turn back from their journey to God's city when they see two lions. The narrator says, "The Lions were chained, but he saw not the Chains."[1] Satan and the forces of hell are on a short leash since Calvary. We are not fighting for victory but rather from victory. The bottom line of spiritual warfare is applying and enforcing the victory of the cross upon the enemy. We cannot overestimate him; neither can we underestimate him.

We are not dualists who believe that God and the devil are equal and struggling for control of man. Satan does not coexist with God. The powers of darkness were conquered at the cross. This tremendous passage in Colossians chapter 2 reaches its climax in verse 15 with a victorious affirmation of Christ's victory: "Having disarmed authorities and powers, He made a show of them openly, triumphing over them by the cross" (MEV).

Most of us see in the cross the sacrifice of Christ for our forgiveness. We see the ultimate example of unconditional love. We see the demonstration of God's love to us. This is certainly true, but there is also an unseen truth about what took place on the cross. There was a cosmic spiritual war waged that day.

This day was the culmination of all of Satan's hatred of Jesus. Satan tried to kill Jesus at His birth using the tyrant Herod. He tempted Jesus in the wilderness to stray from the Father's plan. He set before the Lord the lust of the flesh, the lust of the eye, and the pride of life. He tempted Jesus's body, soul, and spirit. Jesus defeated Him with the Word of God.

We should make no mistake about what the clear purpose of Jesus was in coming into the world. He came to do battle with Satan. The Lord Jesus Christ left heaven and invaded Satan's sphere. He came unwelcomed by the masses and hated by Satan. In Jesus's inaugural address at the synagogue in Nazareth He quoted Isaiah 61:1: "The Spirit of the Lord God is upon Me, because the Lord has anointed Me to preach good tidings to the poor; He has sent Me to heal the brokenhearted, to proclaim liberty to the captives, and the opening of the prison to those who are bound." Jesus saw our world as bound, blind, brokenhearted, and bruised; here were the disastrous effects of Satan's control.

Throughout His ministry Jesus confronted the forces of hell and cast them out. Many times He opened the eyes of the blind—and He still opens the eyes of those blinded by Satan. He still sets the captive free. Jesus saw the destructive work of Satan and did something about it.

The Bible is replete with verses that reveal these truths. In one of the many statements given as to the purpose of the Lord coming into the world, John tells us, "For this purpose the Son of God was revealed, that He might destroy the works of the devil" (1 John 3:8, MEV).

Shortly before the cross Jesus said, "Now judgment is upon this world. Now the ruler of this world will be cast out" (John 12:31, MEV).

When He was arrested, Jesus said to His arresters, "When I was with you daily in the temple, you did not try to seize Me. But this is your hour, and the power of darkness" (Luke 22:53).

The world in which He ministered was a world dominated by Satan: "We know that we are of God, and the whole world lies under the sway of the wicked one" (1 John 5:19).

Again His purpose is stated by the writer of Hebrews: "So then, as the children share in flesh and blood, He likewise took part in these, so that through death He might destroy him who has the power of death, that is, the devil" (Heb. 2:14, MEV).

The apostle Paul had no room for doubt about what took place in the spiritual realm on the day Jesus was crucified. In specific detail the passage in Colossians 2:6–15 gives us a spiritual picture of the cosmic war that raged on Calvary that day and demonstrates to us our victory. Paul says three main things happened at the cross that the natural eye could not see.

THE CROSS DISARMED SATAN

Hostile spiritual powers had reigned over man and the world. This reign had its origin in sin and the Fall. Now Jesus had come to spoil them: "Having disarmed authorities and powers, He made a show of them openly, triumphing over them by the cross" (Col. 2:15, MEV). The word translated "disarmed" means "to spoil," "to strip," or "to rob." It is in the Greek aorist tense in the original, which means it was a once-and-for-all disarming.

There will not be a rematch; the battle has forever been decided. The word picture is that of a fallen enemy who has been stripped of his sword, armor, shield, position, and wealth. The Scripture teaches us that Satan has been stripped of his right, power, and authority over all those who have bowed at the foot of the cross and received the precious blood of Christ as atonement for their sin.

What did Jesus rob Satan of? We see in Romans 8:33–34 that He robbed him of the right to accuse us: "Who shall bring a charge against God's elect? It is God who justifies. Who is he who condemns? It is Christ who died, yes, who is risen, who is also at the right hand of God, who also intercedes for us" (MEV). Satan has been robbed of his right to kill us. We are no longer guilty. He has been robbed of his ownership of us. He has no weapon and no way to keep us.

THE CROSS DISPLAYED SATAN

Christ made a "public spectacle of them" (Col. 2:15). Someone might object to this passage and say, "Wasn't it Christ who was made a public spectacle that day?" Indeed He was. He was stripped of His garments and made a public spectacle before men who cried, "If You are really God, then come down off the cross." But we must remember there was another public spectacle going on in the unseen spiritual realm.

In the spiritual realm Christ made a public spectacle of Satan and all of the demonic forces. Jesus displayed him before the angelic world, the demonic world, the spiritual world, and before "just men made perfect" (Heb. 12:23). They saw him not as an angel of light, as he so often would make himself appear, but rather they saw his true nature. They saw him as a rotten, filthy, lying thief. Satan and all of the demonic forces were viewed in their true nature.

Satan and all of his host flurried themselves in full fury against the seemingly helpless Son of God. Satan came as Apollyon the destroyer. When the smoke of the battle had lifted, however, there was an empty cross and an empty tomb. Jesus defeated Satan on Satan's home field. He was put on display as the defeated foe he really is. The word picture is that of a billboard. They were put on display for everyone to see.

Satan is forever a public spectacle of defeat when God's people enforce Calvary's victory. At His ascension Jesus passed through the atmosphere, declaring that neither the laws of gravity nor the powers of hell could hold Him back.

THE CROSS DEFEATED SATAN

Dr. James S. Stewart, Scottish preacher and former chaplain to the queen of England, stood for the fundamentals of the faith in the Anglican church when it was not popular to do so. Dr. Stewart called for a return to the truth, stating that a cosmic battle took place at the cross. Behind the cross we see the fallen design of man. Human sins such as pride, jealousy, greed, self-righteousness, religion, political injustice, and human apathy brought our Savior to the cross. Yet behind these stood principalities and powers of evil. The people were driven by forces beyond themselves.[2]

Jesus chose to die for His people because He knew the enemy as a strongman had a death grip on them. He came as one stronger to set the captive free. Jesus acted in history not only to reconcile sinners but also to expose the error of dualism. People everywhere feared the gods of superstition. Jesus not only defeated them but also announced that they would bow before Him and acknowledge him as Lord.

> Therefore God highly exalted Him and gave Him the name which is above every name, that at the name of Jesus every knee should bow, of those in heaven and on earth and under the earth, and every tongue should confess that Jesus Christ is Lord, to the glory of God the Father.
> —PHILIPPIANS 2:9–11, MEV

The power of Satan was shattered at the cross. Triumph over Satan has come at last. The verb translated "triumph" means "a complete and irretrievable subjugation."

However, the question remains, "If Satan has been disarmed, displayed, and defeated at the cross, why is my life so far from victorious?" Number one, if you have not been saved, then you are fair game for the attacks and residency of Satan in your life. You cannot have victory over Satan apart from the application of the blood of Jesus to your sins.

Secondly, if you are a believer, then the only way Satan can attack you is if you have given him the right. The Bible warns, "Do not give place to the devil" (Eph. 4:27, MEV). If you have given place to the devil by living in rebellious sin, then you have put out a welcome mat for the enemy to come in and enslave you. Many believers live such defeated, depressed lives that they neither bring honor to the Lord nor serve as an example to others. These believers make up a weak, anemic church that is a blight to what Jesus accomplished on the cross. Did Jesus die for a church full of diseased, depressed people in bondage to the enemy?

There is victory in the cross! The blood has wiped out our sin and left Satan powerless. Every blow that drove the nails into His holy hands was also a nail in the coffin of Satan. Every Christian is set free.

Christ's death was a battle in which God achieved an immortal victory. The conflict was furious and mysterious. Our Lord died to win the battle and rose from the dead to enforce the victory.

There is victory in Jesus every day. When Satan comes, we simply remind him of our Savior. If he accuses us, we point to forgiveness. If he desires to tempt us, we let our Lord's words fell him. If he would touch us, we declare that he has no authority over God's property.

Chapter Thirteen

FOUNDATIONS FOR VICTORY

Second Timothy 2:3–4 describes every Christian as a soldier at war.

If victory is to be enjoyed, then the soldier's battle plan must rest on a solid foundation of sound teaching from the Word of God. The greatest snare of the enemy is in the area of perverting or denying the truth.

God's foundations stand sure, and we must rest our faith, planning, and battle strategy upon three unchanging biblical and spiritual foundations:

1. The finished work of Christ

2. The believer's union with Christ

3. The present work of the Spirit of Christ in the believer

THE FOUNDATION OF THE FINISHED WORK OF CHRIST

All that we have and are able to enjoy in the realm of the Spirit is based upon the glorious fact that the Son of God came in the flesh, invaded this demon-infested world, and wrought the victory through His death and resurrection on the cross.

> How God anointed Jesus of Nazareth with the Holy Spirit and with power, who went about doing good and healing all who were oppressed by the devil, for God was with Him.
>
> —Acts 10:38, mev

How did God win this victory? Read on in Acts 10:39–40: "Whom they slew and hanged on a tree: him God raised up the third day" (KJV).

The late Professor James S. Stewart in the Lyman Beecher Lectures at Yale University in the early 1950s mourned the loss of teaching on the demonic and their defeat only through the cross: "I wish to introduce the theme of preaching the cross by suggesting that if for great numbers of our contemporaries the effect of Newton, Darwin, and Freud has been to banish the divine, it has even more emphatically been to banish the demonic."[1]

He further states, "The elimination of the dimension of the demonic has had its effect upon Christian theology…a usurping personal force alive and tyrannical…not simply some phobia of man or divided self."[2] Jesus Christ's death did at least four things to assure victory.

1. He settled the sin question.

> Therefore, since we have been justified by faith, we have peace with God through our Lord Jesus Christ, through whom we also have access by faith into this grace in which we stand, and so we rejoice in hope of the glory of God. Not only so, but we also boast in tribulation, knowing that tribulation produces patience, patience produces character, and character produces hope. And hope does not disappoint, because the love of God is shed abroad in our hearts by the Holy Spirit who has been given to us.
> —ROMANS 5:1–5, MEV

> There is therefore now no condemnation to those who are in Christ Jesus, who walk not according to the flesh, but according to the Spirit.
> —ROMANS 8:1, MEV

Jesus Christ died as our sinless substitute to once and for all cancel our sin debt and Satan's right to accuse us.

2. He came to make you acceptable.

> To the praise of the glory of His grace, by which He has made us accepted in the Beloved.
> —EPHESIANS 1:6

You now have eternal significance.

3. He came to conquer Satan.

> He has delivered us from the power of darkness and has transferred us into the kingdom of His dear Son.
> —COLOSSIANS 1:13, MEV

> Having disarmed authorities and powers, He made a show of them openly, triumphing over them by the cross.
> —COLOSSIANS 2:15, MEV

> So then, as the children share in flesh and blood, He likewise took part in these, so that through death He might destroy him who has the power of death, that is, the devil, and deliver those who through fear of death were throughout their lives subject to bondage.
> —HEBREWS 2:14–15, MEV

> Whoever practices sin is of the devil, for the devil has been sinning from the beginning. For this purpose the Son of God was revealed, that He might destroy the works of the devil.
> —1 JOHN 3:8, MEV

The atonement death of Christ was the battle of the ages. Unseen victories were being won. Theologian Gustav Aulen declares that Jesus is "Christus Victor."[3] His death was triumphant. P. T. Forsyth has said, "The world's awful need is less than Christ's awful victory. And the devils we meet were [already destined to hell] in the Satan He ruined. The wickedness of the world is, after all, 'a bull in a net,' a chained beast kicking himself to death."[4]

John Calvin, in commenting on Colossians 2:8–15, said, "There is no tribunal so magnificent, no throne so stately, no show of triumph so distinguished, no chariot so elevated, as is the gibbet [cross] on which Christ has subdued death and the devil...[and] utterly trodden them under his feet."[5]

The great German theologian Oscar Cullman, in his book *Christ and Time,* said of Christ's finished work, "The principalities and powers between the Resurrection and the Parousia [Second Coming] are tied to a rope, still free enough to evince their demonic character, but nevertheless bound, since Christ has already conquered all demons: the cross and the resurrection being the decisive battle that has turned the tide of the war and settled the issue, even though Victory Day may still lie in a future, out of sight."[6]

We must always understand that we fight on the foundation of a victory already won!

Christ came to cancel everything we inherited from the first Adam.

> Therefore as sin came into the world through one man and death through sin, so death has spread to all men, because all have sinned. For until the law, sin was in the world. But sin is not counted when there is no law. Nevertheless death reigned from Adam to Moses, even over those who had not sinned in the likeness of Adam's sin, who was a type of Him who was to come. But the free gift is not like the trespass. For if through the trespass of one man many died, then how much more has the grace of God and the free gift by the grace of the one Man, Jesus Christ, abounded to many. The gift is not like the result that came through the one who sinned. For the judgment from one sin led to condemnation, but the free gift, which came after many trespasses, leads to justification. For if by one man's trespass death reigned through him, then how much more will those who receive abundance of grace and the gift of righteousness reign in life through the One, Jesus Christ. Therefore just as through the trespass of one man came condemnation for all men, so through the righteous act of One came justification of life for all men. For just as through one man's disobedience the many were made sinners, so by the obedience of One the many will be made righteous. But the law entered, so that sin might increase, but where sin increased, grace abounded much more, so that just as sin reigned in death, grace might reign through righteousness unto eternal life through Jesus Christ our Lord.
> —Romans 5:12–21, MEV

In the Garden of Eden Satan usurped the inheritance of humanity and enthroned death as the king of the earth. A "second Adam"— Jesus Christ—was called forth to break the grip of these principalities and powers and to rescue the race from extinction (Rom. 5:17). You and I must appropriate the finished work of Christ if we are to enjoy His victory. That brings us to the second foundation.

THE FOUNDATION OF OUR UNION WITH CHRIST

> Jesus answered him, "Truly, truly, I say to you, unless a man is born again, he cannot see the kingdom of God."
>
> —JOHN 3:3, MEV

> And you He made alive, who were dead in trespasses and sins, in which you once walked according to the course of this world, according to the prince of the power of the air, the spirit who now works in the sons of disobedience, among whom also we all once conducted ourselves in the lusts of our flesh, fulfilling the desires of the flesh and of the mind, and were by nature children of wrath, just as the others. But God, who is rich in mercy, because of His great love with which He loved us, even when we were dead in trespasses, made us alive together with Christ (by grace you have been saved), and raised us up together, and made us sit together in the heavenly places in Christ Jesus, that in the ages to come He might show the exceeding riches of His grace in His kindness toward us in Christ Jesus. For by grace you have been saved through faith, and that not of yourselves; it is the gift of God, not of works, lest anyone should boast.
>
> —EPHESIANS 2:1–9

At the new birth (John 3:3), you are made alive by the Holy Spirit (Eph. 2:1–9) and brought into a vital union with Christ. Romans 5:10 says, "Having been reconciled, we shall be saved by His life." Indeed, His death for us secured our salvation. His life in us applies that salvation.

God changes our lives by exchanging our lives for the life of Christ. According to the New Testament, we are now identified with Christ in every aspect of His finished work.

Our death with Christ

> I have been crucified with Christ. It is no longer I who live, but Christ who lives in me.
>
> —GALATIANS 2:20, MEV

Our burial with Christ

Romans 6:4 declares that everything we were in Adam was buried with Christ; baptism is a picture of that burial.

> Therefore we were buried with Him through baptism into death, that just as Christ was raised from the dead by the glory of the Father, even so we also should walk in newness of life.

Our resurrection with Christ

> For if we have been united with Him in the likeness of His death, so shall we also be united with Him in the likeness of His resurrection, knowing this, that our old man has been crucified with Him, so that the body of sin might be destroyed, and we should no longer be slaves to sin.
> —ROMANS 6:5–6, MEV

> And you He made alive, who were dead in trespasses and sins, in which you once walked according to the course of this world, according to the prince of the power of the air, the spirit who now works in the sons of disobedience, among whom also we all once conducted ourselves in the lusts of our flesh, fulfilling the desires of the flesh and of the mind, and were by nature children of wrath, just as the others. But God, who is rich in mercy, because of His great love with which He loved us, even when we were dead in trespasses, made us alive together with Christ (by grace you have been saved).
> —EPHESIANS 2:1–5

Spiritually the saved person has been raised out of spiritual death. Though our bodies have not been raised, the resurrection factor lives by the Holy Spirit in our spirit. In fact, the Holy Spirit is the "earnest" or guarantee of our bodily resurrection. Eternal life dwells in every believer.

> In Him you also, after hearing the word of truth, the gospel of your salvation, and after believing in Him, were sealed with the promised Holy Spirit, who is the guarantee of our inheritance until the redemption of the purchased possession, to the praise of His glory.
> —EPHESIANS 1:13–14, MEV

Our enthronement with Christ

> Even when we were dead in sins, made us alive together with
> Christ (by grace you have been saved), and He raised us up
> together and seated us together in the heavenly places in Christ
> Jesus.
>   —EPHESIANS 2:5–6, MEV

When you look back at Ephesians 1:20–21, you see that when we
take our position in Christ, seated with Him, we are then "far above
all principalities, and power, and might, and dominion" (MEV). Now
everything that was once over our heads is now under our feet. Our
strategic position is identified fully with Christ. First John 4:17 says,
"As He is, so are we in this world" (MEV). This brings us to the final
foundation, the fullness of the Holy Spirit.

THE FOUNDATION OF THE FULLNESS AND POWER OF THE HOLY SPIRIT

The Lord on the earth today is the third Person of the Godhead, the
blessed Holy Spirit. The Holy Spirit indwells every believer. He may,
however, be ignored, insulted, grieved, and quenched. He longs to fill,
gift, and bring forth fruit in every believer.

**The Holy Spirit alone turns the Word of God into the sword of the
Spirit.**

> Take the helmet of salvation and the sword of the Spirit, which is
> the word of God.
>   —EPHESIANS 6:17, MEV

> For the word of God is alive, and active, and sharper than any
> two-edged sword, piercing even to the division of soul and spirit,
> of joints and marrow, and able to judge the thoughts and intents
> of the heart.
>   —HEBREWS 4:12, MEV

The Holy Spirit alone makes effective praying possible.

> Likewise, the Spirit helps us in our weaknesses, for we do not know what to pray for as we ought, but the Spirit Himself intercedes for us with groanings too deep for words.
>
> —ROMANS 8:26, MEV

> But you, beloved, build yourselves up in your most holy faith. Pray in the Holy Spirit.
>
> —JUDE 20, MEV

The Holy Spirit alone gives understanding of the Word of God.

> Therefore I also, after hearing of your faith in the Lord Jesus and your love toward all the saints, do not cease giving thanks for you, mentioning you in my prayers, so that the God of our Lord Jesus Christ, the Father of glory, may give you the Spirit of wisdom and revelation in the knowledge of Him, that the eyes of your understanding may be enlightened, that you may know what is the hope of His calling and what are the riches of the glory of His inheritance among the saints.
>
> —EPHESIANS 1:15–18, MEV

This scripture speaks of the gift of revelation knowledge and understanding by the Holy Spirit. God's Spirit makes it possible to understand and apply spiritual truth.

The Holy Spirit strengthens our inner man.

> That He would grant you…to be strengthened with might through His Spirit in the inner man.
>
> —EPHESIANS 3:16

The Holy Spirit desires to fill every Christian.

Ephesians 5:18 says, "Be filled with the Spirit" (MEV). This fullness is no less than total control of the individual. This is the lordship of Christ active in the life of a Christian. A Spirit-filled believer cannot be defeated by Satan and his demonic forces. When we are filled with the Spirit, we live in a constant state of triumph.

Chapter Fourteen

THE BELIEVER'S POSITION FOR VICTORY

O PERATION DESERT SHIELD IS A CLASSIC EXAMPLE OF BATTLE strategy. No battle was launched until everything and everyone was in the proper position. Then the air attacks began. The Allied planes took the battle to the skies and then to the earth. Then the ground troops moved in to recapture lost territory and set the captives free.

Spiritual warfare uses this same time-tested strategy. Believers must know their enemy, know their strength, and get into battle position. That battle position is described in Ephesians 6:10: "Be strong in the Lord" (MEV). Salvation is Christ in you. Your exalted position is you in Christ!

UNDERSTANDING THE BELIEVER'S EXALTED POSITION

Paul's favorite description of a Christian is "in Christ." Ephesians uses this expression repeatedly to specify the privileges of being a Christian. Christians are to be "faithful in Jesus Christ." The possibility of faithful living is ours because of our presence in Christ. Also, "every spiritual blessing" (Eph. 1:3, MEV) is ours in Christ. Our acceptance in the divine family is secured because "He has made us accepted in the Beloved" (v. 6). In fact, if you read through Ephesians 1, you will discover that all your needs for this life and the life to come are found by understanding what it means to be in Christ. Often the focus is on Christ being in the believer. Yet in Ephesians the believer is viewed as in Christ.

For our purpose in this study it is important to note that the "in

Christ" believer has been exalted and enthroned above all principalities and powers "and raised…up together, and made…[to] sit together in the heavenly places in Christ Jesus" (Eph. 2:6). The heavenly places are where Christ is presently enthroned, "which He performed in Christ when He raised Him from the dead and seated Him at His own right hand in the heavenly places, far above all principalities, and power, and might, and dominion, and every name that is named, not only in this age but also in that which is to come. And He put all things in subjection under His feet" (Eph. 1:20–22, MEV).

When we understand our position in Christ, then we clearly understand that everything that is under His feet is also under the believer's feet. As ambassadors of heaven believers have the authority of the throne of Jesus Christ! Our battle with Satan and his demons takes place in the heavenly places: "For our fight is not against flesh and blood, but against principalities, against powers, against the rulers of the darkness of this world, and against spiritual forces of evil in the heavenly places" (Eph. 6:12, MEV).

You and I have no authority within ourselves over demons. Yet these wicked spiritual forces are fully aware of the authority that is ours in Jesus Christ. Even though an ambassador of our country lives outside of our own country, he still has citizenship; and when he speaks, he speaks with the authority of Washington, DC, and all of the might of the United States. Likewise, we are citizens of heaven, and here on the earth we speak with all the authority of heaven.

UNDERSTAND THE BELIEVER'S ETERNAL PURPOSE

God's eternal purpose for every believer is Christlikeness. Our purpose is not to fight for a victory. Our Lord has already won the decisive battle at Calvary. We fight from His victory. We are here to enforce the victory of our Lord. "Be strong in the Lord and in the power of His might" (Eph. 6:10, MEV).

The verb *be strong in* is a present passive imperative. It is a continuous command. It is passive, indicating that the subject is strengthened by an outside power. It would better be translated, "Go on being strengthened." It is not the believer flexing his spiritual muscles. It is receiving and appropriating God's strength.

God permits Satan to war against believers. Though ultimately this is a mystery, clearly several reasons can be noted.

1. Warfare with Satan sharpens the believer's skill in using Scripture.

2. These earthly battles are freeing us for exalted rule in the next world: "For I consider that the sufferings of this present time are not worthy to be compared with the glory which shall be revealed in us" (Rom. 8:18, MEV).

3. Spiritual warfare teaches us the tragedy of the human condition because of the fall of mankind. Satan's hatred of the human race and his relentless efforts to control human destiny are clearly exposed in spiritual warfare.

4. Man learns his utter helplessness before evil without Christ. C. S. Lewis has said, "Education without values, as useful as it is, seems rather to make man a more clever devil."[1]

5. Spiritual warfare keeps the believer from becoming too comfortable in this world. Regular struggles with the enemy remind us that we are living in hostile territory. Finally, warfare teaches the believer that the servant is not above his master! Our Lord was a soldier. He battled even to the shedding of His blood. He battled and won the victory.

Now it is the believer's duty to enforce the victory Jesus has won. Our Lord was no stranger to warfare, facing Satan at the beginning of His ministry when He was tempted and at the end of His earthly ministry in the garden and on the cross. It is the purpose of God that every believer know how to do battle following His example.

UNDERSTAND THE BELIEVER'S POWER

Once again let me remind you to "be strong in the Lord and in the power of His might" (Eph. 6:10, MEV). When a Christian understands his position, then he can begin to appropriate the power of Jesus. What is "the power of His might"? This same phrase is found in Ephesians 1:19–20. The working of His mighty power is the same power that raised the dead body of Jesus to life. It's the same power that exalted Him above all to the highest position in heaven and on the earth. It is the same power Paul had in mind when he wrote, "I can do all things because of Christ who strengthens me" (Phil. 4:13, MEV).

When a person accepts Christ as Lord, he is initiated into His victory. It is a fierce and terrible war, but we are in the winning position. How do we appropriate and apply this victory? Prayer, the Word, and faith are the way. We appropriate unlimited power when we are willing to live for the Lord. The Spirit-filled life supplies the strength we need.

Satan has two major goals. First, he desires to keep as many people as possible from salvation through Christ. Second Corinthians 4:4 gives us this terrible strategy: "That they cannot see the light of the gospel of the glory of Christ, who is the image of God" (NIV). Satan believes that his only hope of reprieve is to ensnare so many human beings that God would reverse His plan of redemption and then prove to be unrighteous.

Secondly, Satan desires to neutralize believers by defeating and discouraging them. Wake up to the truth! If you do not take your battle position in Christ, the enemy will destroy you.

Right now you can take your exalted position in Christ. Pray the following prayer:

> *Heavenly Father, I bow in praise and ownership before You. I praise You that the blood of Jesus is my covering. I praise You for the Holy Spirit, who indwells and fills my life. I surrender myself anew to You as a living sacrifice. I repudiate conformity to this world and praise You for the transforming work of Christ. I renounce Satan and all his workers and declare that they have no right to interfere with me in this prayer. I am praying to the true and living God, and I refuse any involvement of the enemy in this prayer.*
>
> *I ask You, Lord, to rebuke Satan, and I take now my exalted position in Christ. I recognize that the armor of*

God is none other than Christ! My sword is the Word of God and praise.

I praise You, Jesus, that in this position on Your throne the enemy is under my feet. I reject, repudiate, and renounce all that Satan has brought against me, and I bring the blood of Jesus against you, Satan, and command you to leave in the name of Jesus Christ. I declare that all principalities and powers take notice that I know who I am in Christ. I will live in Christ and over you in His sure victory. In the strong name of Jesus, amen.

Chapter Fifteen

ARMING FOR VICTORY

T HE OLD HYMN "STAND UP FOR JESUS" HAS A LINE IN IT THAT goes like this: "Put on the gospel armor / each piece put on with prayer."[1] This thought reflects what Paul is saying to the church. Having declared the believers' position for battle in Ephesians 6:10 and their posture for battle in verses 11–13, Paul moves to their panoply for battle.

Both verses 11 and 13 command the believer to "put on" the whole armor of God. This once-and-for-all command includes the entire outfit. The Greek word for "whole armor," *panoplia*, comes from *pan*, meaning "all," and *hoplon*, meaning "weaponry." The *panoplia* ("whole armor") includes all of the soldier's equipment. One scholar translates it, "Put on the splendid armor."

When Paul wrote the Book of Ephesians, he wrote from personal knowledge about Roman soldiers. He was chained to one guard when he wrote, "I, Paul, the prisoner of Jesus Christ..." (Eph. 3:1, MEV); "I, therefore, the prisoner of the Lord, exhort you..." (Eph. 4:1, MEV). He described himself as "an ambassador in chains" (Eph. 6:20, MEV). Paul saw in the Roman soldier a wonderful illustration of spiritual truth.

Understand that the armor is symbolic. The armor is no less than Christ Himself. Every believer knows Christ as Savior. The problem comes when we do not appropriate all that our Lord brings with Him. You see, it is not Christ available but Christ appropriated that makes the difference. It would be like someone having a million dollars in the bank but living a life of poverty. If you never make a withdrawal and appropriate the funds, what good does it do you? Romans 13:14 says, "Put on the Lord Jesus Christ, and make no provision for the flesh, to fulfill its lusts." The phrase *put on* is translated from the same Greek word *enduo* that is found in Ephesians 6:11. Paul wrote to Timothy, "Be strong in the grace that is in Christ Jesus" (2 Tim. 2:1, MEV).

In the battles of life Christ is the answer—but His resources must be appropriated.

In the greater context there are three pieces of armor that should always be in place without question: the belt, the breastplate, and the boots (Eph. 6:14–15). The other pieces are to be taken up decisively and finally. The emphasis here is that it is possible to forget these pieces of armor, such as the shield, helmet, and the sword. We are to take these up regularly into the battle. But in this chapter we will focus on the belt of truth.

THE BELT OF TRUTH DISPLAYS AN ILLUSTRATION OF INTEGRITY

The belt served three primary purposes for the Roman soldier. It held all of his weapons and equipment together. The belt was used to tie his robe so that he would not stumble over it going into battle. Plus, it was ornamental, displaying medals or awards for heroism in battle.

Here it is a spiritual weapon, but the functions are the same. It is called a belt of truth; therefore it pictures the Lord Jesus Christ, who said, "I am…the truth" (John 14:6, MEV). It also pictures the written Word of God, which keeps one from tripping over the obstacles in the world. Finally, it pictures the honesty and integrity that ought to characterize the life of all who know Jesus Christ.

THE BELT OF TRUTH EXHIBITS THE INSPIRATION FOR INTEGRITY

As we have already observed, the Lord Jesus Christ is the armor for the believer. Isaiah 11:5 said of Him, "Righteousness shall be the belt of His loins, and faithfulness the belt of His waist."

When Jesus faced Satan, He declared the truth of the Word of God (Matt. 4). He looked at the Pharisees who opposed Him and said, "Which of you convicts Me of sin?" (John 8:46, MEV). Pilate looked at Jesus and asked, "What is truth?" And then he declared, "I find no guilt in Him" (John 18:38, MEV). Even the thief on the cross cried, "This Man has done nothing amiss" (Luke 23:41, MEV).

Our Lord Jesus Christ spoke the truth and lived the truth. He remains the truth today. Revelation 1:12–13 pictures Jesus in His glorified state: He is bound, or girded, by a golden belt. All of our Lord's glory is bound together by His truth.

The belt represents the Lord Jesus Christ and His Word holding everything together in one's life. His truth, His character, and His integrity are to characterize our lives.

A music student walked into his teacher's studio and asked, "What good news do you have today?" The teacher picked up a hammer and hit the tuning fork. He said, "That note is A; it will be A tomorrow; it was A five thousand years ago. It will be A five thousand years from now."

Life can hold together only if it is bound together by unchanging truth. Jesus Christ and His Word are the tuning fork that gives our lives an unchanging reference point to live in harmony in a discordant world.

THE BELT OF TRUTH TEACHES US THE IMPORTANCE OF INTEGRITY

This belt of truth is displayed in the honesty and integrity of the believer. Our lives ought to be lived in such a way that people see the truth. Just as the Roman soldier used the belt to bind his robe to keep from tripping, so the truth of Jesus's Word keeps us from tripping before a watching world.

Also, the believers' medals of victory worn on the belt of integrity are their reputations. Ephesians 4:14–16 warns the believer of false doctrine and deceptive teachers. Verse 15 challenges us to speak "the truth in love" so that we "may grow up in all things."

Let us remember that our enemy can move in to destroy us in the area of honesty and character.

Do you know the truth in a person? Jesus is the truth. You can call on the great philosophers, but Socrates, Plato, and Kant will not answer. You can call on great leaders of the past, and they will not answer. Jesus Christ will answer you today. He proved His truthfulness by rising from the dead. You must admit the truth about yourself and receive the truth of Jesus today. When you do, integrity will characterize your life.

THE HEART OF THE WARRIOR

> Stand therefore... having put on the breastplate of righteousness.
> —EPHESIANS 6:14, MEV

The second piece of armor needed by soldier-saints is the breastplate of righteousness. The Greek word for *breastplate* is *thorax*. This piece of armor was made of metal and leather and fastened around the soldier's body from the neck to the thighs. It protected his vital organs, including the heart and lungs. In the armor of the believer, it is called the breastplate of righteousness. The word *righteousness* literally means "to be made right or to be justified."

The internal organs were considered by first-century people to be the center of the will and emotions. Spiritually, a blow to the mind and emotions is very dangerous. Satan desires to "mess up" your mind. He is an accuser and a slanderer.

What is the righteousness that protects our minds and hearts? First, we will consider what it is not.

Realize there is an impotent righteousness.

> We all are as an unclean thing, and all our righteousnesses is as filthy rags.
> —ISAIAH 64:6, MEV

Romans 3:10 cites several Old Testament passages, declaring, "There is none righteous, no, not one" (MEV). From these passages we know that this righteousness is not self-righteousness.

This righteousness is not a natural human attribute. This righteousness is not religious activity, charitable activity, or human goodness. Our very best behavior is tainted by sin. Human righteousness is the good that is not good enough. Jesus said, "Unless your righteousness exceeds the righteousness of the scribes and Pharisees, you will in no way enter the kingdom of heaven" (Matt. 5:20, MEV). Pharisees lived good lives outwardly. Paul was a Pharisee before his conversion. His testimony in

Philippians 3:4–9 was that as a Pharisee he was religious, had zeal, and was blameless.

What does all of this mean? Simply this: you can never be righteous (right with God) on your own merits! How then can a person be righteous?

Receive an imputed righteousness.

Jesus said, "But seek first the kingdom of God and His righteousness, and all these things shall be given to you" (Matt. 6:33, MEV). His reign and His righteousness are necessary in our lives, so how can we obtain "the righteousness of God"?

Romans 3:19–26 tells us clearly that Jesus Christ is the righteousness of God: "Being justified freely by His grace through the redemption that is in Christ Jesus, whom God set forth as a propitiation through faith, in His blood, for a demonstration His righteousness" (vv. 24–25, MEV).

The only dilemma God ever faced was to be righteous and make sinners righteous at the same time. This dilemma was solved when Christ became the blood sacrifice for the sins of humanity. He died to pay the penalty and bear the curse of the law against all of us.

Romans 3:21–22 declares that the righteousness of God is revealed and received. Then 2 Corinthians 5:21 tells us how this is possible: "For He made Him who knew no sin to be sin for us, that we might become the righteousness of God in Him." Scripture declares that we are righteous because He has imputed His righteousness to us: "If anyone does sin, we have an Advocate with the Father, Jesus Christ the Righteous Ones" (1 John 2:1, MEV). Scripture also says that we are righteous "just as He is righteous" (1 John 3:7).

Romans 5:17–19 declares that this righteousness of God is a gift of God's grace. Further, this gift enables us to reign in life. The righteousness of Jesus marks us as royalty!

All of these scriptures declare that righteousness is a gift of God and a work of God. Righteousness is the Son of God in our lives. You receive this righteousness by faith.

A breastplate was designed to deflect the blow of the enemy. The righteousness of Christ protects the believer in the same way. When you have accepted Jesus and know that He has accepted you, this deflects the arrows of rejection by others. When you know that God sees you as 100 percent righteous, this deflects the put-downs, the guilt, and the accusations of the enemy.

This righteousness protects from inferiority.

Identity with Christ is the key to a healthy self-image. The world says, "You are nothing," but God says, "You are royalty." (See Romans 5:17.) The enemy says, "You have no future," but God is preparing for you to reign with Him in glory.

The devil will tell you that you are unimportant and what you do is insignificant. Someone said, "All born-again believers, as members of the future bride of Christ, are fully as significant, important, and of great consequence in God's ongoing undertakings, adventures, and creative endeavor as any intelligence in the universe."

We cannot control others. Satan will come against us with all kinds of attacks. The only way he can get through is if we react wrongly. When we respond in the wrong way—whether it be in anger, pouting, self-pity, or self-rejection—we have failed to appropriate the breastplate of righteousness.

Only what touches your spirit can really injure you. If you allow what happens to you or what is said to you affect what God has said about you, then you are not using the breastplate.

What motivated the prodigal son to get out of the hog pen? He realized who he was: he was a son! When he came home, his father said, "This son of mine was dead, and is alive again" (Luke 15:24, mev).

The breastplate of righteousness protects from immorality.

When we know that we are righteous in Jesus and will share in His reign, we do not want to live beneath our position. Why should an heir of God want to live like an animal? Why should a saint want to be a reprobate? Why would a king want to live like a slave?

There was a day when a person would live right to protect the family name. When we realize that we have Jesus and that He is our righteousness, then this motivation enables us to live out what we are in Jesus. You are not a sinner saved by grace; you *were* a sinner. Now you are a saint and a family member. Why would you live as less than you are?

By an act of will we can yield our bodies to be controlled by His righteousness (Rom. 6:13). The righteousness of Jesus controls our behavior.

This righteousness protects from insecurity.

> The kingdom of God is not meat and drink; but righteousness, and peace, and joy in the Holy Ghost.
> —ROMANS 14:17, KJV

> Seek first the kingdom of God and His righteousness, and all these things shall be given to you.
> —MATTHEW 6:33, MEV

When Jesus is King in our lives, then we are the beneficiaries of His righteousness. All of the rest of life will fall into place. The things that happen in our lives may be God's way of saying, "Recognize My reign and receive My righteousness."

What do you need to do? Pray the following prayer:

> *Lord, I have no righteousness of my own. I give You my sin for Your righteousness. Lord, I receive Your righteousness as my standing before the Father. I gladly confess that I am now, and forever will be, who You say I am. I confess to being Your child, a saint, an heir of God, a part of Your bride and body. Lord, I yield my body as an instrument of righteousness. I recognize that all I was in Adam is now dead, and that all I am in Jesus makes me Your own. Lord, I accept the Bible as Your very breath of life. I acknowledge 2 Timothy 3:16, which tells us that all Scripture is God-breathed and is profitable for instruction in righteousness. Lord, I thank You that Your death has made me righteous before the Father. In Jesus's name, amen.*

THE WALK OF THE WARRIOR

> And having shod your feet with the preparation of the gospel of peace.
> —EPHESIANS 6:15

Jesus Christ Himself is the armor of God: "Put on the Lord Jesus Christ" (Rom. 13:14, MEV). Putting on the armor is simply realizing who Jesus is, recognizing who you are in Him, and appropriating all He has for your life.

The piece of armor we will examine next is the warrior's shoes. Great generals have said that in warfare an army moves on two vital things: its food and its feet. This was especially true of the Roman army, which had to march great distances over rugged terrain. The Roman battle dress for the feet were thick leather soles with hobnails to serve as cleats. They were tied to the feet and leg with leather laces. These boots served three purposes:

1. *To provide firm footing.* The nails dug into the ground to keep the soldiers from slipping.

2. *To furnish protection.* In those days the enemy would drive pegs into the ground and sharpen the tips. A bare-foot soldier would receive a painful puncture wound in the foot. Infection would set in and disable the soldier.

3. *To give mobility.* These shoes made it possible for the army to move quickly to the place of battle.

Our spiritual shoes serve essentially the same purpose. They help us see clearly what solid foundation is under us and what keeps us moving.

The identity of the shoes

The believer's spiritual warfare shoes are described as "the gospel of peace." We stand on the sure foundation of the gospel. *Gospel* means "good news." What is "good news"? In 1 Corinthians 15:1–4, Paul described the gospel as the death, burial, and resurrection of Christ. Our firm footing is the unchanging message of Jesus Christ. There are still some unchanging and unalterable truths.

Many people are slipping and sliding in their faith. Many substitutes are offered for the gospel. Paul confronted this problem in Galatians 1:6–10. This false gospel had the following marks: it was different, it was perverted, it was accursed, and it pleased men.

Galatians 5:1 says, "Stand fast therefore in the liberty by which Christ has made us free." We have but one gospel and one way to be saved: "Nor is there salvation in any other, for there is no other name under heaven given among men by which we must be saved" (Acts 4:12, see also verses 10–11). This is where we must stand.

The stability of the shoes

This is the day of spiritual tumbleweeds, blown about by circumstance and false doctrine. Shoes give us stability to keep us from stumbling in the battle. It is possible, even in the battleground of this world, to live a stable life. Ephesians 6:15 speaks of the gospel of peace.

The word *peace* is translated from the Greek word *eirene*. The Hebrew word is *shalom*. Peace is a state of well-being, a sense of contentment. I can have peace with God while I am at war with the devil himself.

> Therefore, since we have been justified by faith, we have peace with God through our Lord Jesus Christ, through whom we also have access by faith into this grace in which we stand, and so we rejoice in hope of the glory of God.
> —ROMANS 5:1–2, MEV

When you know that you stand before God at peace with Him because of the blood of Jesus, then Satan cannot worry you to death. W. D. Cornell must have been experiencing God's peace when he wrote the words to "Wonderful Peace."

> Peace, peace, wonderful peace
> Coming down from the Father above.
> Sweep over my spirit forever, I pray.
> In fathomless billows of love.[2]

If you allow the devil to trouble your mind and cause you anxiety, then all of your life becomes unstable. James 1:8 warns, "A double-minded man is unstable in all his ways" (MEV). Don't allow the enemy to take your shoes off. Remember, in Christ you have what the world longs for—peace (Rom. 5:1–2) and true freedom (Gal. 5:1).

The mobility of the shoes

The word *preparation* is translated from a Greek word that means "readiness." The idea is of one being ready to move into battle at a moment's notice.

Already in Ephesians we have learned that the Christian life is a walk:

- We are not to walk wrongly (Eph. 2:2).
- We are to walk in His works (Eph. 2:10).
- We are to walk worthily (Eph. 4:1).
- We are to walk in love (Eph. 5:1–2).
- We are to walk in the light (Eph. 5:8).

You cannot walk properly without your gospel shoes in place. Too many Christians are sluggish and slow-footed. Others who have walked in the world without their shoes on are wounded and crippled. Today the church is paralyzed and muscle-bound.

Before World War II, General Charles de Gaulle wrote a series of essays warning France that a new kind of warfare was coming. The French had built the Maginot Line on their border. This defensive line consisted of powerful weapons in place facing Germany. De Gaulle warned the nation that new weapons, such as fighter planes and tanks, would make their defenses obsolete. No one listened, and France became a captive nation.[3]

Churches that draw their own lines of defense will stand still. We must be ready to advance with the gospel. Our opportunity for service is today. Now we must use our resources for spreading the gospel of Jesus Christ. We must be ready to move to the front, where the battle for souls rages. Let us not flinch in this battle.

We must stand on the secure footing of the truth about Jesus. We must stand with stability of heart, even in the midst of our conflicts. We must be ready to move and stand in the heat of the battles.

Achilles, a hero of Greek mythology, was wounded in his heel. This was the only part of his body exposed, yet the wound killed him. Our feet must not be left unshod if we are to survive and triumph.

THE FAITH OF THE WARRIOR

Above all, taking the shield of faith, with which you will be able to extinguish all the fiery arrows of the evil one.
—EPHESIANS 6:16, MEV

In ancient wars, archers would dip their arrows in pitch, set the tips of the arrows on fire, and launch them toward the opponent. The unwary soldier struck by one of these flaming missiles would receive an agonizing wound. His clothing would often be ignited, and he would be severely burned.

To combat these fiery arrows, the Romans invented a large door-shaped shield. The shields would measure four feet by two feet. Leather would be stretched around the frame, and prior to a battle, the shields were soaked in water. This served to repel the fiery arrows of the enemy.

Paul used this weapon to illustrate faith. He changed the verb in the Greek language from *having* to *taking* to describe the believer's use of the last three weapons (Eph. 6:16–17). You can "take" the shield, the helmet, and the sword. This means that you may choose to appropriate faith or not to appropriate faith.

What is faith? New Testament faith is believing to the point of commitment. Faith is trusting and acting on what God has said. Faith is as valid as the object on which it rests. I may believe a chair is sturdy, but I don't exercise biblical faith until I sit down in that chair. Here faith is said to be a shield. A shield like this was used by the Roman soldier to defend against the enemy as well as to advance against the enemy. If I am to put my faith in a shield, I need to know more about that shield.

The shield taken

In order to take the shield, you must understand what—or rather who—the shield is in Scripture. We discover in Genesis 14 and 15 the identity of our shield. In these chapters, Abraham wins a great victory. The king of Sodom offers him a reward that he wisely refuses. Rather, Abraham pays tithes to Melchizedek shortly after Abraham refused the reward of the world. God speaks to him and says, "Do not fear, Abram. I am your shield, your exceedingly great reward" (Gen. 15:1, MEV).

Abraham put his life in God's hands. God was the shield he needed in order to live in a hostile world.

David also took the shield of faith. He said, "But You, O LORD, are a shield for me" (Ps. 3:3, MEV). In Psalm 84:11 we read, "For the LORD God is a sun and shield; the LORD will give favor and glory, for no good thing will He withhold from the one who walks uprightly" (MEV).

We take the shield of faith when we trust the Lord. Habakkuk 2:4

says, "The just shall live by his faith" (MEV). Habakkuk wrote this at a time when the wicked prospered, the enemy threatened, and the people of God needed revival. He asked God hard questions. God's answer was, "Live by faith."

This verse is quoted in Romans 1:17, Galatians 3:11, and Hebrews 10:38. Faith not only gives us life, but it is also the way we live our lives.

We are saved by faith in God's Word about His Son. We also live by faith: "The life I now live in the flesh, I live by faith in the Son of God, who loved me and gave Himself for me" (Gal. 2:20, MEV). The songwriter Robert Grant expressed his thoughts this way:

> O worship the King, all glorious above,
> O gratefully sing His power and His love;
> Our Shield and Defender, the Ancient of Days,
> Pavilioned in splendor, and girded with praise.[4]

The shield tested

The test of faith reminds us of the wicked one, whom we meet daily on the battlefield of our lives. This should not surprise us or alarm us. Our Lord was tested by the enemy in the wilderness temptation. When the apostle Paul wrote of this shield of faith, he was in prison.

The shield of faith does not protect us from life. Paul faced difficult circumstances, bodily weaknesses, exhausting labors, and agonizing disappointments, yet he had a shield. You may go through trials of faith, but God won't let anything touch you without His permission. The shield is not meant to make you comfortable in this world. The shield is Christ, and we face everything by His grace.

The devil will hurl his fiery darts. They come sometimes as temptations. They come as distractions. They come as accusations. They come as imaginations. They come as depression. Sometimes they come as persecution! All of these flaming arrows of hellish hate can be answered by Jesus. This shield can take care of all that Satan can hurl at you.

How does faith answer the attacks of the enemy? With the Word of God, always! Faith rests on the character of God, the Word of God, and the promise of God.

When Satan accuses you, let the Word of God answer him. Let the cross of Christ answer the enemy. Refuse the flaming missiles of the enemy.

Someone may ask, "What if I can't remember a scripture?" Just cry out for God. When a child is in trouble and doesn't know what to do, the child cries, "Daddy!" Dear friend, when you don't know how to answer, just cry out for God!

The shield triumphant

All that Satan can hurl at a believer, God can take care of. "This is the victory that has overcome the world—our faith" (1 John 5:4). Faith is always victorious.

Often the Roman army would place their best soldiers on the front line. On occasion that line would stretch a mile. The army would advance behind that formation of brave soldiers who would go forward behind the shield.

The church advances behind the mighty shield of faith. Without faith we are defenseless and useless to God. We cannot please Him without faith. Faith alone is the key to victory. Faith is how we live. Faith is "frontline" Christianity. Faith protects us from Satan. Faith appropriates the promises of God. Faith is always victorious.

THE MIND OF THE WARRIOR

> Take the helmet of salvation...
> —EPHESIANS 6:17, MEV

Every believer is a saint and a soldier, a worshipper and a warrior, in the faith and in the fight! As warriors we fight from a position of strength and victory. We wage war in the right posture, for we are told to stand! We are supplied with a panoply of armor that is adequate to carry us through the battlefields of this life.

We face an intelligent, aggressive enemy who targets the crucial areas of our life for attack. The Greek word for "devil" (*diabolos*) means "a traducer, false accuser, slanderer." He is the "one who hurls through." He is an accuser.

God has provided armor with which to defend our faith and defeat our foes. This armor is comprised of the attributes of our Lord Jesus Christ.

- When you receive the *belt of truth*, it is Jesus who says, "I am...the truth" (John 14:6).

- When you receive the *breastplate of righteousness,* it is Jesus who is the righteousness of God (1 Cor. 1:30).

- When you put on the *shoes of peace,* it is Jesus who says, "My peace I give to you" (John 14:27, MEV).

- When you lift the *shield of faith,* it is Jesus alone who can answer every fiery accusation of hell.

Next is the *helmet of salvation.* The Roman helmet, made of metal, covered the head and the cheekbones. It protected against the deathblow of the enemy. The helmet of salvation likewise protects the believer from the deathblow of Satan. Let's look at Satan's attack on the mind.

The attack on the mind

We live in a corrupt world in which people are governed by a "reprobate mind" (Rom. 1:28, KJV). Believers are warned not to walk "in the vanity of their mind" (Eph. 4:17, KJV).

Playwright George Bernard Shaw wrote, "The science I pinned my faith to is bankrupt....For its sake I helped destroy the faith of millions of worshippers...And now look at me and behold the tragedy of an atheist who has lost his faith."[5]

Our world talks about "safe sex" rather than about moral living. Our nation knows a lot about rights and not much about responsibility. Even the church often runs its ministry according to the world. Romans 8:6 says, "To be carnally minded is death" (MEV). *To be carnally minded* means "to think according to the flesh."

In Luke 12:29 Jesus warned us about the confused mind: "neither be ye of doubtful mind" (KJV). This phrase is translated from the Greek word *meteorizo,* from which our English word *meteor* comes. It means to be "up in the air, suspended, unsettled." There are many who have allowed their lives to be without answer.

Philippians 4:6 says, "Be anxious for nothing" (MEV). Much discouragement and depression is caused by needless worry. Our minds must not be filled with deception. Second Corinthians 2:11 warns us about a careless mind: "Lest Satan should take advantage of us. For we are not ignorant of his devices" (MEV). How foolish to live in ignorance of Satan's deceptions. God wants us to think straight.

The assurance of the mind

The helmet is called the helmet of salvation. Salvation is the deliverance of the believers from their lost and condemned position to life in God's kingdom. Salvation has three perspectives:

1. *Salvation is a past event.* In the councils of eternity, at the cross in history, and in one's personal conversion, salvation is an event that begins in the past.

2. *Salvation is a present experience.* Salvation continues in the life of the Christian. "He who began a good work in you will perfect it until the day of Jesus Christ" (Phil. 1:6, MEV). Salvation goes on happening in the life of the Christian.

3. *Salvation is a promised expectation.* Salvation looks ahead to the believer's future hope. Romans 13:11 speaks of that future perspective: "Now our salvation is nearer than when we first believed."

I am convinced that the helmet of salvation is our assurance of God's protection until the day He comes back. In 1 Thessalonians 5:4–9, the helmet is clearly defined as the "hope of salvation." We can keep our heads straight and our minds from being messed up by remembering that the Lord is in control and that He is coming.

Psychiatrists tell us that for good mental health, a person needs someone to love, something worthwhile to do, and something to hope for. This is true on a practical level. Knowing that Friday is coming gets some of us through the week. The knowledge that present pain will end and health will come gets people through illness and surgery.

The hope of heaven and a better life helps to carry us through this life. Titus 2:13 says, "We await the blessed hope and the appearing of the glory of our great God and Savior Jesus Christ" (MEV). Hebrews 6:18–19 says, "That…we might have strong consolation, who have fled for refuge to lay hold of the hope set before us. This hope we have as an anchor of the soul." The forerunner, our Lord, has gone before us to glory and anchored our souls to His throne. There is nothing the world can do that our anchor of hope cannot get us through.

I'm reminded again of another great hymn of our faith, "How Firm a Foundation":

> How firm a foundation, ye saints of the Lord
> Is laid for your faith in His excellent Word...
> That soul, though all hell should endeavor to shake
> I'll never, no never, no never forsake.[6]

The answer of the mind

How do we control, then, our thoughts and minds?

First, you must repent in the mind. *Repentance* comes from the Greek word *metanoia*, which means "a change of mind."

Second, you must receive with the mind. "Let this mind be in you all, which was also in Christ Jesus" (Phil. 2:5, MEV). "We have the mind of Christ" (1 Cor. 2:16, MEV). "Since Christ has suffered for us in the flesh, arm yourselves likewise with the same mind" (1 Pet. 4:1, MEV).

Third, you must renew your mind. "Present your bodies as a living sacrifice, holy, and acceptable to God, which is your reasonable service of worship. Do not be conformed to this world, but be transformed by the renewing of your mind, that you may prove what is the good and acceptable and perfect will of God" (Rom. 12:1–2, MEV). These verses teach us that surrendering our bodies to Him and refusing to be conformed to the world brings the renewal of the mind. This is a daily need.

Steps to a renewed mind

How do you renew the mind? Philippians 4 sets forth the steps to handling troubled thoughts and a messed-up mind.

1. **Rejoice in the Lord.** "Rejoice in the Lord always. Again I will say, rejoice! Let everyone come to know your gentleness. The Lord is at hand" (Phil. 4:4–5, MEV). Praise is a great antidote to trouble. Rejoicing acknowledges the nearness of the Lord.

2. **Request of God.** "Be anxious for nothing, but in everything, by prayer and supplication with gratitude, make your requests known to God" (Phil. 4:6, MEV). Prayer is an antidote to mental agony. Talk to God about your needs.

3. **Rest in Christ.** "The peace of God, which surpasses all understanding, will guard your hearts and minds through Christ Jesus" (Phil. 4:7). Let God's peace stand guard over your mind.

4. **Reflect on the good things of God.** "Whatever things are true, whatever things are honest, whatever things are just, whatever things are pure, whatever things are lovely, whatever things are of good report, if there is any virtue, and if there is any praise, think on these things. Do those things which you have both learned and received, and heard and seen in me, and the God of peace will be with you" (Phil. 4:8–9, MEV). Think good thoughts. Use the Bible to counter the evil thoughts.

5. **Relax in the Lord.** "I rejoiced in the Lord greatly that now at last you have revived your concern for me. Regarding this, you did care, but you lacked opportunity. I do not speak because I have need, for I have learned in whatever state I am to be content. I know both how to face humble circumstances and how to have abundance. Everywhere and in all things I have learned the secret, both to be full and to be hungry, both to abound and to suffer need. I can do all things because of Christ who strengthens me" (Phil. 4:10–13, MEV). God has promised to supply all our needs. Faith thanks God and receives from His hand all that we need.

Are you wearing the helmet of salvation? Are you living in hope? Is your mind clear? Are you thinking straight? Jesus Christ will give you a new mind. Do you need to repent? Do you need to receive? Do you need to renew your mind? Jesus Christ stands ready to help you today.

THE SWORD OF A WARRIOR

Take the helmet of salvation and the sword of the Spirit, which is the word of God. Pray in the Spirit always with all kinds of prayer

and supplication. To that end be alert with all perseverance and supplication for all the saints.
—EPHESIANS 6:17–18, MEV

This section on warfare calls on every Christian to stand against Satan. Now Satan comes at us directly—through the world system in which we live and through our flesh. All of the weapons that we have studied thus far are defensive in nature. With these weapons we can fend off the attack of our enemy.

- With our belt and breastplate we have integrity and identity in Christ. Satan cannot attack our character.
- With our shoes and shield we have balance and belief. Satan cannot penetrate our commitment.
- With our helmet we have assurance and anticipation of the good things of God. Satan cannot destroy our confidence.

James 4:7 tells us, "Resist the devil, and he will flee from you" (MEV). Defensive weapons can hold off Satan, but only offensive weapons can cause him to flee! God has supplied just such a weapon in the sword of the Spirit.

The word *sword* is used of the Roman two-edged sword, one used in hand-to-hand combat. This perfectly balanced weapon was handled skillfully by the Roman soldiers who practiced several hours daily to perfect its use. Let's learn about this weapon and its use.

The sword and the soldier

"Take…the sword." The word *take* is an aorist imperative middle verb in the Greek text. It is a once-and-for-all command for the soldier-saint to take what God has available. The offensive weapon God offers is His Word. The Word of God is to be used to attack our enemy, Satan.

This sword is not of human origin. It was forged by the divine decree. It was not tempered with earthly fire but in the burning flames of the majestic presence of God. The hammer of heavenly inspiration shaped the sword that fits in the hand of the believer.

Hebrews 4:12–13 tell us that the Word of God is a living sword. It is penetrating and powerful. The sharp sword of the Word of God exposes evil. In this passage the sword is in the hand of our great High Priest, the Lord Jesus. Using the sword as a surgical tool, He can cut into our lives and discern the thoughts and intentions. With this sword He performed the surgery of salvation. After using the sword on you, the saint, Jesus places the same sword in your hand.

The secret of King Arthur's fighting ability was his sword, Excalibur. This special sword endowed an ordinary warrior with extraordinary power! So it is with the believer. The sword of the Spirit gives the believer a weapon of unlimited power.

The sword of the Spirit

"Take...the sword of the Spirit." Notice carefully that the sword is connected to the Spirit of God. Having the sword of the Spirit is not simply having a Bible! The Holy Spirit inspired the Bible (2 Pet. 1:21). Only the Holy Spirit can teach you the Bible: "The Advocate, the Holy Spirit, whom the Father will send in my name, will teach you all things and will remind you of everything I have said to you" (John 14:26, NIV). John 16:13 says of the Spirit, "He will guide you into all the truth" (MEV).

Without the Holy Spirit the truths of the Bible cannot be understood: "But the natural man does not receive the things of the Spirit of God, for they are foolishness to him; nor can he know them, because they are spiritually discerned" (1 Cor. 2:14, MEV). The power of the Holy Spirit directs the use of the Word in the life of the believer.

Another way to use the sword is to praise. Psalm 149:6 says, "Let the high praises of God be in their mouth, and two-edged swords in their hands" (MEV). Every one of us needs to take the sword of the Spirit. The Word of God must be loved, learned, and lived out in order for it to be a sword. No part of our lives should be lived without prayer and the Word.

In 2 Samuel 23:10 we are told about Eleazar, one of David's mighty men. He fought the Philistines until the sword stuck to his hand. That sword became an extension of his body. May the Word of God, the sword of the Spirit, be that and more to all who would be good soldiers of Jesus Christ.

Chapter Sixteen

SLAMMING THE DOOR IN THE ENEMY'S FACE

J ESUS CHRIST IS CALLED "THE CAPTAIN OF [OUR] SALVATION" (Heb. 2:10). One of His stated purposes was to set those free who were captive of Satan.

Jesus came to heal all who were oppressed by the devil. As we read in the Book of Acts, "God anointed Jesus of Nazareth with the Holy Spirit and with power, who went about doing good and healing all who were oppressed by the devil, for God was with Him" (Acts 10:38, MEV).

This is the purpose of His church. The first time the church is mentioned in the Scriptures is in Matthew, where we read, "And I tell you that you are Peter, and on this rock I will build My church, and the gates of Hades shall not prevail against it" (Matt. 16:18, MEV). Here is spiritual warfare at the first mention of the church.

The phrase "gates of Hades [or hell] shall not prevail against it" is often misunderstood. We have a picture of us locked behind some gates. Look again at the text. The Greek text indicates that we are attacking the gates of hell! Here is the church on the offensive tearing down the gates of the kingdom of darkness and setting the captives free! You see a militant Christ and a militant church.

We are in an invisible war with a sinister foe. We have weapons of the Spirit that can win. Sadly, many believers live with depression, oppression, fear, habits, family curses, personality changes, addictions, and unexplained illnesses. Where is the victory promised us? What is going on?

Paul speaks of our warfare and satanic attacks on believers in

2 Corinthians 10:3–4. He describes these problems using the term *stronghold*. The Greek word means "fortress." It is derived from a word that means "able, hold, possessed with disease, lack, and need." Strongholds are the way the enemy gains access and control in a Christian's life.

DEFINITION OF A STRONGHOLD

A stronghold is a fortress of wrong thinking that can harbor a demonic entity. This demonic entity can launch attacks from the house our wrong thinking has constructed for him. Yes, indeed, we can actually put a gun in the enemy's hand for him to shoot us. Habits and addictions many times are simply demonically infested strongholds. This is not demon possession but demon infestation. Christians can be oppressed, depressed, tempted, harassed, and buffeted—but they cannot be possessed.

Though believers can never be totally overtaken by Satan and his demons, the sad reality is that many are harassed constantly by wicked forces. Whenever the flesh is in control of a Christian's life, demons are given a place in the believer's mind. This place is usually an unconfessed sin, an unbroken bad habit (obsession), or a wrong attitude. Simply stated, the believer has embraced a lie. Second Corinthians 10:5 says, "Casting down arguments and every high thing that exalts itself against the knowledge of God..." The battle rages in the thinking process of a believer; these wrong ideas, bad attitudes, false assumptions, wrong traditions, and lies can become a doorway for demons into our lives. They also can serve as hiding places that harbor demons.

TWELVE ROOT STRONGHOLDS

1. The *spirit of infirmity* affected a believing woman in the New Testament: "And there was a woman who had a spirit of infirmity for eighteen years and was bent over and could not straighten herself up" (Luke 13:11, MEV). This woman was a faithful attendee of the synagogue. She was a daughter of Abraham, yet demons affected her health. Some examples are disorders of the body, attacks

on male and female identity, allergies, and strange syndromes.

2. The *spirit of fear.* "For God has not given us a spirit of fear, but of power, and of love and of a sound mind" (2 Tim. 1:7). Examples include fright, torment, inferiority, inadequacy, worry, critical spirit, tension, performance, and fear of anything.

3. The *spirit of python*, also called divination. "On one occasion, as we went to the place of prayer, a servant girl possessed with a spirit of divination met us, who brought her masters much profit by fortune-telling. She followed Paul and us, shouting, 'These men are servants of the Most High God, who proclaim to us the way of salvation.' She did this for many days. But becoming greatly troubled, Paul turned to the spirit and said, 'I command you in the name of Jesus Christ to come out of her.' And it came out at that moment" (Acts 16:16–18, MEV). Rebellion, witchcraft, occult practices, and black arts flow from this spirit. Curses follow involvement with these practices.

4. The *spirit of sexual immorality,* called harlotry or whoredoms. "My people ask counsel from their wooden idols, and their staff informs them. For the spirit of harlotry has caused them to stray, and they have played the harlot against their God" (Hosea 4:12). Lust, adultery, pornography, rape, incest, pride, and love of the world are characteristics of this demon. Sexual addiction is also a result of this perverted spirit.

5. An *enslaving spirit* that usually accompanies fear. "For you have not received the spirit of slavery again to fear. But you have received the Spirit of adoption, by whom we cry, 'Abba, Father'" (Rom. 8:15, MEV). Addictions, bulimia, anorexia, wrong relationships, codependency, and other obsessive disorders are worsened by this demon.

6. The *spirit of pride* that normally is accompanied by rebellion. "Pride goes before destruction, and a haughty spirit before a fall. Better it is to be of a humble spirit with the lowly, than to divide the spoil with the proud" (Prov. 16:18–19, MEV). Pride, scorn, mockery, lewdness, egotism, prejudice, arrogance, gossip, and criticism manifest from this wicked spirit.

7. The *spirit of perversion*. "The LORD has mingled a perverse spirit in her; so they have caused Egypt to err in her every work, as a drunken man staggers in his vomit" (Isa. 19:14, MEV). Homosexuality, sexual perversion, and abnormal activities are incited by this spirit.

8. The *spirit of Antichrist*. "And every spirit that does not confess that Jesus Christ has come in the flesh is not from God. This is the spirit of the antichrist, which you have heard is coming and is already in the world" (1 John 4:3, MEV). This demon takes glory away from Christ; denies the supernatural gifts, attributing them to Satan; opposes; harasses; persecutes; and divides true ministries.

9. The *spirit of depression* or heaviness. "...to console those who mourn in Zion, to give them beauty for ashes, the oil of joy for mourning, the garment of praise for the spirit of heaviness; that they may be called trees of righteousness, the planting of the LORD, that He may be glorified" (Isa. 61:3). Depression, abnormal grief, despair, hopelessness, and suicidal thoughts flow from this malevolent demon.

10. The *lying spirit*, one of Satan's favorite tools. "We are of God, and whoever knows God listens to us. Whoever is not of God does not listen to us. This is how we know the spirit of truth and the spirit of error" (1 John 4:6, MEV). Unbelief, deception, compromise, intellectualism, cults, flattery, and legalism flow from this divisive spirit.

11. The *spirit of jealousy*, a relationship-destroying spirit. "If the spirit of jealousy comes on him, and he is jealous

of his wife who has defiled herself, or if the spirit of jealousy comes on him and he is jealous of his wife, though she has not defiled herself..." (Num. 5:14, MEV). Jealousy, anger, rage, cruelty, suspicion, unnatural competition, insecurity, divorce, and division are the results of allowing this spirit to operate.

12. The *spirit of stupor* or slumber. "Just as it is written: 'God has given them a spirit of stupor, eyes that they should not see and ears that they should not hear, to this very day'" (Rom. 11:8). Constant fatigue, passivity, feeling like a wallflower, and self-pity describe this demon. When allowed to control, this spirit blocks success and brings weariness to life.

TAKING DOWN THE ENEMY'S STRONGHOLDS

In order to take down these strongholds of Satan, you must become an armed believer. Revelation 12:11 declares our threefold weapon to overcome our enemy: "They overcame him by the blood of the Lamb and by the word of their testimony, and they loved not heir lives unto death" (MEV).

1. The blood cancels Satan's right to oppress you.

2. The word of your testimony. Yes, take the Word of God as a sword, and release it out of your mouth against the enemy. The truth will set you free.

3. A surrendered life to Jesus. You can appropriate all of Jesus's weaponry, and you must capture every thought of the enemy and cast it down.

We see the atoning blood, the witness of the armed believer, and the life abandoned to the will of Jesus. Satan trembles before the believer with God's weapons. Let me share eight steps to the removal of a stronghold.

- Step one—Be sure you have confessed Jesus Christ as your Lord and Savior.

- Step two—Realize that only God can remove a stronghold.

- Step three—Identify the stronghold.

- Step four—Confess all sins related to strongholds.

- Step five—Thank God for forgiveness.

- Step six—Visualize the destruction.

- Step seven—Ask God to free you from the negative demonic force associated with strongholds.

- Step eight—Make restitution.

After these steps you must possess the reclaimed territory. Confess that you are no longer affected by that area of stronghold and claim God's fullness. Be finished with the sins that enslaved you, and fill your mind with Scripture in order to reinforce the victory.

In the Old Testament, the Jews were told to drive out the enemy and possess Canaan. The territory of your soul, like Canaan, is full of strongholds that must be torn down. As soldiers we must take what is ours. The abundant life awaits those of us who will drive out the enemy and possess the land of our souls. The fortress of Jericho fell down before the people of God. Satan's fortress will crumble before us if we wield our weapons.

> …and being ready to punish all disobedience when your obedience is complete.
> —2 CORINTHIANS 10:6, MEV

When you cast away these strongholds, every demon that has lurked behind these lies, habits, sicknesses, and wrong choices is exposed, and God punishes their disobedience. The Greek word for "punish" is *ekdikeo*—or revenge. When you are full of obedience, then God will take revenge on every demon that has dared to threaten you.

Section Four

Maintaining the Victory Over Your Enemy

Chapter Seventeen

PUTTING THE ENEMY TO FLIGHT

SATAN HAS BEEN STRIPPED OF AUTHORITY IN THE LIFE OF every believer. Satan and his demonic forces fear the authority of the Word of God through Christ. James 2:19 says, "Even the demons believe—and tremble!" A decisive battle was waged and won at the cross and the empty tomb, and that victory stripped Satan and his hosts of authority. Colossians 2:15 declares that Jesus "disarmed principalities and powers [of their authority]."

When Jesus came to the world, it was an occupied, armed camp of Satan. The forces of evil recognized Him (Mark 1:23–25). In Mark 5, evil forces encamped in a man. Enough demons controlled him to fill two thousand swine. But notice that these forces could not move without the permission of Jesus. Jesus defeated Satan and broke his authority at every point.

Satan could not receive Jesus. He could not get Jesus to yield to temptation. Death could not hold Jesus. Satan used every weapon and found them broken under the feet of Christ. The glorious truth is that you and I can enforce that victory. We can put the enemy to flight. We can see Satan in rapid retreat. Here are the simple steps to victory.

THE REQUIREMENT OF SUBMISSION

God resists the proud, but gives grace to the humble.
—JAMES 4:6, MEV

Before a believer can effectively put Satan to flight, he must be under authority himself. God resists the proud. The word *proud* describes a self-sufficient person who runs his own life. The word *resist* means "to arrange an army against." God has placed an army against the self-sufficient.

The key word in James 4:7 is *submit*. It is a military word that means "to place under orders." A believer has authority over Satan by living under the authority of Christ. A rebellious, sinning Christian cannot put Satan to flight. The Christian who lives under God-given authority can put the enemy to flight. Believers must learn to live under authority. The Word of God sets forth God's pattern of authority.

Christians live under the authority of Christ. We also live under the authority of human government (1 Pet. 2:13–15). The wife is to live under the authority of her husband (Eph. 5:22–24). Children are to live under the authority of parents (Eph. 6:1–3). This is for protection and power. All human authority is delegated, but it is invalid if it violates the will of God. "We must obey God rather than men" (Acts 5:29, MEV).

We are told that if we are to defeat Satan, we must be under orders. Jesus lived under the will of the Father in His earthly sojourn. This was the secret of His power. He lived under authority. "He humbled Himself and became obedient to death" (Phil. 2:8, MEV). This was the prelude to victory. This was the path to authority. After His submission came His exaltation. Verse 10 declares that every realm is now under His authority—the spiritual realm, the natural realm, and the demonic realm. Before we can stand in authority, we must submit ourselves to God completely.

THE RESISTANCE OF SATAN

> Therefore submit to God. Resist the devil and he will flee from you.
> —JAMES 4:7

Once we are under authority, we can stand in Christ's authority. Ephesians 1 and 2 declare these truths. Ephesians 1:19–23 declares the authority of the risen, ascended, and enthroned Christ. We must recognize that we have no authority over Satan in our own flesh and power. We are made lower than the angels. But in Christ we have been given His authority over Satan.

Ephesians 2:1–6 declares that we are now fully identified with Christ in His crucifixion, resurrection, ascension, and in being enthroned.

Thus we now share His authority. We are now in Him, elevated above the angelic realm.

We are to *resist* Satan. This word in Ephesians 4:7 is not the same as the word in verse 6. The word in verse 7 implies "to stand alone." It pictures the believer and God against Satan. We stand without human help.

We must learn that we cannot hide from Satan. We cannot run away from Satan. We cannot outrun him, and we cannot get away from him on this planet.

How, then, do we resist Satan?

- Be sure you are living an obedient and clean life under authority.
- Take your stand against Satan in the authority of Christ.
- Stand steadfast in faith, believing God for the victory.
- Verbally attack Satan with the Word of God and the work of Christ.
- Give no place to Satan; give up no ground whatsoever.
- Demand in the authority of Christ that he leave.
- Give thanks and praise to God and watch the devil run.

Chapter Eighteen

TURNING BACK THE ENEMY

THE CHRISTIAN LIFE IS ALWAYS ON A COLLISION COURSE with the agenda of Satan. Once a prince, he is now a usurper— a pretender to the throne of the earth.

Satan's rebellion dates back to the pre-Adamic world. Both science and Scripture affirm a great cataclysm that brought ruin and death to this world before Adam. Lucifer became the malicious Satan lurking in the body of a snake in Eden.

Though Satan is defeated, he awaits his final sentence along with those of the human race who will be sent to hell with him. Jesus defeated our ancient enemy and sentenced him to oblivion, preparing a burning hell for him and his angelic cohorts.

Until the final sentence, he remains in our solar system as "the prince of the power of the air." He has permission to operate in the disobedient. He is part and parcel of this fallen world. Therefore we know that the earth for us is not a playground but a battleground.

Psalm 56 is one of those psalms called a *michtam*, which means "golden song" or "precious song." Its title expresses a longing in David, "The Silent Dove in Distant Lands." This reaches back to Psalm 55:6: "So I said, 'Oh, that I had wings like a dove! I would fly away and be at rest.'"

This psalm was composed when David was being hounded by Saul and fell into the hands of the Philistines. David longed for the days of solitude before the haunting responsibility of leadership fell on him. He had been anointed king, yet instead of a throne, he had war!

This is not unlike our experience: we come to Christ, are anointed by the Spirit, and then the enemy declares war! Yet we know that victory is ours.

Four Ways the Enemy Oppresses

How does the enemy challenge us? His strategy is to put pressure on you on every side. Here is a clear distinction of satanic oppression and how to identify it.

Satan will surround us with people who distract us. In Psalm 56:2 David feels that he is being hounded by lions. You know there are people in your life whose main goal is to waste your time, distract you, criticize you, or confuse you! When Peter tried to "help" Jesus by denying the need for the cross, Jesus said, "Get behind me, Satan."

Sometimes those close to you will hinder you. At other times people will directly attack you! Remember—the enemy will use anyone! "Be merciful to me, O God, for man would swallow me up; fighting all day he oppresses me" (Ps. 56:1). Notice the word *swallow*; it means "to beat, to curb, and to swallow." Sometimes the enemy just wants to crush your spirit and swallow up your purpose! The phrase "all day" is translated from a Hebrew word that means "all the time; the total of everything." Literally it means that Satan attacks the totality of my life's purpose all the time! He is relentless.

We have already learned of Satan's efforts to intimidate. In the first Gulf War the terms "shock and awe" were introduced, describing an attack that went on from the air for days. The purpose was to crush the will of the ones attacked. Our enemy tries "shock and awe" as the prince of the power of the air.

Satan will use slander to defeat us and turn us away from victory. "Every day they twist my words; all their thoughts are against me for evil" (Ps. 56:5, MEV). Satan is the accuser! His goal is to slander and to ruin. Remember his vicious attack on Job. The word *twist* is the Hebrew word *atsab*, which means "to fabricate, to carve, to cut up, to inflict pain." Satan will take what you say and do, fashion it into something that causes pain, and misrepresent you and what you believe!

The word *thoughts* means "to weave or fashion." It is used of wrong judgments. Satan will twist and fabricate in order to thwart God's purpose for your life.

Psalm 56:6 declares that Satan stalks believers to hinder their faith: "They stir up strife, they lurk, they watch my steps, when they lie in wait for my life" (MEV). Here are the final tactics of Satan. Simply notice that more often than not Satan uses people, even believers, to do his dirty work.

Seven Winning Responses to Satan's Challenge

Psalm 56:9 teaches us, "In the day I cry to You [the Lord], then my enemies will turn back" (MEV). In tracking through this psalm we discover seven victorious responses to the enemy.

First, we must trust the Lord as the psalmist did. "Whenever I am afraid, I will trust in You" (v. 3). The word *trust* in Hebrew is *batach*, which means "to be confident, secure, safe, and to trust." Its ancient root means "to be stretched out." Here the wrinkles of worry leave as you get spiritual Botox. It also means "to lie safely on the ground."

Psalm 56:4 gives us the second response, which is to trust God's Word. "In God (I will praise His word), in God I have put my trust; I will not fear. What can flesh do to me?" Here the believer takes refuge in God and His Word. He *hallels* the word! He shouts hallelujah in the middle of the attack because he has a word from God! There He trusts in God while the battle rages.

Third, we can take refuge in a God who cares for us and "number[s] my wanderings; put my tears into Your bottle; are they not in Your book?" (Ps. 56:8). Here is trust! While the enemy stalks, God "number[s] my wanderings." The word *number* is "to keep score in order to celebrate later." God will celebrate our victory with us! The word *wandering* is "exile." The enemy has tried to exile us from our land, but God is keeping score. We will get back all that the enemy has taken. God is keeping the book! Our tears are being kept in a wineskin (bottle). That which is bitter God will turn to fine wine. He will take our tears and turn them to joy.

Fourth, prayer brings God's resources on to the scene. "When I cry out to You, then my enemies will turn back; this I know, because God is for me" (Ps. 56:9). Here is passionate prayer that cries out to God in the face of the enemy. This is bold, loud, demanding prayer. God will hear our prayers when they are offered in urgency.

Fifth, I can rest in absolute assurance according to verse 9: "This I know, because God is for me." Wow! Here the believer expresses supreme confidence. Here the mighty shield of faith is lifted up against the enemy. Romans 8:28 affirms this Old Testament promise: "We know that all things work together for good to those who love God, to those who are the called according to His purpose" (MEV). God is for you—*believe it!*

Sixth, when we honor our promises, God will protect us. "Vows made to You are binding upon me, O God; I will render praises to You" (Ps. 56:12). A direct interpretation of this would read, "I will fulfill my promises to you, O God, even as I lift my hands in praise." *Towdal* means "to lift the hands while praising God." God views this as a solemn promise to keep our vows. When you do what you promise, victory is guaranteed.

Notice the following warning and promise about vows:

> When you make a vow to God, do not delay in fulfilling it because He has no pleasure in fools. Fulfill what you have vowed. Better it is that you do not make a vow than you make a vow and not fulfill it. Do not let your mouth cause you to sin, and do not say before the messenger that it was an error. Why should God be angry with your words and destroy the work of your hands?
> —ECCLESIASTES 5:4–6, MEV

The destroyer comes after broken promises to the Lord. "It is a snare to the man who dedicates rashly that which is holy, and after the vows to make inquiry" (Prov. 20:25, MEV).

Seventh, we give witness of God's mighty power as David did in the closing verse of Psalm 56: "For You have delivered my soul from death. Have You not kept my feet from falling, that I may walk before God in the light of the living?" (v. 13). This closing verse declares that God rescues our lives. God keeps us from falling. The word *falling* means "to be pushed." The word *feet* is journey. God will not allow the enemy to push us down or off a cliff on our journey; we will make it home!

God gives us a fresh, new start. The word *living* means "fresh flesh." God renews your life on Earth as you walk before Him in the *light*, or daylight. This speaks of a new beginning. This is how life was meant to be lived!

Here is a proclamation to turn back the enemy:

- I nullify every satanic prayer by the blood of Jesus, in Jesus's name.
- I nullify every satanic challenge by the blood of Jesus, in Jesus's name.
- I nullify every satanic decree against my life, in the name of Jesus.
- I nullify every satanic desire upon my life by the blood of Jesus, in Jesus's name.
- I nullify every satanic expectation concerning my life, in the name of Jesus.
- I nullify every satanic decision taken against my life, in the name of Jesus.
- I nullify every satanic agreement standing against my life, by the blood of Jesus.
- I nullify every satanic conspiracy in the heavenlies against my life, in the name of Jesus.
- I nullify every satanic conspiracy on Earth against my life, in the name of Jesus.
- I nullify every satanic plan and program for my life, in the name of Jesus.

Chapter Nineteen

LIVING A LIFE OF WORSHIP

L ET'S LOOK BRIEFLY AT DAVID'S TRAINING OF HIS WARRIORS for battle. It is interesting to note that Psalm 18, the "manual of instruction," is framed by praise. Toward the end of the psalm David exclaimed, "The LORD lives! And blessed be my Rock! Let the God of my salvation be exalted" (v. 46, MEV). David knew that the worship of God put the enemy to flight.

WORSHIP 101

Yet another psalm seems to be an instruction manual on the art of praise.

> Praise the LORD!
> Sing unto the LORD a new song,
>   and His praise in the assembly of the godly ones.
> Let Israel rejoice in its Maker;
>   let the children of Zion be joyful in their King.
> Let them praise His name with dancing;
>   let them sing praises unto Him with the tambourine and
>   harp.
> For the LORD takes pleasure in His people;
>   He will beautify the meek with salvation.
> Let the godly ones be joyful in glory;
>   let them sing for joy on their beds.
> Let the high praises of God be in their mouths,
>   and two-edged swords in their hands,
> to execute vengeance on the nations,
>   and punishments on the peoples;

to bind their kings with chains,
    and their nobles with shackles of iron;
to execute upon them the written judgment;
    this is honor for all His godly ones.
Praise the LORD!

—PSALM 149:1–9, MEV

This beautiful psalm tells us that praise isn't just about the music created—it's about the noise of worship. This noise floods the ears of our enemies in battle. It includes laughter, weeping, clapping, and shouting. It even includes the quiet rustle of the breath of the body of Christ when they turn to Him in quiet meditation of His goodness. It is all warfare, the sound of battle in the ear of the enemy.

Worship has even more strength when a whole body of believers does it. This psalm tells us, "Let Israel rejoice." The reference is plural. Something occurs that is powerful during corporate worship where two or three or more are gathered. Jesus promised, "There I am in their midst" (Matt. 18:20, MEV).

We also know from Hebrews 2:12 that when He shows up in the midst and we are singing, He starts singing. If you think your worship does something to demons, wait until the Lord Jesus starts singing along with you and then the Holy Ghost kicks in and then God the Father starts singing back to you!

Worship should reflect or picture the three parts of the tabernacle or temple. We start at the outer court, where the blood saved us, and we praise the name of Jesus for our salvation. We then proceed into the holy place, where there is the table of shewbread and the candlelight. In that place His Word and His guidance illuminate us a little more, and we enter into those gates with thanksgiving and into those courts with praise.

But then we proceed toward the holy of holies, where there is a veil that has been rent. When the highest praises begin, we go into that place of immunity and intimacy with our Lord where no devil of hell can touch us. The psalmist said, "This is honor for all His godly ones" (Ps. 149:9, MEV). At one time, only the priests could enter the holy of holies, but after the cross, Jesus said, "Come on in. You're welcome in this holy place."

Most churches have never entered that place during their corporate worship. They don't know what it is like to get quiet and just lie at His feet and say, "I'm not moving, Lord, until You move. I'm here until You tell me what to do."

Look further at Psalm 149, where the psalmist says that there are many ways to do it. We can play instruments. We can sing. Yes, we can even dance! Verse 3 says, "Let them praise His name with dancing; let them sing praises unto Him with the tambourine and harp" (MEV).

There is more we must learn about worship. Verse 4 continues, "For the LORD takes pleasure in His people." God loves it when you sing. Psalm 22:3 says, "Thou [God] inhabitest the praises…" (KJV). The Hebrew word for "inhabit," *yashab*, means "to dwell with as a husband with the wife he loves." When you begin to sing, He comes not with a whip but with a gift in His hand. When you sing, He comes to kiss you. *Worship* means "to kiss toward." When you sing, God responds as a protector, as a provider, as a lover, as a covering, and as a father.

It doesn't matter if you have a trained voice; God loves to hear you sing! Once in a while my wife, Paulette, will make the request, "Honey, sing to me." My congregation knows that I would never be asked to stand with a microphone and present a special musical offering, but filtered through love, my wife thinks I sound great!

AN EFFECTIVE WEAPON

Our praises of God become a mighty weapon. Psalm 149:6 says, "Let the high praises of God be in [your] mouth, and a [sharp] two-edged sword in [your] hand." Do you long for the power of God's Word to work in your life? Start praising Him!

I often think of David as a youth, running to meet Goliath with stone and sling in hand. The praises of God were on his lips, and the giant couldn't help but laugh, "I'm coming to you as a mighty man, and you send a baby out here." But onward came the singing, praising boy. What Goliath didn't know was that the rock in David's hand was guided by the Rock of Ages, who never misses!

You may feel you have a Goliath arrayed against your life. Pick up the Rock of Ages and begin to praise God. Then take the sword of the Word of God, get that enemy by the hair of its head, and finish it off!

God is restoring the tabernacle of David in these last days. Davidic worship is back. Our churches can incorporate every part of praising God: instruments, choir, soloists, bands, guitars, clapping, dancing, and shouting.

The praise of God accomplishes so much! God says in Psalm 149:7, "To execute vengeance on the nations, and punishments on the peoples" (MEV). When I begin to praise God, the angels of glory go to war for me against every enemy. The next verse states that with this praise, you can bind nobles and kings and put them in chains. You can bind the devil!

Jesus said, "Upon this rock I will build my church; and the gates of hell shall not prevail against it" (Matt. 16:18, KJV). He then continues in verse 19, "I will give you the keys of the kingdom of heaven, and whatever you bind on earth shall be bound in heaven, and whatever you loose on earth shall be loosed in heaven" (MEV).

What are the keys to the kingdom of heaven? The gospel, of course, is the key. The psalmist said, "Enter into His gates with thanksgiving, and into His courts with praise" (Ps. 100:4, MEV). When we do that, we have the keys that will bind the forces of darkness.

At times our praise will bind the spirits that try to harass our lives. The demon of depression will often flee if we just begin to sing. God has promised to give us the garment of praise for the spirit of heaviness (Isa. 61:3). When you feel that darkness start to fall again, just start singing. Victory will come, and He will bind away the devil of depression that has tried to kill you and destroy you.

Music gives you courage. Music has always had a powerful influence on attitudes about warfare. With every war, a theme song seems to arise that becomes the rallying cry. In recent years as America faced a crisis in the Persian Gulf and Iraq, you couldn't go a day without hearing Lee Greenwood's powerful song "God Bless the USA." The tired, weary, and sometimes fearful soul begins to rise and take courage with that music.

Ask Paul and Silas. They were beaten and bloody in the darkness of midnight. "Silas," said Paul, "let's sing!" At the top of their lungs, with pain still coursing through their beaten bodies, they sang, and heaven was torn open. God came down and landed so hard that it burst the doors of the jail open, and the jailer ran in and said, "Sirs, what must I do to be saved?" (See Acts 16.) No sermon…just praise!

Every time David sang, the demons fled out of his life and from those who listened. And Nehemiah—he also knew the power of praising God! He had a ragtag crowd trying to build an incredible wall. Some laughed at the efforts, saying, "Why, if a fox ran up on this wall, the little creature would be able to tear it down!" (See Nehemiah 4:3.) Nehemiah's workers were mocked and made fun of, and they were exhausted beyond imagination. Yet Nehemiah said, "Remember, don't leave your post. If you are weak and tired, the joy of the Lord is your strength." (See Nehemiah 8:10.) Workers began to sing in their own way, and God liked it all.

Strength flowed into their spirits.

Praise Births Revival

If you want true revival, you will need to learn true praise and worship. And it may be messy! A time of praise may interrupt your order of service or make that delicious roast burn because the Sunday service runs past noon. But those are insignificant side effects to suffer when you see the altars flooded with crying, repentant, hurting people and then see the power of God flow through His people.

The devil has tried to rob you of your song. It is time to sing again. The psalmist said, "Weeping may endure for a night, but joy comes in the morning" (Ps. 30:5, MEV). Well, it is now morning! The night is over. Your Father is singing over you. This is a new day.

Chapter Twenty

LOVING OTHERS UNCONDITIONALLY

I BELIEVE THE GREATEST LESSON I'VE EVER LEARNED IN SPIRITUAL warfare is one I found too late for many opportunities I have had in my life. This powerful weapon is one that has never failed anytime I wielded it. This weapon is agape love, the love of God.

If you take time to read the great love chapter of the Bible, 1 Corinthians 13, you will find that in it the Holy Spirit clearly discusses this powerful gift. Hidden within this priceless treasure that "beareth all things, believeth all things, hopeth all things, and endureth all things" (v. 7, KJV) is an explosive power that can topple many spiritual walls. In Romans 8:31–39 (MEV) we read:

> What then shall we say to these things? If God is for us, who can be against us? He who did not spare His own Son, but delivered Him up for us all, how shall He not with Him also freely give us all things? Who shall bring a charge against God's elect? It is God who justifies. Who is he who condemns? It is Christ who died, yes, who is risen, who is also at the right hand of God, who also intercedes for us. Who shall separate us from the love of Christ? Shall tribulation, or distress, or persecution, or famine, or nakedness, or peril, or sword? As it is written: "For Your sake we are killed all day long; we are accounted as sheep for the slaughter." No, in all these things we are more than conquerors through Him who loved us. For I am persuaded that neither death nor life, nor angels nor principalities nor powers, nor things present nor things to come, nor height nor depth, nor any other created thing, shall be able to separate us from the love of God, which is in Christ Jesus our Lord.

The greatest weapon of spiritual warfare is the love of God. That's why God began with it and promised it from the beginning of time.

> For God so loved the world, that he gave his only begotten Son, that whosoever believeth in him should not perish, but have everlasting life.
>
> —JOHN 3:16, KJV

> Behold, what manner of love the Father hath bestowed upon us, that we should be called the sons of God.
>
> —1 JOHN 3:1, KJV

The cross of Calvary was a public demonstration of the agape love of God, of the love that knows no limits, of the love that will not hold back, of the love that will go as far as it has to go to bring back its beloved. It is the theme of the Bible. It is the heartbeat of our own song. It is the centerpiece of the gospel that we preach. It is this feature alone that separates Christianity from Islam, Buddhism, and all the "isms" of the world.

We have a God who loves us no matter what we've done. There is no measure to His love. We can't comprehend the height, the depth, the length, or the breadth of His love. This love of Christ surpasses all knowledge. We can't learn it all. We can't study it all. We can't talk about it all. We can't write enough songs. We can't compose enough poems. We can't preach enough sermons. We can't pray enough to express what the love of God is!

One of my favorite old hymns talks of this powerful love, the final verse of which was found written on the walls of an insane asylum:

> Could we with ink the ocean fill?
>> And were the skies of parchment made,
> Were every stalk on earth a quill,
>> And every man a scribe by trade,
> To write the love of God above,
>> Would drain the ocean dry.
> Nor could the scroll contain the whole,
>> Though stretched from sky to sky.

Chorus

O love of God, how rich, how pure,
    How measureless and strong.
It shall forevermore endure
    The saints' and angels' song.[1]

ELEMENTS OF THE WEAPON

We must clearly understand the many facets of this powerful weapon. It frustrates me to step into churches only to see people going through the motions and playing religious games. I want to just cry out and say, "Do you think God bankrupted heaven to send His beloved Son to hang on a cross for six hours under the noonday sun of Israel and to bleed His life's blood out so you could play some church games? He spent His blood to change you, to heal you inside and out, to transform you forever!" No one who has ever opened his heart and taken Christ's embrace has ever been the same. He changes us.

Love undeserved

As His child, no matter what mistakes you may have made, God is for you. Your marriage may have ended in divorce, but God is for you. You may have made some youthful mistakes, failed at your business, or served time in a penitentiary, but God is for you. He cast His vote at Calvary for you. He loved you before you were born. Before the first wave crashed on the shore, He knew your name and knew your heart and loved you! Nothing can separate you from the love of God. You can't do anything to deserve it. That's what agape love is all about.

When you turn that love around and wield it, you discover something of great power. You can love and serve someone without expecting anything back. You will live in victory.

Love undaunted

"Who shall separate us from the love of Christ?" asks Paul. "Shall tribulation or distress?" (See Romans 8:35.) The answer, of course, is no! Your pressures and problems are just ways God can show you He loves you! "Persecution?" Agape love will outlast every controversy. "Famine, or nakedness, or peril, or sword?" None of these influence the power of God's love.

Love undefeated

Romans 8:37 states boldly, "In all these things we are more than conquerors." This phrase "we are more than conquerors" is one word in the Greek—*hupernikao*—and it appears to be a word the apostle Paul just invented, as it appears nowhere else in Greek literature. You see, the word *nikao*, conqueror, was as strong as you could be. It means you have conquered; you have won. You get the spoils. You are in charge. Your enemies are down. Everything you want is in your hands. There was no stronger word than *nikao*. But Paul added *huper* in the Greek, which is like *super* in English. He wanted to communicate something bigger than conquest when he said, "You are *more* than conquerors."

How can I be more than a conqueror? Because of Jesus, there will be certain battles I'm never going to have to fight again. I may have a struggle or two in life, but I don't have to fight for my salvation. He has already won that battle! I don't have to fight for forgiveness. I don't have to fight for my healing. I don't have to fight for the gifts of the Spirit. I am more than a conqueror!

There is a story of a woman whose husband moved to the Philippine Islands for a short-term business opportunity. The couple had raised three children, who were now almost grown. Only a few weeks into his business venture, he sent her a telegram saying, "I don't love you anymore. I have found someone here. I'm not ever coming back. Good-bye. Your husband."

The businessman married a Filipino girl, and they had a child together. But tragically he soon discovered he had terminal cancer, and he died. The widowed Filipino girl and her baby had nowhere to go, so she wrote the man's first wife: "I was married to your husband. We have a child. I don't know what to do."

Now, this woman was a Christian. "Dearest," she wrote the girl back, "God loves you. Christ died for you. I'm sending you money to come here to the States. We will take care of all the details when you get here. You and the child will live in my house." That is what the power of agape love can do!

Winning and being loved by God does not mean that you won't have pain and be hurt, but it does mean that you will always love. That woman could have simply said, "I'll tell you what, he divorced me. Let his little fling worry about her own self." No, that's how you lose.

Perhaps you are losing your spiritual battle because you cannot forgive. The Bible says, "Love your enemies, bless those who curse you, do good to those who hate you" (Matt. 5:44, mev). It doesn't matter what the response is to our acts of love. If it is agape love, it doesn't matter. Love is going to love anyway. Love went to the cross, and it kept on loving. It was buried in the ground, and three days later it came alive.

In years past a counterfeit gospel was preached. Many have said, "To be a true Christian, it's all about this denomination, belonging to this church, and you have to do this, and you have to be that. You have to dress this way and act that way." But the truth is, the gospel is none of those things. The true gospel is this: Christ loved us, died for us, took our penalty, and loves us anyway in spite of everything. Love wins all the time.

Love undeniable

Paul goes on to write in Romans 8:38, "For I am persuaded…" The word *persuaded* is a passive verb in the Greek. It means "I've been convinced from something beyond myself." It doesn't mean that I've talked myself into it. In the passive voice it means, "I didn't do anything to deserve this. Someone outside of me convinced me." Paul said, "I have enough of it poured on me that I'm absolutely convinced; I am persuaded…"

Paul had been beaten many times. He had been thrown in jail. He had been persecuted. He had been misunderstood. But he said, "I am persuaded." That means in this Greek tense, "I am fully convinced. I will never change my mind. Nothing can rock this in my life. I can't be separated from God's love!" Even death can't separate us from His love.

Until my mother passed away, I called her every Sunday. When I was struggling as a poor freshman college kid, my mama would send me $15 a week. That doesn't sound like a lot now, but in the 1960s, Mama worked for $1.25 an hour. She basically was sending me a day-and-a-half's pay each week!

Looking back, I'm ashamed that I didn't really appreciate it at the time. I watched my mother wear the same dress to church for years. She would clean it up nice so that we could have something new to wear. She gave when it was hard to give. When Daddy was going through all his struggles with alcoholism, I never heard Mama say, "I'm leaving." Long before he came back to God and took the office of a soul-winning deacon the last ten years of his life, my mother was there. She was there when it was tough. Love won!

A Divine Transfer

You may be reading this and have a need to feel truly loved. Ephesians 1 tells you that you have been accepted in the Beloved. It is time for you to quit blaming yourself for everything and feeling guilty about everything. "There is therefore now no condemnation for those who are in Christ Jesus" (Rom. 8:1, MEV). You are loved.

Perhaps you simply need to allow the love that He has given you to be transferred out of your heart and into the lives of those around you. He has poured enough in you that you can let some run out of your life, whether the recipients ever say "I love you" back or not. It is not about getting paid back. Jesus paid it all!

> Oh, the love that drew salvation's plan!
> Oh, the grace that brought it down to man!
> Oh, the mighty gulf that God did span at Calvary![2]

If you will let God's love wash you and flow through you, demons will leave. You will know true victory, for the enemy can't stay where God's love is poured out. Claim your freedom and explode the weapon of His love in your life!

Chapter Twenty-One

TAKING BACK GROUND

THE OLD TESTAMENT OFFERS BEAUTIFUL PICTURES OF NEW Testament truth. These are called types. The greatest picture or type of spiritual warfare is found in the Book of Joshua. The very name Joshua is the Hebrew *Yeshua*, or Jesus, which means "savior" or "deliverer."

The journey of the children of Israel from Egypt through the wilderness to Canaan is a picture of the Christian life. God used all of these experiences to break His people.

THE RESISTANCE WE FACE

In the Christian life we face a threefold enemy: the world, the flesh, and the devil. Deliverance from Egypt pictures our rescue from the world. The wilderness experience breaks the power of the flesh. We have drawn clear parallels between Canaan and the strongholds in our lives.

Canaan is not a "fair and happy land," nor is it heaven. It represents what is rightfully the believers' now! It is the land flowing with milk and honey. It is the abundant life promised by Jesus in John 10:10.

Most believers have escaped from Egypt, but like the tribe of Gad and the half tribe of Manasseh, they have decided to live in a wilderness, never crossing over into the spiritual territory that flows with milk and honey. Most believers settle for less than the promises of God. God has willed that His sons and daughters be soldiers! He gave them the land of Canaan, and yet it was a veritable armed camp of their enemies. It was filled with fortified cities with great kings who had to be destroyed before they could possess their possessions.

THE RICHES THAT ARE YOURS

Do you see that there are spiritual vistas you have never viewed, mountains you haven't scaled, rivers of life you haven't swum in, fruit you've never tasted, harvests you haven't enjoyed, gifts you've never opened, and abundance you have never experienced?

The towering strongholds have frightened you away. God had given the children of Israel the land, yet they had to claim it, to fight for it (Josh. 1:2). So must you!

In Joshua 3:5 God promises to do wonders, to do the supernatural. In Joshua 4:24 the people praise God for the miracle of the parting of the waters of the Jordan. Immediately the enemy was put on notice that God's people were coming for their land!

After you are saved, you must claim every inch of the territory of your soul. Just as the children of Israel had to march over the land, you must take every inch of what Satan would want to take away from you.

THE REINFORCEMENTS THAT ARE YOURS

The minute the children of Israel stepped out in faith, God showed up with invisible resources—"the Commander of the army of the LORD" (Josh. 5:14). What was going on here?

Here we see the Lord's promise. God had promised never to forsake Joshua. Now the Lord has shown up with His army for the fight. We also see the Lord's presence in that the angel of the Lord has his "sword drawn" (Josh. 5:13). This host of invisible warriors had come to the battle. All Joshua could do was worship and obey. Remember, God never commands His children to fight alone. "I am with you always, even to the end of the age" (Matt. 28:20, MEV).

THE REALM THAT IS YOURS

The key passage here is Joshua 6. The children of Israel had to obey the orders to march around Jericho once a day for six days and then seven times on the seventh day. After the seventh time around, they were to blow their trumpets. When this was done, the walls fell and the city was taken. Today if we obey God's commandments, the walls of our strongholds cannot stand against us.

THE RULE THAT IS YOURS

Give the enemy no place. In Joshua 10:8–25, Joshua was given a clear word from God concerning his enemies. God said no enemy of Israel would be left standing. After hearing from God, Joshua took quick and decisive action. After marching all night, the children of Israel did not rest in the presence of their enemies; instead they attacked them.

In the midst of the battle Joshua needed a miracle if he was going to see the word of God fulfilled in the battle. He prayed. God heard his prayer and stopped the sun from going down on the battle. If God has promised victory, He will not allow darkness to overtake the day.

Five mighty kings, those who would stand against the children of Israel, were delivered into Joshua's hands. With a proclamation of victory, not just for the battle at hand but also for future battles, Joshua destroyed the kings.

God will do for you what He did for Joshua. He will give a clear word. Move quickly in that word, and you will be positioned to see a miracle of God. He will deliver your enemies into your hands.

Chapter Twenty-Two

BREAKING CURSES

P ROVERBS 18:21 SAYS, "DEATH AND LIFE ARE IN THE POWER OF the tongue, and those who love it will eat its fruit" (MEV). Life and death are powerfully influenced by what we say, what we hear, and what we receive! Just as confessing the Word of God out of our mouth releases blessings and faith to activate the supernatural and defeat the enemy, so negative words bring curses, activate the demonic, and release destructive forces.

OPEN DOORS

Dr. Henry Malone, in his excellent book *Shadow Boxing*, suggests five open doors that allow negative forces to operate in your life.[1]

Disobedience

Willful disobedience brings you into the captivity of the enemy.

> Do you not know that to whom you yield yourselves as slaves to obey, you are slaves of the one whom you obey, whether of sin leading to death, or of obedience leading to righteousness?
> —ROMANS 6:16, MEV

When thoughts of disobedience are spoken, they lead to strongholds.

> Casting down arguments and every high thing that exalts itself against the knowledge of God, bringing every thought into captivity to the obedience of Christ.
> —2 CORINTHIANS 10:5

We must capture our negative and disobedient thoughts rather than confess them.

Unforgiveness

Unforgiveness is the second door that allows the enemy to work in your life. In order to enjoy the benefits of the kingdom of heaven now, you must forgive those who hurt you. Jesus taught unlimited forgiveness.

> Then Peter came to Him and said, "Lord, how often shall I forgive my brother who sins against me? Up to seven times?" Jesus said to him, "I do not say to you up to seven times, but up to seventy times seven."
> —MATTHEW 18:21–22, MEV

This call to forgive is imperative. Jesus follows it with a parable about debt. A man had a large debt, and his master forgave it. This same forgiven man refused to forgive a smaller debt owed to him. Listen to the verdict of Jesus in Matthew 18:32–35:

> Then his master, after he had called him, said to him, "You wicked servant! I forgave you all that debt because you begged me. Should you not also have had compassion on your fellow servant, just as I had pity on you?" And his master was angry, and delivered him to the torturers until he should pay all that was due to him. So My heavenly Father also will do to you if each of you, from his heart, does not forgive his brother his trespasses.

The tormentors are demons of depression, fear, rage, infirmity, and insomnia. Often, words said or written are the things that people struggle to forgive. Forgiveness is a supernatural act the Holy Spirit does through you.

Emotional trauma

Another tool the enemy uses is emotional trauma, which can result from accidents, abuse, divorce, crime, betrayal, and wrong words. You need healing from things such as fear, unforgiveness, traumas, victimization, and self-pity.

Wrong vows and judgments

Wrong vows and judgments are the fourth avenue used by the enemy. Our wrong words give Satan access.

> But I say to you, do not swear at all: neither by heaven, for it is God's throne; nor by the earth, for it is His footstool; nor by Jerusalem, for it is the city of the great King. Nor shall you swear by your head, because you cannot make one hair white or black. But let your "Yes" mean "Yes," and "No" mean "No." For whatever is more than these comes from the evil one.
> —MATTHEW 5:34–37, MEV

People will swear they will never do something. Satan hears it, and then they will repeat the exact act for which they were victims. Most abusers have been abused—and most swore they would never do to others what happened to them. Also, words of judgment against others open the door for the enemy to release the same problem in your life.

> Judge not, that you be not judged. For with what judgment you judge, you will be judged. And with the measure you use, it will be measured again for you.
> —MATTHEW 7:1–2, MEV

The power of a vow or a judgment will bind you to a fleshly course of action that will control you until the vow is broken. Ecclesiastes 5:5 states, "Better not to vow than to vow and not pay." Be aware of the words "I will never" or "I will always." Until these words are reversed, Satan has ground.

Curses

All of the above can include curses—the fifth open door that allows the work of dark spiritual forces. A curse is an extended evil rope with one end tied to you and one end tied to "who knows what" in the unseen past. You may be living with a curse if it seems that something repeatedly hinders you or creates struggle in a certain area of your life.

Curses, which can also be called habits, affect families, churches, social circles, cities, and nature. They pass down through families if they aren't broken. The invisible realm is where curses operate, and they can be transferred by words or objects.

To determine if you are dealing with a curse, there are several things that may be present in the physical realm if a curse is active in the spiritual realm.

1. **Mental state.** Insanity, personality disorders, and emotional disturbance may be present. "The LORD will make pestilence cling to you until it has consumed you from the land, which you are going to possess" (Deut. 28:21, MEV).

2. **Hereditary afflictions or chronic illness.** "The LORD will strike you with consumption, with fever, with inflammation, with severe burning fever, with the sword, with scorching, and with mildew; they shall pursue you until you perish" (Deut. 28:22).

3. **Female problems and child-bearing difficulties.** While these may have a medical explanation, they can also be the result of a curse. "Your offspring will be cursed along with the fruit of your land, the produce of your herd, and the flocks of your sheep" (Deut. 28:18, MEV).

4. **Family difficulties or division.** "You will give birth to sons and daughters, but you will not enjoy them; for they will go into captivity" (Deut. 28:41, MEV).

5. **Financial shortages.** Financial shortages can be a result of unwise choices, but they also can indicate a curse working in your life. " You are cursed with a curse, your whole nation, for you are robbing Me" (Mal. 3:9, MEV).

6. **Being accident-prone.** Being accident-prone can also be evidence of a curse working in your life. "The LORD will strike you with madness, and blindness, and bewilderment of heart. You will grope at noon, as the blind man gropes in darkness, and you will not prosper in your ways. You will only be oppressed and continually robbed, and no man will save you" (Deut. 28:28–29, MEV).

Once it has been determined that you may be dealing with a curse, the next step in reversing it is to expose it. "Like a flitting sparrow, like a flying swallow, so a curse without cause shall not alight" (Prov. 26:2).

CAUSES AND EFFECTS OF CURSES

Curses are always caused by something or someone in the past or present. There are certain sins that curses consistently follow—such as rebellion and disobedience.

> Samuel said: "Does the LORD delight in burnt offerings and sacrifices as much as in obeying the voice of the LORD? Obedience is better than sacrifice, a listening ear than the fat of rams. For rebellion is as the sin of witchcraft, and stubbornness is as iniquity and idolatry. Because you have rejected the word of the LORD, He has also rejected you from being king."
>
> —1 SAMUEL 15:22–23, MEV

Samuel said that rebellion releases witchcraft. Children's rebellion brings curses.

> Children, obey your parents in the Lord, for this is right. "Honor your father and mother," which is the first commandment with promise, "so that it may be well with you and you may live long on the earth."
>
> —EPHESIANS 6:1–3, MEV

Curses also come with the occult.

> Now the works of the flesh are revealed, which are these: adultery, sexual immorality, impurity, lewdness, idolatry, sorcery, hatred, strife, jealousy, rage, selfishness, dissensions, heresies, envy, murders, drunkenness, carousing, and the like. I warn you, as I previously warned you, that those who do such things shall not inherit the kingdom of God.
>
> —GALATIANS 5:19–21, MEV

Curses follow those who do an injustice to others.

> "Cursed is he who removes his neighbor's landmark." And all the people shall say, "Amen." "Cursed is he who misleads the blind

man on the road." And all the people shall say, "Amen." "Cursed
is he who perverts justice for the foreigner, orphan, and widow."
And all the people shall say, "Amen."

—DEUTERONOMY 27:17–19, MEV

Curses follow sexual perversion. All adultery, fornication, homosexuality, bestiality, incest, and pornography bring curses.

"Cursed is he who lies with his father's wife, for he dishonors his
father." And all the people shall say, "Amen." "Cursed is he who
lies with any kind of beast." And all the people shall say, "Amen."
"Cursed is he who lies with his sister, the daughter of his father, or
the daughter of his mother." And all the people shall say, "Amen."
"Cursed is he who lies with his mother-in-law." And all the people
shall say, "Amen."

—DEUTERONOMY 27:20–23, MEV

Racism and anti-Semitism will bring a curse on those who feel
superior to others.

I will bless them who bless you and curse him who curses you,
and in you all families of the earth will be blessed.

—GENESIS 12:3, MEV

Trusting human potential, strengths, and influence will cause a
curse to fall.

Thus says the LORD: "Cursed is the man who trusts in man and
makes flesh his strength, and whose heart departs from the LORD.
For he will be like a bush in the desert and will not see when
good comes, but will inhabit the parched places in the wilderness,
in a salt land and not inhabited."

—JEREMIAH 17:5–6, MEV

Curses follow stealing and lying.

He said to me, "This is the curse going out over the surface of
all the land. Everyone who steals will be purged according to
the writing on one side, and everyone who swears falsely will be
purged according to the writing on the other side. I will send it

out, says the LORD of Hosts, and it will enter the house of the thief, and the house of him who swears falsely by My name. It will remain in his house and consume it, with its timber and stones."

—ZECHARIAH 5:3–4, MEV

Stealing and lying include robbing God of the tithe.

Will a man rob God? Yet you have robbed Me. But you say, "How have we robbed You?" In tithes and offerings. You are cursed with a curse, your whole nation, for you are robbing Me.

—MALACHI 3:8–9, MEV

Words spoken by those who are in loving authority can result in curses. When you say something in anger to someone under your authority, you curse that person. Seemingly simple and quickly spoken phrases, such as "You are stupid" or "I hate you," bring lasting effects. Jacob's wife Rachel died young as a result of his words: "'With whomever you find your gods, do not let him live. In the presence of our brethren, identify what I have of yours and take it with you.' For Jacob did not know that Rachel had stolen them" (Gen. 31:32).

Lying, gossiping, and idle religious talk release evil.

But if you have bitter envying and strife in your hearts, do not boast and do not lie against the truth. This wisdom descends not from above, but is earthly, unspiritual, and devilish.

—JAMES 3:14–15, MEV

He who turns away his ear from hearing instruction, even his prayer will be an abomination.

—PROVERBS 28:9, MEV

GETTING RID OF THE CURSE

Once a curse has been identified and exposed, the next step is expelling the curse. A critical element in getting rid of curses is to know you are saved! Demons consider your body their home until you are saved.

When an unclean spirit goes out of a man, it passes through dry places seeking rest, but finds none. Then it says, "I will return to my house from which I came." And when it comes, it finds it empty, swept, and put in order. Then it goes and brings with itself seven other spirits more evil than itself, and they enter and dwell there. And the last state of that man is worse than the first. So shall it be also with this evil generation.

—MATTHEW 12:43–45, MEV

Confess aloud your willingness to yield to God. Close all doors and take away Satan's access in your life. Repent of rebellion and disobedience. Forgive those who hurt you. Bring all past hurt and trauma to God. Cancel past vows, judgments, and wrong words, whether spoken by you or to you. Confess aloud that Jesus has borne every sin, hurt, and curse for you!

Christ has redeemed us from the curse of the law by being made a curse for us—as it is written, "Cursed is everyone who hangs on a tree."

—GALATIANS 3:13, MEV

In closing, renounce every spirit that has oppressed your life, and receive deliverance and praise God. Confess Psalm 34 as your prayer:

I will bless the LORD at all times;
    His praise shall continually be in my mouth.
My soul shall make its boast in the LORD;
    The humble shall hear of it and be glad.
Oh, magnify the LORD with me,
    And let us exalt His name together.
I sought the LORD, and He heard me,
    And delivered me from all my fears.
They looked to Him and were radiant,
    And their faces were not ashamed.
This poor man cried out, and the LORD heard him,
    And saved him out of all his troubles.
The angel of the LORD encamps all around those who fear Him
    And delivers them.
Oh, taste and see that the LORD is good;
    Blessed is the man who trusts in Him!
Oh, fear the LORD, you His saints!
    There is no want to those who fear Him.

The young lions lack and suffer hunger;
  But those who seek the LORD shall not lack any good thing.
Come, you children, listen to me;
  I will teach you the fear of the LORD.
Who is the man who desires life,
  And loves many days, that he may see good?
Keep your tongue from evil,
  And your lips from speaking deceit.
Depart from evil and do good;
  Seek peace and pursue it.
The eyes of the LORD are on the righteous,
  And His ears are open to their cry.
The face of the LORD is against those who do evil,
  To cut off the remembrance of them from the earth.
The righteous cry out, and the LORD hears,
  And delivers them out of all their troubles.
The LORD is near to those who have a broken heart,
  And saves such as have a contrite spirit.
Many are the afflictions of the righteous,
  But the LORD delivers him out of them all.
He guards all his bones;
  Not one of them is broken.
Evil shall slay the wicked,
  And those who hate the righteous shall be condemned.
The LORD redeems the soul of His servants,
  And none of those who trust in Him shall be condemned.

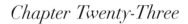

Chapter Twenty-Three

BUILDING HEDGES OF
SPIRITUAL PROTECTION

THE PROPHET EZEKIEL WROTE, "YOU HAVE NOT GONE UP INTO the gaps, nor did you build up the hedge for the house of Israel to stand in the battle on the day of the LORD" (Ezek. 13:5, MEV). A hedge in Bible times was a special barrier or fence placed around grape vineyards. Depending on its design, it was placed to keep insects, bugs, rodents, thieves, or birds from coming in and stealing the harvest.

Spiritually, a hedge is God's wall of protection promised for all those who believe on Him, walk with Him, and trust in Him. As Christians believing in His promises, it is time that we declare, "I've come to get back what Satan stole! I want God's protective barrier around my life and that of my family."

God longs for churches and individuals to have the faith to stand in the broken-down gaps so the enemy will have no right to plunder what He has given.

CAN GOD REMOVE A HEDGE?

The Bible indicates at least two times or two reasons why God Himself may allow a hedge to fail. Sometimes He will take down a hedge in judgment. God sang to Isaiah in chapter 5 and basically said, "I gave My Beloved as a vine, and I cleaned out the stones and planted My people into My choice vineyard. I removed everything." Then God says, "I put a hedge around you to protect you. But when I came in there to get My fruit, instead of a beautiful, sweet cluster of choice grapes, the fruit stunk. It was wild and worthless." God told Isaiah that because of their disobedience, He brought judgment and removed the hedge, allowing destruction to come to the nation.

When God takes down the hedge over a nation, over a church, over a family, or over an individual, deep trouble follows!

God also may take down a hedge to prove Satan is a liar. In the first chapter of Job, the devil shows up. God says to him, "Have you considered My servant Job, that there is none like him on the earth?" (Job 1:8).

The devil replied, "Well, it's no wonder—You have hedged him in. If You will take the hedge down and let me at him, he will curse You to Your face." (See Job 1:10.)

God said, "I don't believe he loves Me just because of what I've done for him. I believe he loves Me with all of his heart." So to prove Satan wrong and prove Job's faithfulness, God allowed Satan to afflict Job for a season. When we find Job on the other side of the removal of hedges, his fortune is gone, his family is gone, his health is gone, and his wife is encouraging him to curse God and die. Even so, Job still says, "Though He slay me, yet will I trust in Him" (Job 13:15, MEV).

Job came through this serious test of faith and lived to see everything returned to him double. That part of his story isn't discussed often enough—we focus so much on his trials that we forget that God rewarded his faithfulness in abundance, above and beyond what had been taken from him.

Job was one of possibly only four men in the Bible whom God could trust with the removal of a hedge. Joseph was another whom God trusted enough to take the hedge down. He allowed him to endure slavery, temptation, imprisonment, and rejection for His glory. Paul also had a hedge down. Thousands were healed under his ministry, but scholars believe his own eyes were his "thorn in the flesh," an infirmity that continued to buffet him unless he be exalted above measure. (See 2 Corinthians 12:7.) God also trusted Jesus enough to take the hedge down and let Him die on the cross, sacrificing Himself for our sins and failures.

IN NEED OF PROTECTION?

Truthfully, some of us with a broken-down or absent protective hedge have not come to it due to our own merit or by being chosen to stand a special test of God. Still others of us have gaps in our protective hedges happen because we have made choices that left us open to enemy attack. Because of these choices, we feel miserable. We are hurt. We are bothered. We are struggling. We are failing, and we are walking through difficulty. The good news is, you can allow God to build a fivefold hedge around you and around your family that the devil cannot touch.

Hedge of prayer

We read in Job, "Now his sons would go and feast in their houses, each on his appointed day, and would send and invite their three sisters to eat and drink with them. So it was, when the days of feasting had run their course, that Job would send and sanctify them, and he would rise early in the morning and offer burnt offerings according to the number of them all. For Job said, 'It may be that my sons have sinned and cursed God in their hearts.' Thus Job did regularly" (Job 1:4–5).

Remember in verse 10 Satan asked God, "Have You not made a hedge around him?" How do you think that hedge got around Job's children? God saw the earnestness of Job's faith. Job wasn't fast asleep, snoring at eight o'clock in the morning—he was up at 4:30 a.m., interceding for his family.

You can imagine those prayers. Perhaps he prayed, "I don't know what my boys and girls have been doing today, but Lord, I'm here with an offering, a memorial to You. God, please put a hedge about my children!"

So many parents feel lost when their children go off to college or move away. It is easy to fall into deep worry and fear about what they are doing at any time of day or night. But here is a practical, tangible way to help them: pray a hedge around them. Lasso them with the Holy Ghost!

Years ago as a young preacher learning lessons from God, I was visiting Natchez, Mississippi. A family put me up for a night, and the mama was a sweet saint of God. This dear woman had a faithful fourteen-year-old girl and an unfaithful twenty-one-year-old son.

About 4:30 a.m. I was returning from getting a drink of water when I heard something that sounded like a wounded animal in an adjacent room. Concerned, I stopped to listen and just caught the broken voice of the saintly mama say, "O God, please save him, Lord. If You have to take my life, Lord, don't let him go to hell. Lord, protect him tonight. I don't know where he is tonight, Lord, but please protect him."

Deeply moved, I went back to bed, but sleep didn't come quickly as I thought of this mother's burden.

The next morning at breakfast, sitting there with her family, I gently said, "I heard you praying last night."

She apologized quickly, "Oh, I'm sorry, Brother Ron. I hope it didn't disturb you."

I said, "No, ma'am, it didn't wake me up, but it sure disturbed me in my own complacent spirit."

She said, "I've been praying for seven years for my son to come out of drugs and alcohol and to come home."

I think back to that story and shake my head to think of how many times we pray five minutes about a worry or a need, and when our answer doesn't come, we throw in the towel and give up our intercession. But this saintly mama was like Job. She said, "I didn't give up." And her faithfulness was rewarded—the very next night her boy staggered into a church and gave his heart to Jesus Christ!

You can build a hedge that will draw your family back to God through prayer. You can throw a hedge around your business. If you begin sincerely praying, you will see an amazing difference. If you wonder why the profits are going down or success is not coming, it is because the devil is a thief who loves to steal success from you. Stand in faith and pray God's hedge about you, binding the devil off of what you own.

Hedge of spiritual leadership

If you have placed yourself under the authority of a local, Bible-believing church led by a pastor who is sensitive to the Holy Spirit, there is protection in that place. Living under the ministry of a man of God will put a hedge around you. Remember Ezekiel 22:30: "I sought for a man among them, that should make up the hedge, and stand in the gap before me for the land" (KJV).

Too many ministries take up the motto, "We don't want to offend anybody." But God places blessing upon church families who stand for the truth of the Word of God.

Hedge of unity

People in unity can build a hedge. You may recall the story of Abraham pleading with God for Sodom and Gomorrah to be spared. Abraham asked, "Would You spare it for fifty righteous people found there?" God said, "I will spare it for fifty." Abraham bargained all the way down to ten. It is sobering to think that ten righteous, praying people would have spared those evil cities! (See Genesis 19.)

Amazing things could happen if we would begin to seriously pray about the governmental issues that are harming families and churches today. What if we began to pray in unity? If ten righteous people living in purity would have spared Sodom, what could a group of interceding Christians today accomplish in our nation?

Hedge of angelic protection

Holy angels will help you place a hedge around your family. Psalm 34:7 says, "The angel of the LORD encamps around those who fear Him, and delivers them." Imagine the grounds around your home with the angels of the Lord encamped all around! Hebrews 1:14 says, "Are they not all ministering spirits sent forth to minister for those who will inherit salvation?"

This truth became more precious to me when I became the parent of a teenager! When your children hit the age of sixteen and get behind the wheel of the car, it seems your whole prayer life changes! I often teased that I was going to have to buy a timeshare in a junkyard just to park the cars my kids wrecked! But I've learned that God's eye is always on my family; He never sleeps. Even when you fall asleep, thank God that He is watching and that the holy angels can be stationed and arranged around your house, around your possessions, and around your children. No distance is too great, for they travel at the speed of light.

The prophet Daniel once was praying for three weeks over a request. God sent his answer on day one, but Daniel didn't see the evidence of the answer until an angel arrived. The angelic creature identified himself and then said, "I would have gotten here sooner, but I've been wrestling with a demon over Persia. I was on my way with your answer." (See Daniel 10.)

Some of you give up too quickly. You are praying, the angels are at work, demons are fighting them, but God is on His way with the answer.

The angels could be bringing that wayward child of yours home even now, protecting him or her all the way.

Hedge of revival

Revival builds a hedge. Psalm 80:14 says, "Return, we beseech You, O God of hosts; look down from heaven and see, and visit this vine." Again in verse 18 is the plea, "We will not turn back from You; revive us, and we will call upon Your name." When revival comes, it puts a hedge around everything going on in the house.

Recall again the picture of a grape vineyard. Those who raised grapes in Bible times valued their vines and protected them at all costs. The protection around their precious crop was multilayered. Often they would first put a stone wall around it. Then they would follow with a thick hedge of thorns. Then, right before the harvest, they would build a fire to keep the flying insects and birds away.

What a thrilling picture for us! First, that stone wall is a symbol of God the Father, who is eternal, unchanging, and a solid foundation. With our families firmly planted upon the Rock of Ages, we can find peace and security in the Father's strength and guidance.

Next, the hedge of thorns is Jesus, whose blood provides everlasting protection for our souls. I think of the lines from the poem by G. A. Studdert Kennedy:

> When Jesus came to Golgotha they hanged Him on a tree,
> They drave great nails through hands and feet, and made a
> Calvary;
> They crowned Him with a crown of thorns, red were His
> wounds and deep,
> For those were crude and cruel days, and human flesh was
> cheap.[1]

Finally, think of the symbolism of the wall of fire. We arrive at harvesttime, when the grapes are ripe, following the long season during which we have waited and waited and waited. The Father has watched over us and the blood has taken care of us, but now the fruit is ripe and the fragrance is wafting. It is when we are at the point of reaping the greatest blessings in our lives that every demon of hell, every insect and fowl bird wants to lodge in the branches! But God says, "I'm sending Holy Ghost fire." And when that fire begins to burn, the smoke of His glory rises, and nothing can come and steal our harvest.

When you are saved and He's your Father, you are living under the blood of the crucified Christ; you are baptized, anointed with the Spirit of God and the baptism of fire. No demon of hell is going to touch anything you have! You have immunity! You are walking in His freedom.

Aren't you tired of the enemy coming around and tampering with what is yours? We have a promise from Almighty God to be our protection against the devil's onslaught. Satan has devoured a lot of harvests in the past, but he cannot penetrate the powerful hedge of God. Our children can be safe within that hedge.

It is time for you to have all the protection He's provided. Just pray this prayer:

> *Lord, build a hedge around me, around my church, around my family, and around our nation. Protect my possessions, Lord, because it all really belongs to You. Lord, let me live long enough to see revival, to taste the new wine. Thank You for the harvest that is coming!*

Chapter Twenty-Four

LIVING IN TRIUMPHANT HOPE

HOW CAN YOU MAINTAIN A BLESSED LIFE? TAKE THESE EIGHT simple steps and discover how the happy life is the antidote to depression!

Do something.

Find something to do. Start serving God! John 13:17 says, "If ye know these things, happy are ye if ye do them" (KJV). Perhaps it could be the simplest task, such as keeping the nursery. In that act of service, you will be happy. Move into action for God, and joy will meet you along the road.

Quit complaining about God's correction.

Job 5:17 states, "Behold, happy is the man whom God corrects; therefore do not despise the chastening of the Almighty." Sometimes difficult times don't come from the devil. At times, God is using those circumstances to firmly correct us. Hebrews 12:6 tells us, "Whom the Lord loves He disciplines" (MEV). He is not a sorry parent like some of us who let our kids get away with anything. He is a loving parent who calls His children back into line, not because He doesn't want us to enjoy life but because He sees the whole picture and wants true happiness for us.

Learn to abide in God's safety.

Deuteronomy 33:29 says, "Happy are you, O Israel! Who is like you, a people saved by the LORD, the shield of your help and the sword of your majesty! Your enemies shall submit to you, and you shall tread down their high places." Christ is your shield. He is the sword of your majesty.

He will put your enemies under your feet. I'll tell you, you can live a life free of depression if you discover your position in Jesus Christ.

Look in the Book!

Become a Bible reader. Proverbs 3:13 states, "Happy is the man who finds wisdom, and the man who gains understanding." God's Word isn't the book of the month; it is the Book of the Ages. This is God's best seller! Within it, there are more than three thousand promises, and all of them are yours. Second Corinthians 1:20 tells us, "All the promises of God in Him are Yes, and in Him Amen." That means they belong to you. Happy are you when you find the treasure. Nearly every depressed person I've ever counseled has lost their devotional life and is not saturating their life with God's promises. If you don't know where to start, begin with the Book of Psalms.

Get your priorities in order.

Psalm 128:1–6 tells us, "Blessed is everyone who fears the LORD, who walks in His ways. For you shall eat the fruit of the labor of your hands; you will be happy.... Your wife shall be as a fruitful vine in your house, your children like olive shoots all around your table. Behold, this man shall be blessed who fears the LORD. The LORD shall bless you from Zion, and may you see the welfare of Jerusalem all the days of your life. Indeed, may you see your children's children" (MEV). Take inventory of your priorities, and nail them to the doorpost or place them on the central bulletin board of your home.

Stop doing questionable activities.

Too many Christians wonder why they are depressed—after they spend hours watching soap operas, "Hell's Box Office," and other questionable television offerings. If this is an issue for you, unplug the cable if you have to! Get some self-control into your life. Quit reading the wrong things. Saturate yourself with the Bible.

Perhaps you are saying, "I don't really believe that some of these things are wrong for me to do or watch." I must argue—if it is making you miserable, it is wrong! Romans 14:22 says, "Happy is he who does not condemn himself in what he approves" (MEV). Here is what this verse is saying: "Happy is the man who doesn't walk in condemnation because of the stuff he is allowing in his life." If you feel guilty about it, quit it, regardless of whether others agree or not. If it is something in your life that shouldn't be there, remove it. Get rid of the horoscopes. Throw off any talisman you are wearing around your neck that honors the devil.

Get rid of any kind of music that glorifies the flesh and the enemy. Begin to get your life in order. Begin to sow into your life things that overflow with joy. If you are still not sure if something is right or wrong, ask yourself these questions: "Can I do this activity without hurting a fellow Christian? Can I maintain my witness to the lost? Can I do it and not live under condemnation?"

Learn to roll with the punches.

James 5:11 says, "Behold, we count them happy which endure" (KJV). I may have battle wounds now and then, but I'm here to tell you that the blood of Jesus is on your side! It is time for Christians to find some backbone, to be among those who will not run every time the devil raises his ugly head and hisses. "Happy are you," James said, "when you can endure the trials that are coming your way."

Finally, remember who is in charge.

Print out Psalm 144:15 and hang it somewhere where you will see it every morning when you get up. It says, "Happy are the people who are in such a state; happy are the people whose God is the LORD!" Your God is in charge! He is Lord over all. Not one thing could happen to topple Him from His throne. We have been given the last chapters of the book, and Revelation 22 reveals that when the whole thing is over, He is still proclaimed to be King of kings and Lord of lords! There has never been a kingdom He is not King over. Your circumstances may be too big for you, but they are not too big for Him.

NOTES

PART ONE
ANGELS

INTRODUCTION

1.   C. H. Spurgeon, "The First Christmas Carol," sermon, Music Hall, Royal Surrey Gardens, Kennington, London, December 20, 1857, http://www .spurgeon.org/sermons/0168.htm (accessed December 5, 2014).

CHAPTER ONE
THE PRESENCE OF ANGELS

1.   Military.com, "The Gulf War: A Line in the Sand," http:// http://www .military.com/Resources/HistorySubmittedFileView?file=history_gulfwar.htm (accessed December 5, 2014).

2.   Malcolm D. Grimes and Donald R. Ferguson, "Joint Publication 3–16, Joint Doctrine for Multinational Operations: 'If You Work With Friends, Bring It Along!'" *Air and Space Power Journal* 18, no. 4 (Winter 2004): 72–73, http://www.airpower.maxwell.af.mil/airchronicles/apj/apj04/win04/grimes .html (accessed December 5, 2014).

CHAPTER THREE
THE MYSTERY OF ANGELS

1.   C. S. Lewis, *Miracles* (United Kingdom: Fontana, 1947).
2.   Francis Collins, *The Language of God* (New York: Free Press, 2006), 124.
3.   Ibid., 205.

CHAPTER FOUR
THE VARIETY OF ANGELS

1.   Francis Brown, S. Driver, and C. Briggs, *Brown-Driver-Briggs Hebrew and English Lexicon* (n.p.: Hendrickson Publishers, 1996).
2.   Billy Graham, *Angels: God's Secret Agents* (Garden City, New York: Doubleday and Company, Inc., 1975, 1995), 30.

CHAPTER FIVE
THE APPEARANCE OF ANGELS

1.   BrainyQuote.com, "Neil Armstrong Quotes," http://www.brainyquote .com/quotes/quotes/n/neilarmstr363174.html (accessed December 5, 2014).

CHAPTER SIX
THE CONFLICT OF ANGELS

1.   G. H. Pember, *Earth's Earliest Ages* (n.p.: Kregel Academic & Professional, 1975).
2.   William Shakespeare, *Macbeth*, 1.5.51–53. References are to act, scene, and line.

CHAPTER SEVEN
WORSHIP—ANGELS AROUND THE THRONE

1.   John Paul Jackson, *7 Days Behind the Veil* (North Sutton, NH: Streams Publishing House, 2006), 28–29.

CHAPTER EIGHT
DESTINY—ANGELS AMONG THE NATIONS

1.   Chuck Ripka, *God Out of the Box* (Lake Mary, FL: Charisma House, 2007), 102–104.
2.   Ibid.

CHAPTER NINE
PROTECTION—ANGELS ON DEFENSE

1.   Bill Bright, "Guardian Angels Watching Over Us," Angel Stories and Miracles, http://www.thoughts-about-god.com/angels/bb_guardian.htm (accessed December 5, 2014).
2.   Al, "Firemen and the Angels Story," Amazing Angel Stories, http://www.angelrealm.com/angels_house_fire/index.htm (accessed December 5, 2014).
3.   FOXNews.com, "Caught on Camera," *FOX and Friends*, December 25, 2008, http://www.foxnews.com/video-search/m/21712317/caught_on_camera.htm (accessed December 5, 2014).

CHAPTER ELEVEN
STRENGTH—ANGELS PLUGGED IN

1.   Angel Stories and Miracles, "Angel Comes to Encourage," http://www.thoughts-about-god.com/angels/surgery.htm (accessed December 5, 2014).

CHAPTER TWELVE
ANGELS OBEY ORDERS

1.   Bart, "Switch Lanes Angel Story," Amazing Angel Stories, http://www.angelrealm.com/switch_lanes_story/index.htm (accessed December 5, 2014).

CHAPTER THIRTEEN
ANGELS RESPOND TO SCRIPTURE

1.   Eugene Merrill, *New American Commentary: Deuteronomy* (Nashville: B&H Publishing Group, 1994), 434–435.

CHAPTER FOURTEEN
ANGELS ANSWER PRAYER

1.   Adapted from "Prayed for God's Angels Story," Amazing Angel Stories, http://www.angelrealm.com/prayed_for_angels/index.htm (accessed December 5, 2014).

2.   Gena, "Angel to the Rescue," AngelsLight: In the Light of Angels, http://www.angelslight.org/angelstory.php?id=gena (accessed December 5, 2014).

CHAPTER FIFTEEN
ANGELS MOVE ON MIRACLE GROUND

1.   Terry Law, *The Truth About Angels* (Lake Mary, FL: Charisma House, 1994, 2006), 41–42.

2.   Taken from the *Agape* Newsletter, Little Rock, AK, May/June 1988, 3. This newsletter is published by Agape Church, pastored by Happy Caldwell, as related in Law, *The Truth About Angels*, 41.

3.   Larry Libby, *Somewhere Angels* (Sisters, OR: Questar Publishers, 1994), 32, as related in Law, *The Truth About Angels*, 42.

4.   Graham, *Angels: God's Secret Agents*, 5.

5.   Victory Church of Christ, "26 Guards," http://victorychurchofchrist.org/otherstuff.html (accessed August 10, 2009).

CHAPTER SIXTEEN
ANGELS EXECUTE GOD'S WRATH

1.   Jim Bramlett, "Angels Discovered Singing End-Time Song in Rural Chinese Worship Service in 1995!" http://www.virtualchurch.org/vchurch/angels.htm (accessed January 9, 2015).

PART TWO
DEMONS

INTRODUCTION

1.   Ted Rowlands and Michael Cary, "Army Honors Dead, Searches for Motive in Fort Hood Shootings," CNN.com, November 7, 2009, http://www.cnn.com/2009/CRIME/11/06/texas.fort.hood.shootings/index.html (accessed December 5, 2014).

2.   Aaron Cooper, Ted Rowlands, Barbara Star, and Brian Todd, "Fort Hood Suspect Charged With Murder," CNN.com, November 12, 2009, http://www.cnn.com/2009/CRIME/11/12/fort.hood.investigation/index.html (accessed December 5, 2014).

CHAPTER ONE
BATTLE BEYOND THE STARS

1.   Sun Tzu, *The Art of War*, trans. Lionel Giles, Project Gutenberg, http://www.gutenberg.org/files/17405/17405-h/17405-h.htm (accessed December 5, 2014).
2.   Joseph DelGrippo, "Cowboys-49ers: Breaking Down the Best 12 Games in NFL's Best Rivalry," BleacherReport.com, August 27, 2009, http://bleacherreport.com/articles/243827-the-dozen-best-games-in-the-nfls-best-rivalry-dallas-and-san-francisco (accessed December 5, 2014).

CHAPTER TWO
THE CONTINUOUS WAR IN EDEN

1.   Book of Jasher 16:11, http://www.ccel.org/a/anonymous/jasher/16.htm; 24:17, http://www.ccel.org/a/anonymous/jasher/24.htm; 28:18, http://www.ccel.org/a/anonymous/jasher/28.htm (accessed December 5, 2014).

CHAPTER SIX
SEVEN DEMONS THAT ATTACK THE CHURCH

1.   Publius Cornelius Tacitus, *Annals* 14.27, trans. Alfred John Church and William Jackson Brodribb, http://mcadams.posc.mu.edu/txt/ah/tacitus/TacitusAnnals14.html (accessed December 5, 2014).
2.   As quoted in sermon "Revival Recovers All" by Dr. Harold L. White, http://www.angelfire.com/az3/hlw1932/1sam3011revrecovers.html (accessed December 5, 2014).
3.   *Lambeth and the Vatican: or, Anecdotes of the Church of Rome, of the Reformed Churches, and of Sects and Sectaries*, vol. 3 (London: Oxford University, 1825), 149.

CHAPTER NINE
UNMASKING THE ENEMY

1.   William F. Arndt and F. Wilber Gingrich, *A Greek-English Lexicon of the New Testament* (Chicago: University of Chicago Press, 1979).
2.   C. Fred Dickason, *Demon Possession and the Christian: A New Perspective* (Wheaton, IL: Crossway Books, 1989).
3.   Kurt E. Koch, *Occult Bondage and Deliverance* (Grand Rapids, MI: Kregel Publications, 1972).

CHAPTER TWELVE
THE VICTORY AT CALVARY

1.   John Bunyan, *The Pilgrim's Progress* (New York: Oxford University Press, Inc., 1996), 45.
2.   James S. Stewart, *A Faith to Proclaim* (London: Hodder and Stoughton, 1962), 95–97.

CHAPTER THIRTEEN
FOUNDATIONS FOR VICTORY

1. Stewart, *A Faith to Proclaim.*
2. Ibid.
3. Gustav Aulen, *Christus Victor: An Historical Study of the Three Main Types of the Idea of the Atonement* (n.p.: Society for Promoting Christian Knowledge, 1945).
4. P. T. Forsyth, "The Fatherhood of Death," in *Missions in State—and Church* (New York: A. C. Armstrong and Son, 1908), http://www.archive.org/stream/missionsinstatec00fors/missionsinstatec00fors_djvu.txt (accessed December 5, 2014).
5. John Calvin, *Calvin's Bible Commentaries: Philippians, Colossians, and Thessalonians*, first published 1847 (n.p.: Forgotten Books, 2007), 161.
6. Oscar Cullman, *Christ and Time* (n.p.: n.p, 1964), 198.

CHAPTER FOURTEEN
THE BELIEVER'S POSITION FOR VICTORY

1. C. S. Lewis Society of California, "Quotes by C. S. Lewis," http://www.lewissociety.org/quotes.php (accessed December 5, 2014).

CHAPTER FIFTEEN
ARMING FOR VICTORY

1. "Stand Up for Jesus" by George Duffield Jr. Public domain.
2. "Wonderful Peace" by Warren D. Cornell. Public domain.
3. NotableBiographies.com, "Charles de Gaulle," http://www.notablebiographies.com/De-Du/de-Gaulle-Charles.html (accessed December 5, 2014).
4. "O Worship the King" by Robert Grant. Public domain.
5. George Bernard Shaw, *Too Good to Be True: A Political Extravaganza* (n.p.: Samuel French, Inc., 1933, 1934, 1960, 1961), 99.
6. "How Firm a Foundation" by John Rippon. Public domain.

CHAPTER TWENTY
LOVING OTHERS UNCONDITIONALLY

1. "The Love of God" by Frederick M. Lehman. Public domain.
2. "At Calvary" by William R. Newell. Public domain.

CHAPTER TWENTY-TWO
BREAKING CURSES

1. Henry Malone, *Shadow Boxing* (n.p.: Vision Life Publications, 2004).

CHAPTER TWENTY-THREE
BUILDING HEDGES OF SPIRITUAL PROTECTION

1. G. A. Studdert Kennedy, "Indifference," in *The Unutterable Beauty* (London: Hodder and Stoughton, 1927), 24.

GOD'S SECRET TO SUCCESS
IN EVERY AREA OF YOUR LIFE

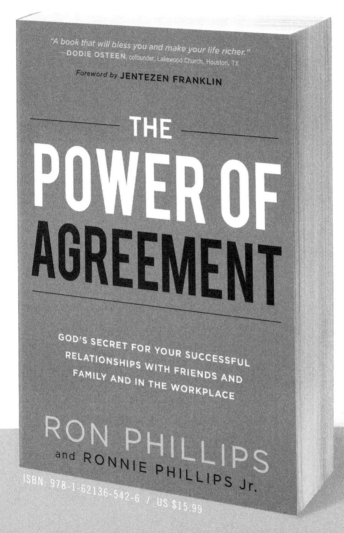

"A book that will bless you and make your life richer."
—DODIE OSTEEN, cofounder, Lakewood Church, Houston, TX

Foreword by JENTEZEN FRANKLIN

THE
POWER OF
AGREEMENT

GOD'S SECRET FOR YOUR SUCCESSFUL
RELATIONSHIPS WITH FRIENDS AND
FAMILY AND IN THE WORKPLACE

RON PHILLIPS
and RONNIE PHILLIPS Jr.

ISBN: 978-1-62136-542-6 / US $15.99

In *The Power of Agreement* Ron and Ronnie Phillips use examples from the Bible along with moving stories of successes and failures from their own lives to show you the key to having a successful life. It all comes down to agreement.

Order today!

  Facebook.com/CharismaHouse | Twitter/CharismaHouse   12935

CHARISMA
HOUSE

SUBSCRIBE TODAY

Exclusive Content

Inspiring Messages

Encouraging Articles

Discovering Freedom

CHARISMA MEDIA

FREE NEWSLETTERS

to experience the power of the *Holy Spirit*

Charisma Magazine Newsletter
Get top-trending articles, Christian teachings, entertainment reviews, videos, and more.

Charisma News Weekly
Get the latest breaking news from an evangelical perspective every Monday.

SpiritLed Woman
Receive amazing stories, testimonies, and articles on marriage, family, prayer, and more.

New Man
Get articles and teaching about the realities of living in the world today as a man of faith.

3-in-1 Daily Devotionals
Find personal strength and encouragement with these devotionals, and begin your day with God's Word.

Sign up for Free at nl.charismamag.com